Youth Offending in Context

Identifying and exploring the challenges in understanding and responding to youth crime, this book investigates the different contexts which contribute to youth offending as well as those which either help or hinder effective youth justice responses to it.

Supporting readers to evaluate traditional understandings and responses to youth offending, this critical, evidence-based text engages with a variety of international case studies, practice examples and expert perspectives from academic researchers in the field.

Delving into theoretical, conceptual, empirical, policy and practice issues, *Youth Offending in Context* will be of great value to students of youth justice, youth offending, youth crime, crime prevention, and criminal justice.

Stephen Case is Professor of Youth Justice at Loughborough University. His research and scholarship has focused on the promotion of positive, 'children first', rights-based and anti-risk management approaches to working with children in conflict with the law. He has published numerous books including *Youth Justice: A Critical Introduction* (Case 2021 – Routledge), *Positive Youth Justice: Children First, Offenders Second* (Haines and Case 2015) and *Understanding Youth Offending: Risk Factor Research, Policy and Practice* (Case and Haines 2009 – Routledge).

Youth Offending in Context

Challenges and Solutions

Stephen Case

Routledge
Taylor & Francis Group
LONDON AND NEW YORK

Designed cover image: Getty Images

First published 2025
by Routledge
4 Park Square, Milton Park, Abingdon, Oxon OX14 4RN

and by Routledge
605 Third Avenue, New York, NY 10158

Routledge is an imprint of the Taylor & Francis Group, an informa business

British Library Cataloguing-in-Publication Data
A catalogue record for this book is available from the British Library

ISBN: 978-1-032-80679-2 (hbk)
ISBN: 978-1-032-80678-5 (pbk)
ISBN: 978-1-003-49810-0 (ebk)

DOI: 10.4324/9781003498100

Typeset in Sabon
by Deanta Global Publishing Services, Chennai, India

Contents

Youth offending 'in context': Challenges and solutions 1
Explaining the 'problem' of youth offending 3
Youth offending and youth justice as constructed realities 6
Why understand youth offending in context? 6
The structure of 'Youth offending in context: Challenges and solutions' 8

1 The problem of decontextualised youth offending 12
Individual explanations of youth offending: Classicism 13
Individual explanations of youth offending: Individual positivism 14
Individual explanations of youth offending: Biological positivism 15
Biological positivism: Physical characteristics 15
Individual explanations of youth offending: Psychological positivism 20
Individual positivism: A conceptual journey towards theoretical, explanatory integration 23
Integrated explanations of youth offending: Integrated individual positivism 23
Integrated individual positivism: Social control theory 24
Integrated individual positivism: Biopsychosocial theory 26
The reductionist explanations of individual positivism: Partiality 'take five' 28
Individual explanations of youth offending: Artefactual risk factor theories 28
Developmental risk factor theory 29
Integrated developmental risk factor theory 32
Contextual challenge: The reductionist definition of 'context' 40

The reductionism of artefactual risk factor theories: Partiality 'take five' 41
Summarising the problem: Decontextualised explanations youth offending 41

2 **The problem of decontextualised youth justice** 44
Youth justice across the globe: Models, rationales and principles 45
Contextual challenge: Systemic contextual influence on youth justice systems 46
The 'punitive turn' across Western youth justice systems 47
Developing youth justice models in the Western world: Five steps towards decontextualisation 49
The 'punitive turn': Constructing young people who offend as presenting risk 50
Neo-correctionalist risk management 51
The risk factor prevention paradigm: Linking explanation to response 53
Contextual challenge: Responding to risk 'in context' 57
Algorithmic Risk Assessment: The new kid on the block 60
Adverse childhood experiences: A Trojan Horse for risk management? 61
Risk management: Five steps towards decontextualised youth justice 63
From 'nothing works' to 'What Works' as effective youth justice 63
'What Works': Perpetuating partiality 66
The proliferation of 'What Works': Five steps towards decontextualised youth justice 67
Summarising the problem of decontextualised youth justice 68

3 **Explaining youth offending 'in context'** 72
Sociological positivism 73
Sociological positivism: The early years 74
Sociological positivism: Concentric zone theory 74
Sociological positivism: Strain theory 76
Sociological positivism: Subcultural theory 77
Evaluating sociological positivism: Tentative contextualisation 'take five' 78
Contextual challenge: Is 'centrism' justified when explaining youth offending? 79

Quasi-contextualised risk factor theory 80
Age-graded life course theory: Crime in the making 80
Age-graded life course theory: The Edinburgh study of youth transitions and crime 84
Evaluating age-graded life course theory: Five steps towards quasi-contextualised explanations of youth offending 86
Constructivist pathways theory: Explaining risk in socio-structural context 87
Constructivist pathways theory: Pathways into and out of crime 87
Constructivist pathways theory: The Teesside studies 89
Evaluating constructivist pathways theory 90
Constructivist pathways theory: Five steps to contextualised explanations of youth offending 92
Critical criminology 93
Critical criminology: Labelling theory 94
Evaluating labelling theory 97
Critical criminology: Marxist criminology 98
Contextual challenge: Explaining offending by young people from ethnic minority groups through processes of 'racialisation' (Webster, in Case 2021) 99
Critical criminology: 'The New Criminology' 100
Critical criminology: Gendered theories 101
Evaluating critical criminology 102
Critical criminology: Towards contextualised explanations of youth offending in five bold steps 103
Left realism 104
Contextual challenge: Right realism's deliberate explanatory decontextualisation 105
Evaluating left realism: Criticising the critic in five easy steps 107
Addressing the problem of decontextualised explanations of youth offending 107

4 Responding to youth offending 'in context' 111
The increasing complexity of Western youth justice 112
Social crime prevention: Contextualised youth justice prevention 114
Community crime prevention with young people 115
Evaluating CCP as 'effective' with young people 117

Five context-related lessons from community crime prevention 119
Realist synthesis: Evaluating contextualised youth justice intervention 120
EMMIE: Effects, moderators, mechanisms, implementation and economics 121
Realist synthesis: Contexts-mechanisms-outcomes of interventions 121
Realist synthesis: Challenging reductionist youth justice intervention in five contextualised pieces 124
Child-friendly Justice in children's rights context 124
Youth justice in a context of children's rights: Conflict, ambivalence and avoidance 127
Child-friendly justice as political rhetoric, not contextual reality? Five contextualised arguments 129
'Child First' youth justice 129
From 'CFOS' to 'Child First' 131
Child first as an expansionist principle, not a reductionist model 133
Child first in five contextualised pieces 138
Addressing the problem of decontextualised youth justice 138

5 Reimagining youth offending and youth justice 'in context' 141
Understanding youth offending and youth justice in context 141
The challenges of resilient evidential, explanatory and responsive reductionism 144
Bifurcation as reductionist partiality, not expansionist evolution 146
The opportunities of emerging evidential, explanatory and responsive expansionism 147
The contextualising promise of 'Child First' 149
Integrating contextualised youth justice perspectives: Aligning child first with rights-based child-friendly justice 151
Conclusion: Reimagining youth offending and youth justice in context 153
Five 'solutions' for understanding youth offending in context 154

Appendix 1: Explaining youth offending by girls (adapted from Case 2021) 157
Appendix 2: Explaining youth offending by boys (adapted from Case 2021) 159
Appendix 3: Contextualised youth justice intervention through Realist Synthesis 161
Bibliography 165
Index 185

Youth offending 'in context'

Challenges and solutions

This book takes up the neglected challenge of understanding youth offending 'in context.' It explores both the contexts which help to explain youth offending and those which help or hinder the effectiveness of formal youth justice interventions responding to youth offending. Throughout the book, 'context' is conceptualised using two complementary, but substantively different, narratives:

- Static: Context understood as the observable features (space, place, people, things) that trigger or block youth offending and youth justice interventions; assuming that context operates at one moment in time and sets in motion a chain reaction of events.
- Dynamic: Context understood as the relational dynamic features that shape the mechanisms through which youth offending occurs and through which youth justice interventions work (and fail), thus assuming that context operates in a dynamic, emergent way over time multiple different levels of the social system.

(after Greenhalgh and Manzano 2021)

In order to develop an 'in context' understanding of youth offending and youth justice, the book follows a 'CASE studies' framework. This involves **C**ontextualising and **A**nalysing established, dominant explanations and responses to inform **S**olutions for constructing complex, contextualised and innovative explanations/responses that **E**volve knowledge and understanding of youth offending and youth justice (CASE). These overarching CASE studies' aims are pursued by challenging and contextualising the arguments presented throughout the book.

Challenge: This critical, evidence-based textbook will help readers evaluate the explanations of youth offending (e.g. measures, definitions, theories) and youth justice responses (e.g. interventions, programmes) to it that have dominated youth justice systems across the globalised Western world.[1] Challenge adopts a critical 'lens' (i.e. perspective, way of viewing) to understanding youth offending and youth justice as complex, constructed and contextualised. It coheres around the golden thread of criticism that

DOI: 10.4324/9781003498100-1

explanations of and responses to youth offending have been dominated by conceptual, methodological and practical 'reductionism.' This central concept refers to a tendency towards oversimplification that is mobilised by strategies of 'partiality' (i.e. bias and incompleteness), 'individualisation' (i.e. exclusive or predominant focus on the individual) and 'decontextualisation' (i.e. ignoring or marginalising the influence of broader, dynamic, non-individualised contexts). Accordingly, the most common and 'hegemonic' (i.e. dominant) explanations and responses have been founded on evidence bases generated using narrow, restricted quantitative, experimental methodologies. Such reductionism has encouraged linear, deterministic and decontextualised understandings of youth offending that individualise 'criminogenic' (i.e. crime-causing) influences and rely on presumptive conclusions regarding how these influences determine the effectiveness of youth justice interventions. Partial explanations of how and why youth offending occurs and how and why youth justice responses may 'work' are reinforced by/reinforce cultural, disciplinary, socio-structural and power-based biases in the creation of knowledge, evidence and understanding of youth offending, notably:

- Ethnocentrism: bias towards knowledge, evidence and understanding created within, by and for (typically white) populations in Western societies;
- Androcentrism: bias towards knowledge, evidence and understanding created within, by and for male populations;
- Class-centrism: bias towards knowledge, evidence and understanding created by and for the middle class, prioritising study and understanding of the working class from the middle-class perspective;
- Adult-centrism: bias towards knowledge, evidence and understanding created by and for adults, prioritising the study and understanding of children and young people from the adult perspective.

With these biases in mind, therefore, partial explanations of and responses to youth offending should not be accepted as unequivocal facts. Rather, they should be understood as the dynamic, contingent and contested 'social constructions' (i.e. creations, inventions) of powerful individuals, groups and institutions at particular times in particular places and as shaped by influences operating at different levels or 'contexts' of the social system, namely:

- Macro: e.g. socio-historic and socio-economic change, inter/national and local cultures, global, national and local politics and agendas, media mis/representations;
- Meso: e.g. organisational cultures, professional and interpersonal relationships;
- Micro: e.g. individual/professional expertise, experience.

The contextualised conceptual framework outlined above follows 'Ecological Systems Theory,'[2] which depicts a young person's environment as a dynamic (not static) constellation of interconnected contexts and settings within which their development unfolds and is shaped via increasingly complex interactions (Bronfenbrenner 1995; see also France, Bottrell, and Armstrong 2012). Consequently, the CASE studies' aim of this book will be pursued through consistent critical challenge and contextualisation.

Contextualise: This text will identify and explore the inherent challenges to understanding and responding to youth offending 'in context.' As outlined above, it will focus on the contextual influences on youth offending and youth justice operate within and between multiple levels of the social system, including dynamic, contextualised structures, processes, relationships, organisations, places, times, people and situations. Therefore, rather than pursuing understanding of youth offending through reductionist and decontextualised lenses, analytical focus will be placed upon progressive, evidence-based arguments that explore the potential for more dynamic, contextualised perspectives of youth offending and youth justice. These perspectives have the potential to evolve traditionally static and situated understandings of the role and influence of youth offending within children and young people's lives and to articulate a range of appropriate and potentially effective youth justice responses to offending behaviour. Consequently, analyses will prioritise the significance of context, which will be understood as the relational (interacting) and dynamic (changing) features or 'forces' that shape the mechanisms through which youth offending and youth justice are constructed and experienced, rather than conceptualising context in more reductionist terms as observable features (space, place, people, things) that are static and linear in influence (see Greenhalgh and Manzano 2021). Evidence-based arguments will outline new, innovative, progressive understandings, responses and solutions to the perceived 'problems' of increasing youth offending and increasingly ineffective youth justice responses to it. The explanations and responses developed as solutions to these constructed problems are intended to evolve knowledge and understanding towards considerations of more holistic, dynamic, child-centric, constructed and contextualised evidence, knowledge and understandings, thus providing a necessarily complex, comprehensive and valid paradigm for addressing the contemporary social issue or 'problem' of youth offending.

Explaining the 'problem' of youth offending

'Youth offending,' variously labelled at different times in different places as 'juvenile offending' and 'juvenile delinquency,'[3] is a social construction created to categorise criminal behaviour by children and young people.[4] In turn, 'youth justice' can be defined as the label given to the formal, systemic responses to offending behaviour by children and young people, including philosophies, theories, systems, structures, policies, strategies, processes and practices (Case 2021). The concept of youth offending has been socially constructed and reconstructed over time and place through the activities of (typically powerful) social, cultural, economic, political, professional, academic and media influences and influencers. The social construction of youth offending as a distinct behavioural category meriting bespoke examination occurred across Western societies over 200 years ago as a means of differentiating the attitudes, behaviours, experiences and appropriate treatment of children and young people who offend from those relating to adult offenders[5] (Case 2021). Since its initial construction, understanding 'youth offending' has been a highly problematic endeavour. Successive generations of adults have struggled to reconcile their traditional constructions and explanations of children and young people as innocent, vulnerable and in need of care and protection with emerging constructions and explanations of this same group when they offend as highly problematic, threatening, dangerous and in need of control and management. Accordingly, for over two centuries, youth offending has been depicted by powerful social groups (e.g. the ruling- and middle-classes, politicians, media, adults) in the globalised Western world as an ever-growing and increasingly harmful social 'problem' that needs to be 'solved' through youth justice measures in order to protect communities from anxiety and harm, to appease the general public and to save money (Pearson 1983; Arnull and Fox 2016). An associated, perennial claim has been that the problem of youth offending has never been properly addressed or solved due to the perceived ineffectiveness of formal youth justice responses such as sentences, punishments, preventive interventions and rehabilitative programmes (see Pearson 1983; Case 2021). As such, the evolution and exaggeration of youth offending from a social issue into a social 'problem' can be seen as the deliberate social construction of powerful groups, often as a manipulation to meet their agendas, such as gaining political appeal, increasing newspaper readership, appeasing public anxieties and being seen to be 'doing something' about social issues (McAra 2023). Emergent youth justice 'solutions' have typically involved targeting, controlling, managing and otherwise adversely affecting the lives of young people who offend. Individualising the 'problem' of youth offending in this way has encouraged decontextualised[6] examinations of the lives of young people who offend, a cohort disproportionately likely to face socio-structural and systemic disadvantage and discrimination due to their demographic characteristics (e.g. working-class status, black and minority ethnicity) and life experiences (e.g. traumatic and adverse childhood experiences, being victims of crime).

In focus: The social construction of official statistics on youth offending and youth justice

Evidence of the extent and nature of the social 'problem' of youth offending and the systemic 'problem' of ineffective youth justice responses to it across the globalised Western world has been founded in another social construction or 'social product' (Box 1983), official statistics. Statistics are typically labelled (constructed) as 'official' if they represent data on youth offending behaviour and youth justice responses that have been recorded (constructed) by government departments (e.g. UK Ministry of Justice, USA Office of Juvenile Justice and Delinquency Prevention, Australian Bureau of Statistics) and youth justice agencies, for example, police, courts, youth justice teams, probation and prison services. Despite the socially constructed nature of official statistics, examining statistical trends and patterns in the extent and nature of officially recorded offending by young people over time can be an extremely useful form of analysis for achieving a better understanding of youth offending and youth justice. For example, it establishes baseline measures of the trajectory and development of 'official' youth offending over time within and between countries and demographic sub-groups within and between these countries (e.g. categorised by age, gender, ethnicity). Equivalent analyses of youth justice can examine trends and patterns in the extent and nature of out-of-court and court sentencing within formal youth justice systems (Case 2021).

Official statistics are inherently reductionist and limited in scope, however, because they do not measure the 'dark figure' of unreported and unrecorded crime. This omission can render them partial in the sense of bias (towards reported and recorded crime), incomplete and potentially invalid (inaccurate). In addition, whilst they are not necessarily unreliable in a sense of being inconsistent or non-replicable, official statistics *can* be unreliable and incomplete if the recording practices of official agencies change over time or vary within and between countries. For example, at the national level in the UK, there was widespread inconsistency in police recording statistics between local force areas until 2002, which fostered partial and unreliable analysis of local and national trends in the extent and nature of official youth offending. Internationally, problems of reliability and validity emerge when making cross-cultural/national comparisons if recording practices differ between nation-states (Dunkel 2014). International comparisons are made even more problematic by socio-historical and contemporary/current cross-national differences in the construction of 'youth offending,' for example, regarding how different countries have legislated their minimum age of criminal responsibility.

Youth offending and youth justice as constructed realities

Youth offending and youth justice are presented as the contextualised social constructions by powerful institutions, organisations and people in specific societies during specific historical periods, often through deciding on the definitions, explanations, labels and measures allocated to the specific behaviours of other, less powerful groups and individuals. Therefore, what is understood to be 'youth offending' and 'youth justice' in a given context at a given time is inherently and necessarily constructed and complex in the sense of:

- *Dynamic:* varying wildly and rapidly over time and place;
- *Contingent:* dependent on (dynamic) historical, cultural, social, economic and political contexts;
- *Contested:* subject to (dynamic and contingent) debate, disagreement and differences/lack of consensus across history and between and within countries, organisations, professions and individuals.

Consequently, youth offending and youth justice are best viewed as 'constructed realities,' rather than as unequivocal facts, because the social, organisational and individual realities of what is understood as youth offending and youth justice are subject to construction at a given point in time and can be subject to reconstruction in the future. It is instructive, therefore, to conceptualise youth offending and youth justice as social constructions for at least three key reasons, which combine to enhance knowledge and understanding of both:

1. **Validity:** Examining youth offending and youth justice as social constructions provides the most accurate, comprehensive and realistic understanding of what the phenomena actually are – the complex products (constructed realities) of a series of dynamic, contingent and contested influences, rather than universal facts that can be uncritically accepted;
2. **Reliability:** If stakeholders and interested parties are clear about exactly how these concepts have been 'operationalised' (i.e. defined, measured, categorised), then they can be consistent/replicable in how they are analysed, explained and understood;
3. **Explanatory utility:** Understanding youth offending and youth justice as dynamic, contingent and contested social constructions provides the intellectual, analytical and professional space to explain these behaviours and responses differently in different contexts (i.e. in contextualised ways) and permits analyses of the range of potential historical, economic, cultural, political, professional, intellectual, media and public influences and influencers that have shaped these constructions.

Why understand youth offending in context?

With the previous discussions in mind, there may be an internal validity[7] issue with claims that Western society has suffered from a perennial youth crime 'problem.' In fact, it has been argued that the widely accepted and long-standing problematisation of youth crime has been founded on reductionist understandings grounded in narrow, over-simplified, partial and decontextualised evidence-bases (see Chapters 1 and 2). Indeed, youth offending and youth justice are likely to be highly complex, dynamic and contextualised social 'issues' (not necessarily 'problems') that necessitate similarly complex, dynamic and contextualised investigation, knowledge-bases, evidence-bases and understandings. Therefore, employing a critical analytical lens of complexity, construction and contextualisation could significantly improve understanding of youth offending, which, in turn, could be employed to inform more effective, efficient, economical and evidence-based youth justice responses and solutions. Alternative, improved understandings of youth offending can provide valuable perspective and context around a complex issue and can enhance systemic and professional youth justice responses to it, whilst potentially reducing the extent and nature of youth offending, youth justice sanctions and interventions, and the harm, fear and cost to communities, victims and young people who offend (Case 2021).

There remain significant challenges, however, to progressing understandings of youth offending and youth justice 'in context' through a focus on potentially criminogenic influences that are contextualised and their potential interactions with criminogenic influences that are individualised. Challenges to developing contextualised understandings of youth offending and youth justice are typically located within the structural, systemic, organisational and professional levels of the social system that influence their social construction (see earlier). Politically, in national and local contexts, there can be inevitable resistance to exploring external, non-individualised criminogenic influences that governments and politicians may be in some way held responsible for causing, exacerbating and 'ameliorating' (i.e. treating, making better) through the investment of time, money and political capital. Academically, there are long-standing, embedded disciplinary barriers across the social sciences, such as theoretical, methodological and conceptual biases, combined with reticence and resistance to challenging the 'status quo' of established paradigms, knowledge-bases, evidence-bases and understandings (see Chapter 1) that have informed political and policy-based constructions of youth offending and youth justice. Publicly, there are existential and psychological challenges to adding necessary complexity to established and accepted understandings because human nature seeks clarity and simplicity, especially when explaining social issues that cause anxiety and require control/management. Such simplicity is often achieved by substituting uncertainty, nuance and evidence for so-called common sense, heuristics (short-cuts), lazy stereotypes and sensationalised generalisations (e.g. to drive mass media viewer/readership, to win political favour with the general public). In other words, reductionism and decontextualisation.

The structure of 'Youth offending in context: Challenges and solutions'

Chapter 1 analyses 'The problem of decontextualised youth offending' by critically exploring the explanations of youth offending that have dominated criminological understandings across the 20th and 21st centuries in the globalised Western world. Critical discussion focusses on the 'Classical/Neo-Classical,' Individual Positivist,' 'Integrated' and 'Artefactual Risk-Based' explanatory theories that have situated the causes of youth offending primarily within the individual. It is argued that such individualising theories are 'reductionist' because they reduce, minimise and narrow potentially complex, comprehensive and contextualised explanations of the criminogenic influences on youth offending to a focus on over-simplified, partial and decontextualised factors operating in linear, deterministic ways. The chapter evidences how this 'explanatory reductionism' and partiality towards micro-level criminogenic influences have been privileged at the expense of examining the role of a broader range of macro-level economic, political, socio-structural, cultural and demographic criminogenic influences, meso-level situational, relational, interactional, systemic and experiential criminogenic influences and the (macro-level) ethnocentric and androcentric biases inherent to the construction of these dominant theories.

Chapter 2 follows logically from the opening chapter by exploring 'The problem of decontextualised youth justice.' The chapter asserts that the ways in which youth offending has been discussed, theorised and understood are critical to the construction of youth justice responses, notably interventions seeking to prevent and reduce it. The chapter begins with a detailed exploration of the overarching 'models,' rationales and principles that have shaped social constructions of youth justice in international, westernised youth justice systems historically, charting their trajectory from a long-standing, dominant 'welfare versus justice debate' into more punitive, neo-liberal and neo-correctional models underpinned by developmental, individualising explanatory theories and youth justice interventions. There follows an analysis of 'evidence-based' youth justice and its realisation through actuarial risk management animated by the quasi-experimental 'Risk Factor Prevention Paradigm' and the closely associated 'What Works' framework for evaluating the 'effectiveness' of youth justice interventions. The chapter concludes that adopting a developmental, individualising, risk-based lens to shaping 'effective' responses to youth offending has perpetuated a decontextualised focus on 'treating' and 'correcting' problems and deficits located in individualised, psychosocial domains of young people's lives, rather targeting broader, contextualised influences that can be criminogenic in their own right and can interact with and/or exacerbate psychosocial influences leading to youth offending.

Chapter 3 follows up and evolves the arguments from chapter one by 'Explaining youth offending in context,' emphasising four categories of explanatory/aetiological theory that incorporate contextual considerations to varying degrees. Firstly, there is an evaluation of 'Sociological Positivist theories' with explanatory foci that are sociological/immediate social, socio-systemic and socio-structural, so situating criminogenic influences as external to the individual young person. Then, 'Quasi-Contextualised Risk Factor Theory' is discussed as offering explanations that have begun to incorporate contextual considerations of the criminogenic interactions between psycho-social risk factors, structural context, in/formal social controls and critical life events, whilst also considering that young people can construct, make meaning of, negotiate and resist their exposure to risk and thus shape their pathways into/out of crime. Thirdly, theories of 'Critical Criminology' are interrogated in terms of their central argument that 'crime' is a socially constructed product born of unequal power relations in society, which typically disadvantages less powerful groups. As such, critical theories are presented as having challenged the Classical-Positivist orthodoxy and the way in which it constructs 'crime' and the 'problem' of youth offending. The chapter ends with a critique of critical theories from a fourth theory, 'Left Realism,' which asserts that Critical Criminology romanticises, idealises and underestimates the realities of youth offending and its real-world impacts on victims and communities. Consequently, this chapter provides an exploration of contextualised criminogenic and criminalising influences situated at different levels of the social system (e.g. macro, meso, micro), including the influences upon how youth offending is constructed and reconstructed in different contexts at different times.

Chapter 4 considers ways of 'Responding to youth offending in context.' It explores the academic, political and professional contextualised responses to youth offending that have expanded upon the asserted theoretical, methodological and ethical limitations of their predecessors, thus providing a degree of 'expansionism[8]' that directly challenges the reductionism of decontextualised responses to youth offending in the Western world. Following the discussion of the emerging complexity and hybridity of approaches to constructing youth justice in contemporary westernised youth justice systems, emphasis is placed upon four categories of contextualised youth justice response. Initially, there is a critical review of the application and 'effectiveness' of 'Social Crime Prevention' in the form of 'Community Crime Prevention' interventions that focus on individuals and the social contexts within which they offend, in order to identify the social causes of crime, rather than trying to treat or correct its symptoms. There follows a critical review of the contextualised 'Realist Synthesis' and 'EMMIE' approaches to designing, administering and evaluating crime prevention programmes by unpacking 'what works for whom, in what circumstances, in what respects, and how?' (Pawson 2013). There is then a critical review of 'Child-Friendly Justice' as a progressive and expansionist approach to youth justice that is explicitly situated within a children's rights context advocating for bespoke structural and systemic contexts and processes for young people who offend, notably welfare-based and prevention-focused minimum necessary intervention delivered in youth justice systems that are distinct from adult criminal justice systems. Finally, the principle, strategy and model of 'Child First' justice is presented as an expansionist challenge to reductionist youth justice that has been mobilised by a series of principles/tenets promoting broader evidence-based understandings of and responses to youth offending. This includes a discussion of a range of macro-level (e.g. cultural, structural, systemic) and meso-level (e.g. relational, interpersonal, procedural) contextual influences that have shaped the development and evolution of Child First, including expanding evidence-bases, principled debates, consideration of socio-economic changes and socio-political dynamism, often resulting from major national and global events. The chapter concludes by emphasising how contextualised methodologies and perspectives enable professional stakeholders (e.g. academics, policymakers, practitioners) to better articulate and conceptualise the criminogenic influences in children's lives and the ways in which youth justice interventions are expected to work.

The Discussion chapter revisits the central challenge of this book, that of 'Reimagining youth offending and youth justice in context.' It begins with a summary of the four main thematic chapters of the book, which sought to understand youth offending and youth justice 'in context' by unpacking and critically reviewing traditionally dominant, reductionist explanations of youth offending (Chapter 1) and youth justice intervention responses to youth offending (Chapter 3). These reductionist explanations and responses are compared with contemporary expansionist, contextualised explanations (Chapter 2) and youth justice intervention approaches (Chapter 4). There follows a summary review of the extent and nature of evidential, explanatory and responsive reductionism in dominant understandings of youth offending and effective youth justice in Western youth justice systems, focussing on the risk resilience, cognitive dissonance and bifurcation that continue to shape understandings and approaches. This leads into a critical discussion of the emerging evidential, explanatory and responsive expansionism across youth justice systems, with an emphasis on the contextual promise of Child First justice, the structural, systemic and practical challenges and opportunities it faces, and the potential for its constructive alignment with rights-based Child-Friendly Justice. The chapter concludes by offering a set of '5Cs' as potential 'solutions' to meeting the challenge of understanding youth offending in context: Challenge, complexity, construction, child-centrism and contextualisation.

Notes

1 That is, the United Kingdom and Ireland, Europe, North America, Australasia and parts of Asia, most notably Japan and South Korea.

2 Bronfenbrenner subsequently outlined two further levels of the social system: *exosystems* comprising the connections and interactions between two or more settings that are outside the young person, yet which have a direct impact upon processes within their immediate setting (e.g. between a young person's home life

and a parent's criminal activities); and *chronosystems*, understanding time as not only an aspect of the growing person but also of their surrounding environment, manifested in changes in family structures, employment or housing status, and even 'the degree of hecticness and ability in everyday life' (Bronfenbrenner 1995: 40).

3 In their review of non-Western world juvenile justice systems, Friday and Ren (2006) distinguished between 'delinquency' and 'youth offending.' They assert that in non-Western juvenile justice systems, for example, delinquency is the label given to less serious offending behaviour committed by a young person in need of protection, whereas youth offending is considered more serious and deserving of punishment. However, the authors cautioned that 'the fine distinction between youthful offender and delinquent and between the need for help and the demand for punishment is cultural' and that 'definitions and interpretations are fluid' (Friday and Ren 2006: 16).

4 In terms of social construction, what constitutes a 'child' or 'young person' has differed within and between Western societies over time. Similarly, the social construction of 'youth offending' has differed historically within and between Western societies and youth justice systems, for example, in terms of the minimum age of criminal responsibility. However, for the purposes of consistency and alignment with the social construction of 'youth offending' in most places at most times (although see the discussion of 'Child First' in Chapter 4), the term young people will be most commonly employed throughout this book.

5 This followed the social construction of 'childhood' and 'adolescence' as distinct developmental periods requiring bespoke explanation and treatment (Muncie 2021), constructions that offered societies a framework for understanding the behaviour of children and young people differently from adults (Case 2021).

6 The decontextualisation of 'youth offending' and 'youth justice' is not a modern phenomenon; rather, it is embedded within the socio-historical trajectories of westernised youth justice systems (see Case 2021). Indeed, the elimination from academic and empirical understandings of youth offending and youth justice of contextualised criminogenic influences, such as the young person's socio-structural background and the critical life events they have experienced, can be traced back to nascent constructions of the 'young offender' in the late 18th- and early 19th-century United Kingdom (May 1973), the USA (Soung 2011) and Australia (Cunneen 2008).

7 The extent to which an argument accurately represents reality and/or supports a claim.

8 In this context and henceforth in the book, 'expansionism' relates to the broadening of constructions of 'children,' 'youth offending' and 'youth justice' in terms of how they are conceptualised, operationalised, explained, examined, evidenced and understood, in order to explicitly challenge and evolve the traditional reductionism in these areas. Expansionism is most definitely not intended here, however, to relate to the turn of the 21st-century neo-liberal project of deliberately increasing the numbers of young people sucked into youth justice systems through 'net-widening' and subject to an increasing range, frequency and intensity of intervention through the strategy of 'interventionism' (see Case 2021; Goldson 2010).

1 The problem of decontextualised youth offending

This opening thematic chapter critically explores the theories that have dominated criminological explanations and understandings of youth offending throughout the 20th and 21st centuries in the globalised Western world. Focus is placed upon Classical, Neo-Classical, Positivist and Artefactual Risk-Based theories, each of which are 'aetiological' (i.e. explanatory, focused on the causal origins of behaviours) and each of which situates the causes of youth offending primarily within the individual young person. It will be argued that such individualising theories are reductionist because they reduce and minimise potentially complex, comprehensive and contextualised explanations of the 'criminogenic' (i.e. crime-causing) influences on youth offending to a narrow focus on over-simplified, partial and decontextualised factors that influence youth offending in linear and deterministic ways (see Introduction chapter). This 'explanatory reductionism' and its inherent partiality towards micro-level, 'psychosocial' (i.e. psychological and immediate social) criminogenic influences dominate Western world theories of youth offending, at the expense of examining a broader range of macro-level economic, political, socio-structural, cultural and demographic influences and biases (e.g. ethno-, andro-, class- and adult-centrism) that could contribute to explanations of youth offending (Cox 2021; Myers, Goddard, and Davidtz 2021). Furthermore, a range of potential meso-level criminogenic influences has been marginalised in explanatory theories of youth offending, including the role of immediate situation/environment, relationships, interactions, system contact and young people's constructions of their personal experiences. Therefore, to explain youth offending with an appropriate degree of complexity and completeness, the reductionist partiality and decontextualisation of dominant aetiological explanations must be identified, unpacked, evaluated and addressed, most obviously, by seeking to understand youth offending 'in context.'

Criminology has spawned many theories of crime causation that have fluctuated in popularity over time, all of which originated in the globalised Western world and most of which have been focused on children and young people (Bruinsma 2016). Notwithstanding the multiplicity of explanatory theories across the historical trajectory of criminological thought, the explanations of youth offending that have dominated academic criminology and

DOI: 10.4324/9781003498100-2

youth justice system responses in the Western world have largely located the causes of crime within the individual young person and can be categorised as 'individual' explanations. This chapter explores these individual theories of youth offending,[1] starting with a discussion of the earliest explanatory theories from the Classical school of criminological thought, which assert that individuals offend due to rational choice, free will and their desire to maximise the personal benefits/rewards of crime and to minimise the costs (e.g. punishment). It will be acknowledged that these explanations have subsequently been updated through the 'Neo-Classical Compromise,' which accommodated the possibility for the rational choices of young people to be restricted, bounded and mitigated to a degree by external factors outside of their control. There follows a detailed examination of the explanatory theories from the Positivist school, which studies the social world and identifies the causes of human behaviour using the methods of the natural sciences. It will be argued that theories of Individual Positivism dominated early criminological understandings of youth offending and have been advocated as scientific, empirical (verifiable by observation or experience) and evidence-based theories to challenge the non-evidenced 'armchair theorising' of Classical theories (Hopkins-Burke 2016). Finally, the chapter explores the contemporary Artefactual Risk Factor Theories that have gained explanatory popularity since the 1990s, typically through integration and reformulation of Neo-Classical and Individual Positivist explanations in order to identify 'predictors' of youth offending as targets for preventative interventions in youth justice systems.

Individual explanations of youth offending: Classicism

The original academic explanations of offending in the social sciences came from the Classical school in the 18th century, mainly from two criminologist philosophers: Cesare Beccaria (1738–1794) in Italy and Jeremy Bentham (1748–1832) in England. Both Beccaria and Bentham asserted that all individuals (including young people) are rational actors (Hopkins-Burke 2019) possessing free will and the capability of making rational choices whether to offend or be law-abiding, based on balancing the benefits of committing crime against the costs of being caught and punished (Cornish and Clarke 1987; see also Bruinsma 2016; Akers 2017). Bentham believed that offending contravened the principle of 'utilitarianism' – that an action should deliver the greatest good to the greatest number of people. Early Classical explanations agreed on free will and rational choice as the cause of offending and looked no further for more complex explanations; neither were they concerned with conducting research to provide evidence to support their theories. Their main objective was to inform appropriate criminal justice responses, which led to recommendations for proportionate, certain and speedy punishment (Beccaria 1963/1767) that outweighed the benefits of crime (Bentham 1970). Classicism argues that certain individuals will inevitably offend if given the chance and if the benefits of offending are considered sufficient to take the risk. Consequently, Classicism advocated a deterrence approach to criminal justice – the need to increase the perceived risk of offenders being caught and punished in order to deter (dissuade) them from offending (Akers 2017). Classical school recommendations (e.g. deterrent punishment) supported a crime control response to offending, understanding the behaviour as inevitable and thus needing to be controlled, rather than seeking to identify and treat its supposed causes, which may span beyond personal choice. Crucially, Classical theorists asserted that young people have the same capacity for free will and rational thought and considered decision-making as adults. This assumption has been the subject of much criticism in light of subsequent theoretical and empirical/evidential developments in understanding children's cognitive development (Piaget 1932, in Case 2021) and moral development (Kohlberg 1958, in Case 2021) as maturing more slowly than that of adults. These critical challenges have raised serious questions over whether young people should be held fully responsible for their offending behaviour and, if so, at what age.

Subsequent 'Neo-Classical' explanatory theories[2] (with 'neo' meaning new, revised and updated) have questioned the degree to which offending and *youth* offending specifically are influenced by rational choice as opposed to biological and psychological factors (see theories of Individual Positivism – this chapter) or socio-structural factors (see theories of Sociological Positivism – Chapter 3) and systemic factors (see theories of Critical Criminology – Chapter 3). These critiques, combined with the natural tendency of academic theories to evolve through test and challenge, ultimately led the Classical school to re-evaluate its reductionist, overly simplistic explanations of offending. Accordingly, Neo-Classical theorists have reconstructed the role of free will and rational choice as only one (albeit significant) element of more holistic, multi-factor, integrated explanations since the 1980s (e.g. the Rational Choice Theory of Clarke 1987; the Routine Activities Theory of Cohen, Kluegel and Land 1981). This 'Neo-Classical Compromise' position advocates that free will and rational choice are 'mitigated' (i.e. addressed, alleviated, made less influential) by other factors in the lives of 'vulnerable' groups such as young people, the mentally ill and the learning disabled (e.g. Akers 1991; Wilson and Herrnstein 1985). As such, Neo-Classical explanations occupy a compromise position between the explanatory theories of Classicism and Individual Positivism.

Individual explanations of youth offending: Individual positivism

A theoretical challenge to Classicism emerged in the second half of the 19th century from the Positivist School of Criminology, which advocated the use of research methods adopted from the natural sciences (chemistry, biology, physics) to collect quantitative (numerical, statistical) data and evidence regarding the causes of behaviour such as (youth) offending. This data and evidence were considered to be 'empirical' – obtained via study and direct experience using experiment and observation. Positivists produced aetiological explanations of crime, which were then employed to inform responses that targeted these causes through treatment, rehabilitation and preventative intervention. In direct contrast to Classical explanations based on free will and rational choice, Positivist theories viewed offending as predetermined by biological and psychological factors that were internal to the individual (typically young males), along with sociological factors external to the individual (see discussion of Sociological Positivism in Chapter 3). As such, Positivists perceive individuals who offend as 'predetermined actors,' those whose actions are predestined when exposed to certain internal or external influences, rather than as rational actors who choose to offend (Hopkins-Burke 2019). Like the Classicism they challenged, Positivist explanations took the definition of crime for granted as an agreed 'fact,' rejecting any consideration that 'youth offending' can be a dynamic, contested and contingent social construction created and shaped by historical, global, cultural political, academic, professional and media influences (Case 2021).

Individual explanations of youth offending: Biological positivism

The initial Positivist theories of offending were individual in nature (hence 'Individual Positivism'), concentrating on the internal biological and psychological (also known as 'biopsychological') influences on offending, typically identified through the 'class-centric' (i.e. dominated by a focus on the working class) research with young working-class males in the globalised Western world. Biological Positivism focussed mainly on the criminogenic potential of physical characteristics and genetic inheritance, moving towards latterly neuroscientific considerations of the role of brain development. From the early 20th century onwards, theories of Psychological Positivism began gaining in popularity and overtook Biological Positivist theories as the dominant aetiological explanations of youth offending.

Biological positivism: Physical characteristics

The seminal Biological Positivist theory of offending was provided by Cesare Lombroso in his book 'L'Uomo Delinquente' or 'On Criminal Man' (Lombroso 1875). Lombroso compared the physical characteristics of a group of imprisoned adult offenders with those of a group of non-offenders (at least, men who had not been formally identified or convicted as offenders). He observed that the imprisoned offenders were more likely to have larger ears, sloping foreheads, crooked noses and long arms than their non-offender comparison group. These 'atavistic' (i.e. less-evolved, primitive, throwback) characteristics were correlated statistically with established definitions/measures of 'offending' (with no consideration that the category may be socially constructed) and viewed as criminogenic.

Towards the middle of the 20th century, other criminologists began to consider the potential influence of physique on offending behaviour. Notably, William Sheldon (1949) utilised somatotyping, the categorisation of the human physique, to conclude that physique is correlated with individual temperament and mental well-being, all of which could influence criminality. Sheldon studied 200 boys who had been housed in a reformatory school in Boston, USA, and found that boys with the more muscular and athletic mesomorph physique were most likely to have an aggressive and violent personality correlated with offending. In contrast, boys with small, weak, fragile ectomorph physiques were more likely to be intellectual and introverted, whilst the heavier, softer endomorphs were more likely to be friendly and sociable in personality. Sheldon's conclusion, therefore, was that offenders were more likely to have the mesomorphic physique linked to aggression and violence.

Although Lombroso's 'scientific' methodology seems rather crude by today's standards, at the time it was a groundbreaking and innovative means of criminological investigation, and an advance from the non-evidenced 'armchair theorising' of Classical criminologists (Hopkins-Burke 2016). Lombroso's seminal form of Biological Positivism was the first criminological theory to utilise controlled comparisons in order to identify the differences between 'offenders' and 'non-offenders'; differences that were then explained as potential causes of offending. Sheldon's somatotypes did likewise, categorising and differentiating individuals by the physique, then correlating these differences with offending behaviour. As such, both studies employed a 'quasi' (partly, almost) experimental method, but without direct manipulation of the variables under examination (physical characteristics) to generate evidence-based theories.

However, the methods of both Lombroso and Sheldon can be criticised as inherently biased (partial) because their so-called 'experimental' groups had already been formed and officially constructed through individuals being identified, convicted and placed in a prison or reformatory for reasons unconnected to their physical characteristics. Consequently, neither Lombroso nor Sheldon was able to conclusively determine whether physical characteristics exerted any causal influence on offending behaviour. Instead, the physical characteristics of their 'experimental' groups were simply correlated with offending behaviour in the sense of being present at the same time as offending behaviour in the lives of offenders. But correlations are not causes (see Wikström and Treiber 2017; Case et al. 2017). Indeed, certain physical characteristics may even have been symptoms themselves caused by imprisonment (e.g. obtaining a broken nose in a prison fight, developing a muscular physique whilst in custody doing manual work), they may have been the products of other influences (e.g. biological, psychological, sociological) or they may have had no relationship with offending behaviour at all. Consequently, it could be argued that Lombroso's and Sheldon's conclusions were largely based on supposition, rather than conclusive proof of any tangible relationship with offending, causal or otherwise. Finally, early theories of Biological Positivism focussing on physical characteristics can be criticised for lacking a degree of relevance as contemporary explanations of youth offending because they simply did not focus on young people specifically. It could be argued, therefore, that their 'ecological validity' (i.e. the ability to accurately represent real-world behaviour) is significantly diminished because young people are yet to fully develop into adults physically (not to mention psychologically or emotionally), so they may lack the (full) physical characteristics that Lombroso and Sheldon identified as criminogenic. In addition, the explanatory utility of early theories of Biological Positivism is restricted to explaining offending by white, westernised males and, as such, can be accused of androcentrism and ethnocentrism.

Biological positivism: Genetic inheritance

Towards the end of the 19th century, the focus of Biological Positivism turned to genetic inheritance and the potential for 'pathological' (i.e. causing disease, illness, behavioural disorder) genes to be passed down through families (Azeredo et al. 2019). In 1877, Richard Dugdale published his study of the Jukes family from New York. Having traced over 1000 family members, Dugdale concluded that over a quarter of the family members studied were criminals, implicating some influence of genetic inheritance. These early suggestions that genetic inheritance could be criminogenic were consolidated by Goddard's (1914) study of the family of Martin Kallikak, who had an illegitimate son by a woman of 'low birth.' Goddard found that the relations of Kallikak's illegitimate son were more likely to be criminal than those of his 'legitimate' family. The common conclusion from these formative biological studies of genetic inheritance was that it was possible to inherit undesirable genetic characteristics that predisposed an individual to crime (Hopkins-Burke 2019; see also Azeredo et al. 2019). However, like Lombroso and Sheldon before them, these (individual) Biological Positivist studies employed a quasi-scientific method with preformed groups (families) and identified biological correlates with offending, not direct causes, despite the manner in which the researchers presented their findings. Furthermore, genetic inheritance studies to that point could neither rule out nor account for the criminogenic influence of socio-environmental and sociological factors (nurture), nor their potential influence on biological factors (nature).

Subsequently, twin studies gained popularity in the 1970s as a method of addressing the perceived limitations of family studies in pinpointing the causal influence of inheritance on youth offending. Initially, twin studies were advocated as more effective in isolating the genetic factors associated with crime as they were able to explore differences in criminality between monozygotic (MZ) twins (identical twins) and dizygotic (DZ) twins (fraternal twins). Two twin studies provided particularly strong evidence that genetic inheritance could play a role in offending behaviour. The first major criminological twin study by Christiansen (1974) found a 52% correlation in criminality between MZ twins (i.e. in 52% of the cases where one twin had offended, so had the other twin) compared to a 22% correlation between DZ twins. The second study reviewed twin research conducted from 1929–1961, identifying a 60% correlation between MZ twins in terms of criminality (i.e. both twins had offended) compared to a 30% correlation between DZ twins (Mednick and Volavka 1980). The main finding was that MZ twins were more prone to offending than DZ twins, concluding that this was due to them sharing a greater proportion of genetic make-up. Comparatively, twin studies were better able to control for genetic differences than family studies, and so researchers felt more confident in concluding a genetic influence on youth offending. However, precisely what was inherited and how this influenced offending remained unclear (see Rutter and Giller 1983).

The perceived methodological limitations of twin studies led criminologists to advocate for adoption studies as a more effective test of the genetic inheritance of criminal predisposition (see Mednick, Moffitt and Stack 1987). The rationale was that twins often shared the same environment, which could in itself contribute to their criminality (i.e. nurture), instead of, or in addition to, the contribution of their biology (i.e. nature). Therefore, studying the criminal outcomes of adopted children with a biological parent who had offended enabled the influence of a shared environment to be eliminated. Following a study of 14,000 adoption cases in Denmark, Mednick and his colleagues (Mednick, Moffitt and Stack 1987) identified that adopted children with a biological parent who had offended were more likely to have offended themselves compared to children with biological parents who had not offended. The logical conclusion was that there must be a degree of genetic inheritance (e.g. a 'criminal gene') that was passed on biologically between parent and child, as the role of shared environment could be excluded in adoption studies – although environmental influences more generally could not.

Although the extent and nature of genetic influence on youth offending appear impossible to pinpoint from these studies, arguments for potential genetic causes of offending have gained credence from successive biological studies of families. As they have progressed, studies of genetic inheritance have sought to rule out or override socio-environmental influences (relating to the physical and social settings in which people live) on offending through the use of twin and adoption studies. However, the socio-environmental context and associated influences can never be entirely ruled out for several reasons. For example, twins are highly likely to share the same environment, whilst the adopted children of criminal parents will still be exposed to environmental factors that could increase their likelihood of committing crimes, whether operating as standalone influences or interacting with biological propensities. Genetic inheritance studies, by their very nature, have seldom considered, measured or analysed environmental (non-individualised) influences. Furthermore, genetic inheritance studies have seldom considered that individuals from 'non-offending' comparison groups (e.g. law-abiding twins, non-offending biological parents of adopted children) may have actually offended but that this behaviour had not been identified, reported, recorded or convicted (i.e. the so-called 'dark figure' of crime – see Introduction chapter) so they had not been constructed/labelled as 'offenders.' This possibility introduces a validity issue in the quasi-experimental comparisons used in genetic inheritance studies. Notwithstanding reductionist limitations in methodological scope and explanatory utility, Biological Positivist studies indicate that genetic inheritance has at least a degree of influence on offending, particularly by young people.

Biological positivism: Neuroscientific theories

Biological Positivist theories of (youth) offending waned in popularity over the course of the 20th century, losing explanatory dominance to theories of Psychological Positivist (see next section). However, the late 20th century and early 21st century evidenced a return to the spotlight for Biological Positivist explanations, due in large part to the growing popularity of neuroscience as a means of physically differentiating the brains of youths from adults and its utility for explaining their (offending) behaviour. New imaging technologies emerged to map human brain development from childhood to adulthood (Bishop and Farber 2007). For example, computerised tomography (CT) scanning enabled the identification of abnormalities in the body, positron-emission tomography (PET) scanning captured radioactive tracers moving through the bloodstream to understand brain functions, the electroencephalogram (EEG) recorded electromagnetic fluctuations in various parts of the brain and functional magnetic resonance imaging (fMRI) could detect changes in brain function when performing specific mental tasks.

Technological advances in brain imaging precipitated significant discoveries about the process of adolescent brain development relative to adult brains (Mercurio et al. 2020; Beckman 2004). One of the first major neuroscientific discoveries was that the adolescent brain massively overproduces 'grey matter,' the brain material responsible for thought, so needs to prune it back. The brain follows this pruning with a myelination process that produces 'white matter' to insulate it and enhance its efficiency (Giedd et al. 1999). Secondly, neuroscientists have discovered that the brain's frontal lobe, which is associated with cognitive reasoning, changes most dramatically during adolescence and is the last region of the brain to fully develop (Sowell et al. 1999). These discoveries indicated that youths are not fully developed physically in relation to their brains and, therefore, are also underdeveloped cognitively, psychologically and socially (Soung 2011). Other neuroscientific studies have demonstrated that stress, trauma and threatening treatment by adults can produce neurochemical changes in adolescents (youths) that can affect their attention, impulse control, ability to form healthy relationships and capacity for remorse and empathy (Mercurio et al. 2020; Perry 2001), all of which can be viewed as criminogenic with regard to youth offending.

These findings support the 'use it or lose it' principle of neuroscience, which argues that adolescent brains become hardwired during a certain time period and in the absence of key experiences and stimulants, their neurological pathways may be lost and their capabilities compromised, which could also have an influence on offending behaviour (Akers 2017; Greenough, Black and Wallace 1987). The implications of these findings for youth justice intervention responses (see Chapters 2 and 4) are conflicted. For example, some neuroscientists view adolescents as developing individuals in need of care and protection, but others view adolescents as hardwired during their formative years and so requiring control and punishment. The implication of this conclusion is that social care and treatment interventions would be wasted on adolescents and so should be reserved for younger children (Soung 2011).

In summary, neuroscientific research in the late 20th and early 21st centuries has identified that cognitive and reasoning processes develop more slowly in adolescence than previously thought. Clearly, such conclusions (if accepted) could have significant implications for how we choose to respond to youth offending, in particular, where we set the appropriate age of criminal responsibility and the degree to which youth justice responses should hold young people responsible for their behaviour. Unlike the Biological Positivists before them, neuroscientists do not claim that biological factors are exclusive explanations for offending behaviour (Jones et al. 2009), instead asserting that biology (especially genetics) and environment both play significant roles in shaping the minds, brain development and behaviours of adolescents (Beckman 2004). Therefore, although neuroscience has focused predominantly on biological brain development, it heralds this as a significant, but not exclusive, influence on youth offending.

Individual explanations of youth offending: Psychological positivism

The emergence of psychology as the dominant social science in the first half of the 20th century increased the popularity of the Positivist method in Criminology, and with that came a new focus on identifying the psychological influences on crime (see Case et al. 2017). A form of Individual Positivism known as Psychological Positivism emphasises how the dynamic cognitive (mental, psychological, thought) processes and characteristics that constitute individual learning and personality could be criminogenic – arguably more so than biological influences. This section examines two main categories of Psychological Positivism related to explaining youth offending: Personality Theory and Learning Theory.

Psychological positivism: Personality theory

Personality Theory explains youth offending as resulting from criminal predisposition and/or criminogenic personality traits that encourage offending (Gungea, Jaunky and Ramesh 2017). One of the earliest (bio)psychological explanations of youth offending was the 'storm and stress' theory of adolescence (G. Stanley Hall 1904). Hall likened the newly constructed developmental period of 'adolescence' to 'storm and stress' – a storm of biological and psychological stressors (e.g. puberty, hormonal and biochemical changes) impacting the adolescent's personality, cognition, emotion and behaviour. Consequently, the developmental stage of adolescence was considered criminogenic due to young people's inability to cope with the significant stressors they experienced. Evidencing exactly how adolescent personality traits led to offending seemed less important to Psychological Positivists than asserting (presuming) that they did. Prioritising assertion over explanation in this way, however, promotes explanatory reductionism and invalidity, blinding researchers to other potential influences on offending, including biology, psychological learning, socio-structural factors, systemic issues and, of course, the role of context.

Later in the 20th century, Hans Eysenck produced a psychologically based, multi-factor explanation of offending that he later applied to youth offending. Eysenck (1970) identified three dimensions of personality: Extroversion (lacking inhibition, impulsive, risk-taking), neuroticism (anxious, nervous, moody) and introversion (passive, reserved). He proposed that individuals are born with a particular structure to their brain's cortex, which affects their ability to learn from and adapt to environmental stimuli. Consequently, extroverts are more prone to offending behaviour because their cortex is under-aroused and so they require more stimulation, which they obtain through impulsive behaviour (e.g. offending). Extrovert children are more difficult to condition (learned/taught through behaviour modification) and have difficulty learning from their environment; deficits which can encourage criminality. In conclusion, Eysenck's Personality Theory combines notions of biological determinism (i.e. behaviour as predetermined through exposure to biological influences) with conditioning (psychological learning) through exposure to socio-environmental factors (Robertson and Azaola 2021; Muncie 2021). However, he never convincingly identified either a direct correlation between extroversion and criminality or a causal link – a common limitation of the confident, yet presumptive, conclusions from theories of Individual Positivism (Hopkins-Burke 2016).

In summary, Personality Theory offers a set of deterministic explanations of abnormal behaviour that have subsequently been applied to explaining youth offending. In this case, it is the undesirable criminogenic traits within an individual's personality (sometimes transient traits, such as in adolescence) that encourage youth offending, rather than learnt behaviour (Robertson and Azaola 2021). The earliest forms of Personality Theory were exclusively psychological, whereas later versions attempted to integrate biological determinism with sociological influences such as social learning. However, aetiological theories highlighting personality as criminogenic (like most theories of Individual Positivism) tend to be limited by reductionist presumptions that statistical correlations equate to real-life causality.

Psychological positivism: Learning theory

Learning Theory explains offending as the result of learning processes favouring committing criminal acts over law-abiding behaviour (e.g. Akers 2017; see also Bruinsma 2016). Early Learning Theory focused on behavioural 'conditioning' (i.e. learning, teaching) in animals through stimulus-response (Classical Conditioning – Pavlov 1927/1960) and through positive and negative reinforcement (Operant Conditioning – Skinner 1938). However, these theories offered little explanation of human behaviour, including offending (see Hopkins-Burke 2016). The influence of learning on offending was initially hypothesised by the Psychodynamic School of Psychology, largely associated with the works of Sigmund Freud and Carl Jung. Theorists from the Psychodynamic School argued that all behaviour results from tensions between the individual's unconscious drives (id) and their conscious understandings of self (ego), morality and social order (superego). Consequently, offending is an outward expression of a psychic conflict when the individual does not learn sufficient measures of self-control to enable them to channel their unconscious drives into socially acceptable acts (Case et al. 2021). Relevant to the central focus of this book, Aichhorn (1925) asserted that children and young people have an underdeveloped ego and superego, which means that they cannot control the 'pleasure principle' driven by the id, which encourages offending behaviour.

The potential role of psychological learning in offending, particularly violent youth offending, was explicated by Albert Bandura's (1973, 1986) 'Social Learning Theory.' Bandura provided explanations based on an integration of Conditioning and Sub-cultural theories, arguing that aggressive behaviour can be learnt by children in social situations through imitating the behaviour of adult role models. Bandura's famous 'Bobo Doll' experiment placed children in a room with a large inflatable doll. An adult entered the room, verbally and physically attacked the doll and was then confronted by the experimenter, who either chastised them or positively reinforced (praised, rewarded) their behaviour. If the child witnessed the adult being positively reinforced, then they were more likely to imitate the aggressive behaviour later in the experiment (due to identifying positively with that adult), suggesting that violent behaviour (e.g. violent offending) can be learnt in childhood through imitation of and identification with adults (Telzer, van Hoorn, Roger and Do 2018).

In summary, the notion that criminal predisposition can be learnt and taught (as opposed to being developed from predisposed personality traits) has been advocated by Psychological Positivism, citing the influence of subconscious learning (Psychodynamic Theory) and learning through imitation (Social Learning Theory). Neither theory explicitly examined offending behaviour, but the principles of both theories have been applied (logically and neatly) to explaining offending and are particularly relevant to the explanation of youth offending due to their basis in explaining young people's 'abnormal' behaviour. Furthermore, whilst Learning Theory typically offers exclusively psychological explanations, Differential Association Theory broadened psychological theorising by integrating explanations to understand how psychological processes could be criminogenic in the young person's social context.

Individual positivism: A conceptual journey towards theoretical, explanatory integration

It has been argued in this chapter that early Positivist explanations of youth offending were individualised in several ways by focussing on individual young people, individual schools of explanatory thought and individual criminogenic influences. However, it must be noted that this generalised overview is itself reductionist, as it oversimplifies a more complex theoretical landscape. Most contemporary Classical and Individual Positivist theories have developed with at least some acknowledgement and even integration of concepts and arguments from other competing theories. For example, Neo-Classical Compromise positions acknowledge that a person's capacity to make fully rational choices is influenced by biological, psychological and sociological factors (Agnew 2011). The forefather of Individual Positivism, Lombroso, eventually accepted that social factors can be far more influential on crime than biological factors. The forefather of Psychological Personality Theory, Eysenck, integrated biological determinism, sociological influences and socio-environmental factors. Sutherland ultimately linked psychological learning with socio-structural (sub-cultural) elements to produce a more integrated theory of youth offending influenced through differential association.

Integrated explanations of youth offending: Integrated individual positivism

A subsequent body of integrated (although still largely individual in focus) Positivist theories has addressed the explanatory and practical weaknesses and limitations of traditional 'individual' theories and built on their tentative nods to integrated explanation to offer more holistic (complete) and potentially valid (accurate) explanations of youth offending. Notably, the resurgence of Biological Positivism in the guise of neuroscience has catalysed the emergence of a range of new, Integrated Biopsychosocial theories offering explanations of crime that combine individualised biological and psychological influences with sociological and environmental (socio-environmental) influences as part of multi-factor, integrated approaches (see Bernard et al. 2015; Vold, Bernard and Snipes 2002). The development of these integrated Positivist and quasi-Positivist explanations is best illustrated by its three most prolific strands of theory: The Social Control Theory of the late 1960s and onwards, the Biopsychosocial Theory of the late 1970s–1980s and 21st-century Biopsychosocial Risk Factor Theory (discussed later in this chapter).

Integrated individual positivism: Social control theory

In contrast to most (indeed, most explanatory theories of offending), Social Control Theory focusses on explaining why people do not commit crimes. Social Control Theory integrates elements of Neo-Classical rational choice with explanations from Psychological and Sociological Positivism to produce a set of associated explanatory theories based on arguably the largest body of empirical evidence in Criminology (Hopkins-Burke 2019; see also Robertson and Azaola 2021). Building on the mid-20th century psychological control theories concerned with the psychological influences (e.g. personality) controlling people's behaviour and stopping them from offending (e.g. Reiss 1951; Nye 1958), 'Social Control Theory' has examined the social factors that bond people to the norms of a given society (e.g. socialisation in the family, school and peer group).

The forefather of Social Control Theory was Travis Hirschi (1969), who produced the original theory to explain why some people obey the law and why others don't. Hirschi (1969: 16) explained that 'delinquent acts result when an individual's bond to society is weaker or broken,' so being law-abiding results from a strong social bond to the rules and norms. Social Control Theory divides this social bond into four elements (see Case et al. 2021):

- Attachment to significant, important people, organisations and institutions (e.g. relationships);
- Commitment to traditional, normal behaviours and actions (e.g. rational choice to conform);
- Involvement in conventional behaviours and activities (i.e. being too busy to commit a crime);
- Beliefs in the importance of normal behaviour and in the other elements of the social bond.

The emphasis on social bonds produced a hybrid, holistic, integrated explanation of offending that fused Rational Choice Theory with elements of Psychosocial and Sociological Positivism (e.g. Strain Theory). As with other explanatory theories, critics have tended to focus on what the theory cannot explain, such as the extent and nature of offending behaviour that may result from weak social bonds (Agnew 2005), the nature of influence that delinquent friends may have and the influence of historical and structural contexts on social bonds and offending behaviour (Case et al. 2021).

Hirschi's original Social Control Theory was extended by Elliott, Ageton and Canter (1979), who argued that offending is the product of weak social bonds resulting from inadequate socialisation in a child's early life. Therefore, strong social bonds and non-offending are the result of effective socialisation. According to Elliott, Ageton and Canter (1979), social bonds are further weakened/strengthened by later socialisation experiences in the home, school and community and especially exposure to delinquent peer groups. Elliott,

Ageton and Canter (1979) added a structural element to Social Control Theory by suggesting that blocked opportunities, social disorganisation, unemployment and economic recession can further weaken social bonds and function as criminogenic, thus integrating arguments from Strain and Social Learning theories.

A subsequent group of theories has been developed since the turn of the 20th century to modify and augment Social Control Theory, including:

- Power Control Theory: This strand of Social Control Theory integrates considerations of gender to argue that patriarchal attitudes in the home can explain gender differences in offending (Schulze and Bryan 2017; Bates, Bader and Mencken 2003). Bates, Bader and Mencken (2003) propose that girls are controlled socially far more than boys in the family setting (usually by mothers who were themselves controlled as girls) and so are less likely to take risks and commit crimes. Offending by girls occurs if the balance of power in controlling the child is shared more equally between parents, and girls are not subjected to excessive control (Bates, Bader and Mencken 2003; see also Hagan 1989).
- Control Balance Theory: Offending results from imbalances in the amount of control an individual has over their own behaviour and the behaviour of others (Tittle 2000, 2018). If a person is subjected to excessive amounts of control (i.e. they experience a 'control deficit'), this can lead to resentment, anger, weak social bonds and ultimately to offending. An excess control over others and over their environment produces a 'control surplus' that can lead to greed, corruption and an obsession with dominance, all of which can lead to offending. Control Balance Theory introduces a need versus greed dichotomy – the need to alleviate a control deficit versus the greed to extend a control surplus.
- Differential Coercion Theory: Offending is the product of exposure to coercion – the pressure to behave in a certain way (Colvin 2000; see also Zavala, Curry and Morales 2020). High levels of consistent coercion, actual or threatened, in the family (e.g. removal of social support), school (e.g. physical force) and neighbourhood (e.g. gang violence, poverty, unemployment) can produce psychosocial deficits that encourage criminal behaviour. Such deficits include weak social bonds (see also Hirschi 1969), low self-control (see also Gottfredson and Hirschi 1990) and an increased commitment to using coercion to achieve personal goals, a process known as 'coercive ideation.'
- The General Theory of Crime: Hirschi collaborated with Michael Gottfredson to produce the 'General Theory of Crime' (Gottfredson and Hirschi 1990), also known as 'Self-Control Theory,' which is an attempt to offer a universal explanation of 'all crimes, at all times' (Gottfredson and Hirschi 1990: 117). The central explanatory mechanism is low self-control, namely that individuals with low self-control are considered more likely to make rational choices to offend, especially

> when they also experienced ineffective parenting during childhood (see also Boccio, Schwartz and Beaver 2022). This single factor cause, low self-control, allegedly provides a universal explanation for all types of crime. However, the general theory of crime largely ignores sociological influences in favour of psychological motivations and immediate rational choices producing low self-control and leading to crime. Due to this very specific explanation, the theory has much more difficulty explaining white-collar and corporate crimes, which are typically the product of long-term, detailed, patient and considered planning, characteristics that seem incompatible with the immediate rational choices implied by the low self-control hypothesis.

As arguably 'the most tested theory of crime causation' (Hopkins-Burke 2019: 218), at least comparable to Artefactual Risk Factor Theories (see next section), Social Control Theory (and its spin-off theories) has an impressive amount of empirical/evidential support, indicative of a reliable/replicable set of explanations that are appropriate, relevant and valid to a range of populations (see Case et al. 2021). These strengths may be attributable (at least in part) to the wide range of criminogenic influences identified, which include socio-structural factors that have been traditionally overlooked or downplayed by Positivist explanatory theories. However, critics assert that Social Control Theory offers an oversimplified and reductionist explanation of crime (Downes and Rock 1998); one that reduces offending to the gratification of basic appetites, either acquisitive (to obtain goals, property), aggressive or sexual (see Hopkins-Burke 2019).

Integrated individual positivism: Biopsychosocial theory

The potential for explaining crime as the result of interactions between biological, psychological and socio-environmental factors (Schwartz, Walsh and Beaver 2019) was introduced by Sarnoff Mednick, who argued that 'the value of biological factors is more limited in predicted antisocial behaviour in individuals who have experienced *criminogenic* social conditions in their rearing' (Mednick, Moffitt and Stack 1987: 68). Mednick's main argument was that humans have natural, biological instincts and urges to commit crime but that most can control these urges. Those who do commit crimes are more likely to be vulnerable in some way, for example, due to their age and lack of physiological and psychological development. They are also likely to experience a combination of biological problems, such as their autonomic nervous system responding slowly to external stimuli such as punishment (Bedoya and Portnoy 2022) and socio-environmental problems, such as inadequate learning of appropriate behaviour in the family and interactions with criminal peer groups. Mednick's Biopsychosocial Theory suggests, therefore, an interaction between nature (biological and psychological factors) and nurture (socio-environmental factors). Subsequently, C. Ray Jeffery (1977) added more psychological factors into the explanatory mix with his Biopsychosocial Theory of crime. Jeffery offered a two-pronged, two-directional ('bifurcated') theory suggesting that the biological and psychological characteristics that people are born with (i.e. nature) can be criminogenic in their own right or can interact with socio-environmental processes such as socialisation (upbringing, being taught social norms) in the family and school (i.e. nurture) to cause offending. For example, biochemical imbalances in the brain could cause youth offending in their own right, but they could also interact with and be exacerbated by socio-environmental factors such as poverty and its associated problems (e.g. poor diet, increased exposure to pollution), which could then lead to behavioural problems and offending (see also Bedoya and Portnoy 2022).

The biopsychosocial interactions proposed by Mednick and Jeffery in the late 1970s were extended in explanatory terms by Wilson and Hernnstein (1985), who concluded that most crime is committed by young men and that, therefore, this group should be the focus of explanations of crime (i.e. explicitly endorsing androcentrism and the neglect of explaining offending by females). Relatedly, 'Right Realism' (see also Chapter three) views crime by young men as the product of an interaction between biological and sociological factors, asserting that:

> It is likely that the effect of maleness and youthfulness on the tendency to commit crime has both constitutional and social origins: that is, it has something to do with the biological status of being a young male and with how the young man has been treated by family, friends and society.
>
> (Wilson and Hernnstein 1985: 69)

In short, the theory argues that being 'male' in terms of both biological 'sex' and sociological and cultural 'gender' means that you may experience different treatment and interactions in society compared to being 'female.' The theory argues that individuals carry certain biological characteristics into the social world (e.g. gender, age, intelligence, personality) that positively or negatively affect their ability to learn the norms of behaviour and to learn from any reinforcement or punishment of behaviour (Robertson and Azaola 2021). The assertion is that some people (e.g. young males) are less likely to receive reinforcement for positive behaviour, but may be more likely to be rewarded for negative behaviour, so they are more likely to choose to become criminals (in a given situation) and to persist with criminal behaviours. Essentially, the Right Realist form of Biopsychosocial Theory integrates rational choice and biopsychosocial explanations in order to recommend the prevention, treatment and punishment of crime by influencing the rational choices of young males to commit crime and to comply with social norms (i.e. their self-control).

So, taken together, what is the extent and nature of the explanatory utility of individualised (Individual and Integrated Individual) Positivist theories of youth offending? Moreover, are there limitations to this explanatory utility if we are seeking comprehensive, valid and contextualised explanations of youth offending to inform effective responses to this behaviour through youth justice and youth crime prevention? A critical overview of theories of Individual and Integrated Individual Positivism highlights five crucial elements of reductionist partiality that narrow, restrict and problematise these explanations:

The reductionist explanations of individual positivism: Partiality 'take five'

1. **Psychosocial bias:** Privileging individualising biological and psychological influences on youth offending neglects the exploration of socio-structural contextual influences and social interactions.
2. **Ignoring 'centrisms':** Ethnocentric, androcentric and class-centric biases in knowledge creation encourage explanations of youth offending that are inherently narrow, biased and unrepresentative of the populations.
3. **Limited explanatory utility:** Static, linear, deterministic explanations and presumptive (e.g. conflating correlation with causality) explanations lack necessary dynamism, flexibility and nuance.
4. **Narrow methodological lens:** Privileging experimental methods and quantitative data over qualitative methodologies and data that explore socially constructed influences and experiences inherently limits the explanatory scope of aetiological theories, as does understanding 'youth offending' as an uncontested fact, not as a dynamic, contested and contingent social construction.
5. **Ignoring context:** Continued neglect of meso-level, relational influences and macro-level socio-structural influences (albeit with some tentative exploration in latter integrated theories), compounded by a lack of consistent explanatory focus on young people, produces decontextualised and adult-centric explanations of youth offending that lack applicability to their target population (young people) and to particular groups within it (e.g. based on ethnicity, gender).

Individual explanations of youth offending: Artefactual risk factor theories

Since the 1990s, a movement of quasi-Positivist, quantitative and 'artefactual' risk-based theories has come to dominate westernised explanations of and responses to offending by children and young people (Case 2022; Case and Haines 2009). These risk-based theories explain youth offending as the result of exposure to damaging and deterministic influences and experiences in early life (e.g. childhood, early adolescence) that are predominantly located in individual domains of life: Biological, psychological and immediate social (e.g. family, education, neighbourhood) and that are predictive of offending in later life (e.g. later adolescence, adulthood). As such, risk-based theories can be characterised as 'developmental' in explanatory terms as they conceptualise the causes of offending as developing in influence as the individual grows older. Within Artefactual Risk Factor theories (ARFTs), criminogenic (typically) psychosocial influences and experiences are quantified into numerical, statistical 'factors' or 'artefacts' (hence these theories are 'artefactual' – Kemshall 2008) and commonly labelled 'risk factors.' ARFTs can be considered quasi-Positivist because they typically employ surveys to generate explanatory evidence (not the empirical experiments and observations favoured by individual Positivists) to identify predictors of offending (not causes of offending) – characterising the influence of these predictors as deterministic (i.e. quasi-causal). ARFTs retain the Positivist claim to being based on 'scientific,' objective and value-free research and retain the Positivist explanatory focus on the individual, rather than looking further afield for more contextualised, socio-structural and systemic explanations of youth offending. Two central categories of individual ARFTs can be identified: Developmental Risk Factor Theory and Integrated Developmental Risk Factor Theory.

Developmental risk factor theory

This form of ARFT explains the criminogenic influence of biological, psychological and sociological (i.e. immediate social influences, such as those within family, education, community, peers) factors across childhood and adolescence; hence, it is labelled as 'developmental.' Equivalent theories tracing the criminogenic influence of such factors into adulthood are called 'Life Course' or 'Developmental Life Course' theories. The most influential versions of Developmental Risk Factor Theory have been 'Multi-factor Developmental Theory' and the 'Criminal Careers Model.'

Developmental risk factor theory: Multi-factor developmental theory

The seminal (Developmental) Risk Factor Theory in Criminology was the 'Multi-Factor Developmental Theory' of Sheldon and Eleanor Glueck (1930, 1950). In '500 Criminal Careers,' Glueck and Glueck (1930) investigated 510 young male adults imprisoned in the Massachusetts Reformatory (USA) from 1911–1922, conducting observations and interviews with the men and their families and tracing their life histories before sentencing, during their imprisonment, whilst on parole and for five years post-completion of their sentences. For the Gluecks, the reformatory was failing in its objectives due to an 80% reoffending rate amongst young people post-parole. They questioned whether there were factors identified in the young men's life histories (e.g. prior to incarceration) that predisposed them to reoffend and so should be addressed by reformatory and post-parole programmes (see also Case and Haines 2009). From their interviews, the Gluecks identified common psychosocial characteristics, circumstances and experiences in the lives of the young men prior to their incarceration. Having quantified (factorised) these characteristics/circumstances/experiences into factors using ratings and categorisation tables, the researchers found that the most influential were located in the psychosocial domains of family (e.g. parental criminality), school (e.g. educational underachievement), lifestyle (e.g. keeping bad company) and individual/personality (e.g. low intelligence). They concluded that exposure to certain factors in early childhood and adolescence increased the risk of later (recorded) offending – the original 'risk factors' for offending (Glueck and Glueck 1930). The Gluecks also concluded that the main influence on desistance from offending was maturation; young people stopping offending was evidenced as a natural consequence of ageing and growing up. This finding raises serious questions over the subsequent popularity of increasing levels of intervention with young people in youth justice systems (see Chapter two), as opposed to using minimal necessary intervention (see Chapter two) whilst most young people mature out of offending.

In their follow-up study, 'Unraveling Juvenile Delinquency' (Glueck and Glueck 1950), the Gluecks researched 500 officially delinquent and 500 officially non-delinquent white males aged 10–17 years from lower-class neighbourhoods in Boston, USA, studying their lives prospectively (from present to future) over a 14-year period. The groups were matched on key demographic and psychosocial characteristics: Age, race/ethnicity, measured intelligence and residence in underprivileged neighbourhoods. The Gluecks collected a wide range of biopsychosocial data through official records and interviews with the boys and their significant others (e.g. parents, teachers, neighbours, criminal justice staff). Once the data had been quantified or 'factorised' (i.e. converted to a quantitative factor), it was cross-tabulated with officially recorded offending to identify a series of risk factors that were biological (e.g. physique), psychological (e.g. personality, attitudes, thinking) and immediate social (e.g. parental influence), reflective of their previous findings.

Developmental risk factor theory: The criminal careers model

The most influential and longest-running risk factor study in the globalised Western world produced the 'Criminal Careers Model' explanation of youth offending. The 'Cambridge Study in Delinquent Development,' better known as the 'Cambridge Study,' began in the UK in 1961 under the supervision of Donald West, who was later joined by David Farrington. It aimed 'to investigate the development of juvenile delinquency in a normal population of boys ... (and why) certain groups, identifiable at an early age, are peculiarly vulnerable' (West and Farrington 1973: xiii). The Cambridge Study aimed to enhance the explanatory utility of existing biopsychosocial, developmentally focussed theories by:

- Focusing on ordinary children, not experimental comparisons between identified offenders and a non-offending control group;
- Employing a prospective longitudinal design to identify risk factors prior to offending behaviour and tracing their development into the future, not

using retrospective bias to identify influential factors in the past lives of identified offenders.

(West and Farrington 1973, 1977)

A sample of 411 working-class males born in South London in 1953–1954 was identified and tracked prospectively from the age of 8 years old. Using a multi-method approach of regular interviews with sample members and their peers, psychological testing and secondary data analysis of official records, they measured the impact of life events and risk factors for youth offending. The researchers identified risk factors in childhood (between 8–10 years old) in the psychosocial domains of family, school, neighbourhood, peer and individual that were associated with offending across the life course, thus extending the existing developmental focus of risk factor theories beyond adolescence and into adulthood (West and Farrington 1977). The Cambridge Study linked risk factors to the 'criminal career,' the young person's 'trajectory' (i.e. course, pathway) of offending over the life course. This criminal career was seen to consist of different elements including onset, duration, frequency, continuity, escalation, specialisation and desistance (Farrington 2000; see also Basto-Pereira and Farrington 2020). The resultant 'Criminal Careers Model' suggested that certain individuals have lifelong offending trajectories and that their extent and nature are shaped by exposure to biopsychosocial risk factors (see Joliffe et al. 2017). The strongest predictors (identified at 8–10 years old) of official and self-reported offending (measured at 14–15 years old) were poor parenting, family criminality, family poverty, academic underachievement, hyperactivity/impulsivity/attention deficit and antisocial behaviour (West 1982). Subsequently, the researchers investigated the role of 'protective factors,' which allegedly insulate young people against future offending and against the harmful impact of exposure to risk factors (West 1982). Thus, protective factors can be understood as the polar opposites (dichotomies) of risk factors (Case and Haines 2011).

The Cambridge Study has been celebrated as 'a point of reference for discussion of juvenile delinquency and criminal behaviour for many years to come' (Radzinowicz, in West and Farrington 1973: v) and as 'among the most complete studies of the relationship between risk and offending' (Armstrong 2004: 105). There is little doubt that the study has been hugely influential in explanatory and policy terms (Case and Haines 2009). The Cambridge Study established and popularised ARFTs and has become the touchstone for youth justice prevention policy and practice with young people in the UK, especially since the 1990s (see Chapter three). It continues to this day and is currently tracing the influence of early risk factors on the adult lives of the children and grandchildren of the original sample.

In summary, Developmental Risk Factor Theory introduced an innovative, quasi-Positivist approach to explaining youth offending as the inevitable, predetermined outcome of exposure to individual, biopsychosocial risk factors in early life. Whilst retaining the individual, quantified, scientific and deterministic emphases of Individual Positivism, Developmental Risk Factor Theory offered more integrated, comprehensive, multi-factor explanations of youth offending. There are, however, several methodological and explanatory issues with the Developmental Risk Factor Theory, each indicative of reductionism. Firstly, the nature of the predominantly white, male, working-class samples in each study demonstrates an androcentrism, ethnocentrism and class-centrism that limits their explanatory utility, especially where explanations have been applied/generalised uncritically (i.e. 'out of context') to non-white, female and middle-class populations. Secondly, the quantification of 'risk' within Developmental Risk Factor Theory could be seen as an act of reductionism that (over)simplifies complex experiences by converting them into over-generalised and excessively crude numerical measures that cannot hope to represent the (qualitative) realities and context-dependent meanings that young people attach to their experiences of risk (France and Homel 2007). Thirdly, the overriding biopsychosocial focus can be perceived as a reductionist, psychosocial bias – privileging psychosocial influences on offending over other potentially important explanatory influences such as socio-structural factors (e.g. poverty, unemployment – see Webster et al. 2004), criminogenic interactions with youth justice agencies (McAra and McVie 2007), young people's personalised constructions of their risk experiences (Case 2021) and, inevitably, the overriding significance of context. Finally, these (and other) ARFTs have prioritised the identification of psychosocial deficits measured through statistical calculations and statistical relationships with offending outcomes. This methodology uncritically detaches the individual young person from the structural influences (particularly family, neighbourhood, demographic characteristics) and their own formations of identity and self – decontextualised processes that Young (2016) labelled 'voodoo Criminology.'

Integrated developmental risk factor theory

Whilst early Developmental Risk Factor Theory was essentially 'integrated,' it retained an individual focus. Subsequent Developmental Risk Factor Theory evolved the field in terms of explanatory utility by integrating neo-Classical, 'immediate' (i.e. individualised and static, not dynamic or relational) contextual and socio-structural influences into their explanations to supplement the focus on biopsychosocial risk factors. In this way, ARFTs evolved in explanatory terms from individualised to integrated (although still largely individual) foci, equivalent to the evolution of Positivist theories of youth offending. Four theories are most notable for evolving developmental risk factor explanations in a more integrated direction: The 'Social Development Model' (Hawkins and Weis 1985; Catalano and Hawkins 1996), 'Ecological Theory' (Wikström and Loeber 2000), the 'Causes and Correlates' studies (Thornberry and Krohn 2003) and 'Rational-Contextual' theories (Farrington 2007; Wikström 2008).

Integrated developmental risk factor theory: The social development model

Since the mid-1980s, the 'Social Development Model' has provided a theoretically integrated explanation of how risk factors influence youth offending. Initially, David Hawkins and Josef Weis (1985) at Washington University, USA, conducted a secondary analysis of prevention programme data provided by the National Center for the Assessment of Delinquent Behavior and its Prevention. They identified multiple 'correlates and causes' (i.e. risk factors) associated with youth offending and located them in the psychosocial (not biological) risk factor domains of family, school, peer groups and community. Hawkins and Weis (1985) integrated Social Control Theory (Hirschi 1969) and Social Learning Theory (Akers 1985) to assert that correlates and causes differ in importance between developmental stages of young people's lives. Socialisation processes in the family and school were identified as potential causes of both youth offending and prosocial behaviour/conformity (linked to Social Control Theory), implicating them as correlates functioning as both risk factors and protective factors (which allegedly insulated young people against the negative effects of exposure to risk). Reinforcement was the process by which youth offending was learnt or extinguished (linked to Social Learning Theory), adding elements of dynamism, change and flexibility to previous deterministic explanations of the static influence of risk factors. The original Social Development Model hypothesised that interactions between four mutually reinforcing, interdependent (risk) factors influence offending behaviour:

1. Perceived opportunities for involvement and interaction with significant others in conventional activities;
2. Degree of involvement and interaction;
3. Skills of the young person to participate in these involvements and interactions;
4. Perceived reinforcements for behaviour that determine whether association with family, school or peers produces a strong bond (Hawkins and Weis 1985).

In 1996, Richard Catalano joined Hawkins in revising and extending this explanatory model by integrating ideas from Differential Association Theory (Sutherland and Cressey 1960) to identify distinct causal pathways for antisocial behaviour/offending. The enhanced Social Development Model included three new sets of variables to expand its explanatory breadth:

1. Constitutional and physiological traits (biological) – cognitive ability (reading, verbal), difficult temperament, aggression, depression, hyperactivity, attention-deficit (influencing skills), low arousal of the nervous system (influencing the ability to perceive reinforcement);

2. Socio-structural status (demographic) – age, gender, race and socio-economic status affecting available opportunities for involvement and interaction with significant others in conventional activities;
3. External constraints (exogenous[3]) – social reactions to behaviour (see labelling theories later) that can be formal (police and other official sanctions) or informal (ridicule, ostracism, disapproval); the clarity of rules, laws and expectations for behaviour; the monitoring of behaviour affecting the degree of perceived reinforcement for involvement in behaviour.

(Catalano et al., in Farrington 2005)

The Social Development Model evolved Developmental Risk Factor Theory towards more integrated explanations of youth offending based on more developmentally sensitive, process-focussed and holistic understandings of the interactions between biopsychosocial risk factors and socio-structural risk factors (Catalano et al. 2017). In the words, it 'organizes a broad range of risk and protective factors into a model specifying causal hypotheses to capture key elements of socialization' (Hawkins et al. 2003: 279). Importantly the model does so beyond adolescence and into adulthood, thus expanding from a developmental to a life-course approach (see also Chapter three). However, despite tentative examination of the potential role of contextual influences, the model continues to employ reductionism – both in how it privileges the deterministic (i.e. pre-determined) influence of psychosocial risk factors and in how it narrows the definition of contexts into static and quantifiable factors rather than qualitative, negotiated and constructed processes.

In focus: Positive Youth Development

The 'Positive Youth Development' Model, founded in the USA in the early 21st century, evolved from the Social Development Model. It highlights the psychosocial characteristics of young people that are associated with their positive development, thus challenging the negative focus on risk and problem avoidance that had dominated youth crime prevention research up to that point (Catalano et al. 2004). Meta-analysis of Positive Youth Development programmes (Catalano et al. 2004) concluded that a common aetiology of individual, family, school and community factors typically predicted both positive outcomes (e.g. academic success) and negative outcomes (e.g. delinquency) for young people, indicating a potential for intervention programmes to simultaneously create positive developmental pathways and prevent the occurrence of problems. Although a clear and consensual definition of 'positive youth development' was not evident across the programmes evaluated, in general, they aimed to foster, strengthen and promote similar positive behaviours and outcomes, such as social, emotional, cognitive behavioural and moral competencies, self-efficacy, self-determination, a clear and positive identity, opportunities for (rewarded) participation in positive activities, bonding, resilience, belief in the future and prosocial norms and standards for behaviour[4] (Catalano et al. 2004; see also Butts, Pelletier and Kazemian 2018).

The Positive Youth Development Model represented a significant cultural and conceptual shift in understanding and responding to offending by young people. The research focus evolved from the dominant deficit-based identification and targeting of risk factors towards a 'whole child' examination of a broader range of interactional, contextual and socio-structural influences. The exploration of a common aetiology introduced the potential for protective factors to exert promotional and prosocial influences, rather than simply protecting the child against negativity and risk. However, Positive Youth Development programmes remain somewhat reductionist, unwilling to break free from the quasi-Positivist, psychosocial shackles of ARFTs and their related research. Despite good intentions, Positive Youth Development (like the Social Development Model before it) has been more concerned with preventing and reducing problems (i.e. negatives) than with promoting development, apparently presuming that positive youth development occurs naturally in the absence of problems (Butts, Pelettier and Kazemian 2018; Pittman et al. 2003). This common hypothesis assumes that risk and protective factors are functional dichotomies/opposites (see Kraemer et al. 2001; Pollard, Hawkins and Arthur 1999) or are 'causally reciprocal' (Thornberry 1987). This exemplifies the 'restricted evolution of the protective factor' (Case and Haines 2011) as understood entirely in relation to risk (factors), rather than as potentially independent, 'promotive' factors exerting influence on a range of positive behaviours and outcomes that are themselves potentially independent from negative behaviours and outcomes (Prelow et al. 2007; McCarthy, Laing and Walker 2004; Ashcroft, Daniels and Hart 2004). Indeed, any nascent promotive focus 'has been grounded in the somewhat uncritical importation of established lists of risk factors into concepts of protection and promotion limited to the psychosocial domains … [and] has retained risk, deficit and problem behaviour as its normative touchtone' (Case and Haines 2009: 41–42).

Integrated developmental risk factor theory: The 'Causes and Correlates' studies

A group of integrated 'interactional' developmental risk factor theories emerged from a large-scale longitudinal research project in the USA known as the 'Causes and Correlates' studies. These studies have developed the existing body of integrated, developmental risk factor explanations of youth offending through an innovative focus on reciprocal interactions between risk factors and offending in mutually reinforcing relationships. In 1986, the Office of Juvenile Justice and Delinquency Prevention in the USA began the 'Causes and Correlates studies,' with the central aim 'to improve the understanding of serious delinquency, violence, and drug use by examining how youth develop within the context of family, school, peers, and community' (Browning 1999: 1). The project was an integration of three prospective longitudinal studies: The Rochester Youth Development Study (Thornberry 1994; see also Thornberry et al. 2023), the Denver Youth Survey (Huizinga and Espiritu 1999; see also Huizinga 2017) and the Pittsburgh Youth Study (Loeber and Hay 1997; see also Ahonen et al. 2021), each of which is discussed in depth in the edited text 'Taking Stock of Delinquency' (Thornberry and Krohn 2003).

The Causes and Correlates studies were designed to investigate the criminogenic causes and correlates related to 'delinquent behaviour' (youth offending). The programme subsequently expanded to investigate additional issues such as the 'antecedents' (i.e. precursors, causes) of prosocial behaviour and developmental trajectories and transitions in adulthood (see Thornberry and Krohn 2003). The compatibility of design across the projects, employing prospective longitudinal, shared self-reported offending inventory and interviews exploring similar groups of risk factors, was a deliberate attempt to identify universal, generalisable risk factors across the studies. The Causes and Correlates studies evolved the explanatory utility of Developmental Risk Factor Theory to that point by (purportedly) identifying causal risk factors and pathways shared by young people, whilst also considering the potential interactional relationship between these risk factors and offending – the possibility that risk factors might influence one another within and between different risk domains. The authors have laid claim to 'the largest and most comprehensive investigation of the causes and correlates of delinquency ever undertaken' (Thornberry et al. 2004: 1). Their examination of the temporal precedence of risk factors has (allegedly) enabled the Causes and Correlates studies to address Farrington's concerns that there has been an absence (in risk factor theories) of understanding of the 'processes or developmental pathways that intervene between risks factors and outcomes' (Farrington 2000: 7). However, in reality, the largely quantitative study methods have not broken free from the static risk factor – offending relationships identified by traditional developmental, ARFTs. Most notably, the notion of explanatory and causal risk factors appears to be an invalid extrapolation from the restricted methods and analyses employed (see Case and Haines 2009).

Integrated developmental risk factor theory: Ecological theory

From the late 1990s, the integrated developmental 'Ecological Theory' emerged to address the perceived relative neglect of neighbourhood/community and socio-structural factors within ARFTs, both in terms of their standalone criminogenic effects and their potential influence on psychosocial risk factors (Wikström and Loeber 2000). Ecological Theory argued that previous ARFTs had a limited, reductionist focus on the interactions between individual/family characteristics and community contexts (i.e. biopsychosocial risk factors), which has precluded comprehensive explanations of youth offending. Accordingly, Wikström and Loeber (2000) decided to examine interactions between risk factors located in the individual and the broader community and social structure in current life, such as immediate social context and changes in community structural characteristics (Wikström and Loeber 2000, in Case and Haines 2009). They outlined four potentially influential, yet relatively neglected, domains of risk that could contribute to more 'holistic' explanations of youth offending:

- Individual disposition: impulsivity, guilt;
- Individual social situation: family, school, peers;
- Immediate social context: environmental elements that affect individual decisions to offend, such as temptations (e.g. attractive commodities), provocations (e.g. insults, threats), risk of punishment (in/formal sanction);
- Community structural characteristics: poverty, high residential mobility, population heterogeneity, family disruption.

(after Wikström and Loeber 2000: 1114)

Consequently, Ecological Theory addressed a noticeable oversight in previous versions of Developmental Risk Factor Theory by examining the influence of interactions between individual and contextual risk factors, including an innovative focus on the influence of risk factors on present-day (rather than retrospective) experiences and behaviours. The theory also encouraged ARFTs to pay closer attention to the role of mediated agency (see also the 'Neo-Classical Compromise'), for example, young people's choices/decisions to offend being constrained and shaped by individual and neighbourhood risk factors. However, since its inception, Ecological Theory has remained largely theoretical rather than evidence-based, at least until Wikström expanded upon its ideas with his 'Situational Action Theory' (discussed below).

Integrated developmental risk factor theory: Rational-contextual theories

Two integrated developmental theories emerged in the 21st century to extend the explanatory scope and lens of ARFTs, each prioritising closer examination of interactions between psychosocial risk factors and rational choice in different situational contexts. These contemporary 'Rational–Contextual' theories were developed by two of the foremost, established artefactual risk factor theorists, David Farrington (see Criminal Careers Model) and Per-Olof Wikström (see Ecological Theory).

Farrington's 'Integrated Cognitive Antisocial Potential' (ICAP) theory focused on the interaction between criminal potential (a long-standing priority of Developmental Criminology) and the commission of offences (a much-neglected topic within Developmental Criminology), thus seeking to integrate developmental and situational theories of (youth) offending (Farrington 2020). The ICAP theory (Farrington 2005) synthesised/integrated elements of established Classical and Positivist explanations, including Rational Choice, Social Learning, Strain, Social Control and Labelling theories, asserting that young people's 'antisocial potential' is determined by the nature and extent of everyday exposure to risk factors. According to Farrington, the antisocial potential is 'actualised' (i.e. made real, brought to life) by cognitive processes (e.g. thinking, decision-making), which are themselves influenced by situational contexts (e.g. opportunities to offend, availability of victims). This precipitates rational choices to offend the young person. The ICAP theory distinguishes between two types of antisocial potential:

- 'Long-term antisocial potential' is latent until it is actualised by risk factors such as impulsiveness, strain, criminogenic socialisation processes and negative life events such as losing a job or relationship. It is further energised/activated by the desire for material possessions, status-seeking and the pursuit of excitement (e.g. sexual satisfaction). Conversely, positive attachments, pro-social socialisation and positive life events (e.g. marriage, obtaining a good job) are protective (factors) against the actualisation of long-term antisocial behaviour;
- 'Short-term antisocial potential' is shaped by exposure to sociological and socio-structural risk factors (e.g. academic failure, unemployment, low income), which are energised/activated into offending behaviour by exposure to individual risk factors (e.g. boredom, anger, drunkenness, peer pressure) combined with situational/contextual risk factors, including suitable opportunities to offend and available victims.

The ICAP theory explains long-term antisocial potential as activated in later life by the choices that young people make, whereas short-term antisocial behaviour is activated by interactions between active risk factors, agency, cognition and situational factors (Farrington 2005). Therefore, youth offending, operationalised as 'antisocial behaviour,' is the product of rational choices made during interactions between individual characteristics (e.g. short- and long-term antisocial potential) and environmental influences (situational and contextual factors). Consequently, the ICAP theory elaborated on Developmental Risk Factor Theory explanations by offering an innovative focus on young people's current lives and by extending developmentally deterministic explanations by considering the role of agency and contextual (i.e. immediate situational) elements as triggers for youth offending in current life (Farrington 2020).

The other significant integrated Rational-Contextual theory is 'Situational Action Theory' (SAT), which purports to have addressed the neglected problem of determining causality within ARFTs by identifying the causal mechanisms (rather than simple statistical correlates or predictors) linking risk factors with offending in different social situations (Wikström, Treiber and Roman 2024; Wikström and Butterworth 2006). Unlike the ICAP, the SAT is evidence-based, underpinned by data drawn from the cross-sectional 'Peterborough Youth Study' of nearly 2,000 school children aged 14–15. The study extended Ecological Theory's individual-contextual understanding of risk factor influence by studying the relationships/interactions between family social position (e.g. parents' occupational social class, family structure and family ethnicity), the adolescents' social situation (e.g. family and social bonds), individual dispositions (e.g. morality, inability to exercise self-control) and lifestyles (e.g. peers' delinquency, their own substance drug use). Analyses of self-reported offending and interview data highlighted a group of 'explanatory factors' located within young people's routines, lifestyles, dispositions and the social situations to which they were exposed (Wikström and Butterworth 2006; see also Wikström, Treiber and Roman 2024). For instance, young people who had limited involvement with their family or school, but who spent time with delinquent peers in high-crime environments, were being exposed to an increased situational risk of offending. Psychosocial risk factors were concluded to be indirect causes of crime, influencing young people's capability to perceive alternative courses of action or 'action alternatives' in different situations and to take decisions to commit a crime. The SAT researchers concluded that:

> Adolescent offending is best interpreted as the consequence of perception of action alternatives and processes of choice made against the background of the interplay between the youths' individual characteristics and their behavioural contexts
>
> (Wikström and Butterworth 2006: 241)

Therefore, the SAT explains youth offending as the result of an intersection/interaction between the individual (i.e. their current characteristics and experiences) and the setting (i.e. the people, objects, events and locations to which the young person is exposed and reacts). These interactions are influenced and activated by situational mechanisms, all of which influence and determine the young person's perception of alternative actions (i.e. alternatives to crime) and their process of choice (i.e. whether or not to commit a crime). Young people's perceptions of alternative actions and processes of choice are allegedly affected by the situational settings/contexts in which they find themselves. According to Wikström and Butterworth (2006), these settings consist of two potentially criminogenic influences: Temptations (i.e. perceived opportunities to satisfy their desires unlawfully) and provocations (i.e. perceived attacks on the person, property or self-respect that precipitate a criminal response), whilst the process of choice is influenced by individual elements such as self-control and morality (Wikström, Treiber and Roman 2024; Pauwels, Svensson and Hirtenlehner 2018; Wikström and Treiber 2017). It has been asserted that the SAT provides a dynamic 'theory of action' that is animated by 'explanatory' risk factors for youth offending (Wikström and Treiber 2017), but that also integrates considerations of rational choice (e.g. morality, self-control) and situational context. This allegedly progresses reductionist psychosocial and deterministic explanations that identify risk factor correlates with/predictors of youth offending towards identifying the causal pathways and mechanisms that can usefully be targeted by youth justice interventions, thus moving 'beyond risk factors' (Wikström and Treiber 2017; see also Chapter two).

Contextual challenge: The reductionist definition of 'context'

Despite the apparent consideration of the criminogenic influence of 'context' presenting as a welcome updating and evolution of contemporary ARFTs, do Rational-Contextual theories flatter to deceive? Could critics argue that these theories have defined and operationalised context in reductionist, quasi-decontextualised ways as simply immediate situations or circumstances, akin to traditional understandings of context as static, observable features such as places, spaces, people and things operating at a single point in time (see Greenhalgh and Manzano 2022)? Indeed, the static and individualised nature of these explanations of youth offending is implicated by the emphasis on 'circumstance' in the title of Wikström's new book 'Character, Circumstances and Criminal Careers' (Wikström, Treiber and Roman 2024). Therefore, it could be argued that the allegedly dynamic theories of action offered by Rational-Contextual theories are anything but dynamic in the sense of understanding context as dynamic and emerging over time at multiple levels of the social system (see Sutton et al. 2022).

The foregoing debates indicate that the privileging of quasi-Positivist, developmental ARFTs (Stephenson and Allen 2018) and their associated explanatory mechanisms (i.e. predictive, psychosocial risk factors) over alternative explanatory mechanisms, paradigms and evidence-bases has fostered partiality (bias and incompleteness) in the nature and scope of dominant explanatory theories of youth offending. Therefore, taken together, what is the extent and nature of the explanatory utility of individualised ARFTs of youth offending? Moreover, what are the limitations to this explanatory utility if we are seeking comprehensive, valid and contextualised explanations of youth offending to inform effective responses to this behaviour through youth justice intervention? A critical overview of individualised ARFTs highlights five crucial elements of reductionist partiality that narrow, restrict and problematise these explanations.

The reductionism of artefactual risk factor theories: Partiality 'take five'

1. **Psychosocial bias:** Privileging individualising biological and psychological influences on youth offending overlooks considerations of socio-structural contextual influences and social interactions (like Individual Positivism).
2. **Ignoring the biasing 'centrisms':** Ethnocentric, androcentric and class-centric biases in the knowledge creation that enable understandings of youth offending encourage explanations that are inherently narrow, biased (e.g. discriminatory) and unrepresentative (like Individual Positivism).
3. **Limited explanatory utility:** Static, linear, developmentally deterministic presumptive (e.g. conflating correlation with causation) explanations, combined with limited analyses of interactions between risk factors, neglect the necessary dynamism, flexibility and nuance needed for comprehensive, valid and contextualised theorising of youth offending.
4. **Narrow methodological lens:** Privileging survey methods and quantitative data over qualitative methodologies/data that explore social constructions (e.g. how 'youth offending' is conceptualised) and young people's experiences inherently limits the explanatory scope of aetiological theories (as with Individual Positivism).
5. **Decontextualisation:** Continued neglect of meso-level, relational influences and macro-level socio-structural influences (albeit with increasing exploration in later integrated theories) and the restricted construction of context as static, immediate and situational engenders decontextualised explanations lacking in applicability to young people (like Individual Positivism) and also to specific groups of young people (e.g. different ethnic groups, girls).

Summarising the problem: Decontextualised explanations youth offending

This opening thematic chapter has introduced and critically examined the aetiological theories that have come to dominate criminological explanations of youth offending in the Western world. The evidence presented suggests that the nature of these hegemonic theories and their explanations has been overwhelmingly reductionist, individualising criminogenic influences by constructing them developmentally and deterministically as rational choices, biopsychological causes or artefactual 'risk factor' predictors (i.e. not causes). Consequently, these reductionist, individualising explanations have largely decontextualised understandings of youth offending by marginalising and narrowing potentially criminogenic contextual influences, be they macro-level (e.g. socio-economic, cultural, socio-structural, political) or meso-level (e.g. dynamic interactions with youth justice systems, dynamic relations with youth justice professionals, immediate situational factors). Furthermore, individualised and decontextualised theories and explanations of and responses to

Table 1.1 Summarising the extent and nature of contextualisation in dominant explanatory theories of youth offending

Explanatory category	*Theory*	*Criminogenic influences*	*Psychosocial bias?*	*Contextual influence?*
Individual Classical	Classical	Rational choice, free will	Yes	No
	Neo-Classical compromise	Bounded rational choice, free will	Yes	Limited – cursory consideration
Individual Positivism	Biological Positivism	Physical characteristics, genetic inheritance, neuroscience	Yes	No
	Psychological Positivism	Personality, learning	Yes	No
Integrated Positivism	Biopsychosocial Theory	Biopsychosocial	Yes	
	Social Control Theory	Attachment, commitment, involvement, beliefs	Yes	Limited – constructed as static and immediate social
ARFTs: Developmental	Multi-Factor Developmental	Biopsychosocial	Yes	
	Criminal Careers Model	Biopsychosocial	Yes	Limited – constructed as static and immediate social
ARFTs: Integrated Developmental	Causes and Correlates	Biopsychosocial interacting	Yes	Limited – constructed as static and immediate social
	Ecological Theory	Biopsychosocial interacton with socio-structural context and socio-structural characteristics	Yes	
	Rational-Contextual	Rational choice mediated by immediate situational contexts	Yes	
	Social Development Model	Biological traits, socio-structural status, external constraints	Yes	Yes, but reductionist (quantified) measurement

youth offending have largely neglected to examine the contexts of knowledge creation in which they have been constructed, in particular, the reductionist partialities of their inherent ethno-, andro-, adult- and class-'centrisms,' which have been compounded by partiality towards evidence generation through (quasi) experimental methodologies collecting quantitative data. Nevertheless, an argument for evolving explanatory utility can be made on the basis that theories of Individual Positivism and ARFTs have begun to develop into more integrated, complex and contextualised forms by combining biological, psychological and sociological factors with agentic (rational choice) factors and tentative considerations of situational and socio-structural contextual influences. However, even these more expansionist, open-minded theories still appear wedded, at least to a degree, to more individualising explanations that privilege biopsychosocial criminogenic influences and that tend to conceptualise 'context' in narrow, reductionist ways as static, immediate situational influences on young people's allegedly rational choices and/or factorised forms of socio-structural influence. This precludes explanations that construct context as a series of complex, multi-level, dynamic, relational influences on explanatory mechanisms that can change the behaviour of individual young people.

By way of conclusion, Table 1.1 summarises the extent and nature of the (de)contextualisation discernible within the individual and associated integrated (although still largely individualised) explanatory theories of youth offending reviewed thus far.

Notes

1 It is impossible across the scope of this book to explore in detail every aetiological theory offered to explain youth offending over the long history of Western Criminology. Therefore, the critical review in this chapter (also in Chapter 3) inevitably relies on the author's expert judgement and experience with the most common, popular, well-evidenced and influential explanatory theories available.
2 These include 'Right Realism' and 'Situational Action Theory' (see Chapter 3).
3 The external, exogenous variables that increased the likelihood (risk) of offending behaviour were understood as 'mediated by other social development model constructs' (Catalano and Hawkins 1996: 160) at different developmental stages (e.g. primary, elementary, middle and high school).
4 There are similarities here with the adult-focused Good Lives Model (Ward, Yates and Willis 2011; Ward and Maruna 2007), a strengths-based rehabilitation theory that aims to equip clients with internal and external resources to live a 'good' or 'better,' socially acceptable and personally meaningful life. The Good Lives Model targets criminogenic needs (risk factors) as internal or external barriers against living a good life, which are addressed within a broader strengths-based framework and need-focused approach that motivates 'offenders' to desist.

2 The problem of decontextualised youth justice

The opening chapter critically examined the Classical, Positivist and Artefactual Risk Factor theories that have dominated criminological explanations of youth offending in the Western world for over 150 years, each of which locates criminogenic influences within the individual. This second thematic chapter explores the academic, political and professional contexts of established, dominant youth justice *responses* to identified youth offending, each of which has been guided and shaped by the dominant explanations explored in Chapter 1. For analytical purposes, 'youth justice' is operationalised here as the formal intervention responses to identified youth offending delivered by youth justice systems,[1] in out-of-court contexts, community and custodial contexts following court sentence. Chapter 2 follows logically from its predecessor by asserting that the ways in which youth offending is discussed, explored and understood (i.e. constructed) are critical to the construction of youth justice responses, notably through the interventions that aim to tackle and prevent it (see Gray, Jump and Smithson 2023). Accordingly, it will be argued that youth justice is a dynamic, contingent and contested social construction shaped by a range of influences and influencers (Case 2024).

The chapter begins with a detailed exploration of the overarching 'models,' rationales and principles that have shaped social constructions of youth justice in international, westernised youth justice systems historically, charting their trajectory from the long-standing, dominant 'welfare versus justice debate' (Smith 2005) into more punitive, neo-liberal and neo-correctionalist models and approaches underpinned by individualising and developmental explanatory theories and evidence (see Chapter 1). There follows an analysis of the emergence of 'evidence-based' youth justice and its realisation through actuarial risk management animated by the 'Risk Factor Prevention Paradigm' and the closely associated 'What Works' framework for evaluating the 'effectiveness' of youth justice interventions. The chapter concludes that adopting an individualising, developmental, risk-based lens to shaping and determining 'effective' responses to youth offending perpetuates a reductionist, decontextualised focus on 'treating' and 'correcting' problems and deficits located in individualised, psychosocial domains of young people's lives. This bias often comes at the expense of targeting broader, contextualised influences

DOI: 10.4324/9781003498100-3

that may be criminogenic in their own right and that may also interact with and/or exacerbate psychosocial influences leading to youth offending.

Youth justice across the globe: Models, rationales and principles

Following a detailed comparative review of national approaches to youth justice across the globalised Western world, Hazel (2008) concluded that it is possible to identify distinct system 'models.' However, he cautioned that these models are 'ideal types' that are not replicated exactly internationally and do not necessarily determine policy formation nationally or locally.[2] Instead, they should be viewed as broad, fluctuating philosophical approaches and/or cumulative patterns of youth justice. Hazel (2008) asserted that every identifiable model of youth justice globally, no matter how complex and 'hybridised' (i.e. representing a mixture of different types and influences), has emerged from, and can be linked to, either welfare or justice models, which can be defined as:

- **Welfare:** This approach emphasises addressing the unmet personal and social (welfare) needs and well-being of young people who offend. Children are not viewed as (micro-level) rational, self-determining responsible agents or actors (in line with individualising explanations), but rather as subject to and products of the (macro- and meso-level influence within) environments and contexts in which they live. Consequently, youth justice responses should identify, treat and cure the underlying social causes of offending, rather than inflicting punishment for the offence itself (Alder and Wundersitz 1994; McAra and McVie 2010). The focus of the welfare model, therefore, is on the needs of the dependent child, diagnosis, treatment, informal processes and indeterminate (not fixed) sentences. The model has been particularly evident in the youth justice practice of Norway, Sweden, France, Germany and Japan (Cavadino and Dignan 2013; Dunkel 2014).
- **Justice:** In direct contrast to the more contextualised welfare perspective, young people are understood in the justice model as either rational agents who are fully responsible for their offending (the Classical view) or semi-rational agents largely responsible for their offending (the Neo-Classical and Individual Positivist views). Contextual influence is typically limited to the impact of immediate situational and social environments on young people's decisions to offend (see the discussion of Rational-Contextual theories in Chapter one). The justice approach emphasises legal rights, due process and accountability for crimes, whilst favouring formal justice and proportionality in sentencing and the deterrent aims of punishment in youth justice responses (McAra 2010). The model is evident internationally, for example, in the youth justice approaches adopted by different states of the USA post-1960 (Cavadino and Dignan 2013) and in the 21st-century youth justice systems of Russia (Dunkel 2014) and

Australia (e.g. Queensland – Walsh and Fitzgerald 2022; Fitzgibbon and O'Brien 2019).

Following his cross-national comparative review, Hazel reasserted the caveat that the identified welfare-justice models are only 'ideal types' of youth justice approaches, arguing that no individual country conforms exactly to every characteristic of either model at any point. Instead, they will tend to oscillate between the two poles of welfare and justice over time, a phenomenon exemplified globally (Hagell and Hazel 2001) and nationally in England and Wales in the 1960s and 1970s (Harris 1985) and in South Australia (Alder and Wundersitz 1994). The 'welfare versus justice debate' (Smith 2005) regarding which should be the dominant priority principle for shaping the responses of Western youth justice systems illustrates the longstanding conflict and ambivalence around how to understand children (who offend) as simultaneously vulnerable/innocent and threatening/dangerous (McAra and McVie 2010; Smith and Ecob 2007). According to McAra (2023, 2010), conflict and ambivalence surrounding appropriate youth justice responses have both encouraged and been exacerbated by competing system objectives for youth justice, which can be dichotomised as:

1. To help troubled young people change, develop and overcome their problems;
2. To deliver a firm, prompt and appropriate response to youth offending that protects the public.

Ongoing conflict and ambivalence have encouraged an increasing complexity and diversity of youth justice models across Western systems. This trend was highlighted by Dunkel (2014) following his review of youth justice models employed across Europe, in which he identified three 'trends' that extend youth justice beyond traditional welfare and justice concerns: Neo-Liberalism/Neo-Correctionalism (e.g. evident in the youth justice systems of England/Wales, France, Netherlands – Dunkel 2014), Restorative Justice (e.g. evident in certain states in Australia, New Zealand – Cunneen and Goldson 2015) and Minimum Necessary Intervention/Diversion (e.g. evident in Germany, Switzerland, several Central and Eastern European countries). These different youth justice rationales, philosophies and strategies have been mobilised within different youth justice structures, indicative of how macro-level national contexts and macro/meso-level systemic contexts of youth justice in specific countries can influence the construction and execution of youth justice policy and practice (see below).

Contextual challenge: Systemic contextual influence on youth justice systems

Youth justice systems globally have developed different structures (e.g. institutions, organisations, processes) with which to animate the requirements of legislation, conventions, national philosophies and strategies for youth justice. These structures can be viewed as the 'architecture of youth justice' (McAra, in Smith 2010) and include:

System types: Youth justice structures in different national contexts may be part of 'generic systems' that respond to children and young people who offend and those considered in need of care and protection (e.g. as in England and Wales for long periods until the Crime and Disorder Act 1998). Conversely, youth justice services nationally and locally may be part of 'specialist systems' dealing only with offenders and those at risk of offending or be embedded within adult criminal justice systems.

Sentencing structures: Some youth justice systems have court-based structures for dealing with youth crime (e.g. youth courts in England and Wales), which may operate inquisitorial, participatory or adversarial procedures. Others have non-judicial decision-making bodies for 'young offenders' (e.g. the Children's Hearing System in Scotland), which may vary in terms of the inclusion and distribution of (trained) lay members of the public and experts, along with the involvement of victims and families in decision-making processes.

There can be discernible, logical relationships between certain macro-level structures and philosophies/models of youth justice, such as the indeterminate nature of welfare interventions being decided by non-judicial bodies or determinate justice-based sentences being better suited to court structures. However, the relationship between youth justice structures and philosophies can be a flexible, mix-and-match affair, such that 'there is no necessary causal relationship between principle and architecture' (McAra 2010: 290; see also Gray and Smith's 2024 distinction between the 'archaeology' and the 'architecture' of youth justice). Furthermore, there is an important contextualised distinction to be made here between the structures within which youth justice decision-making is situated and the nature of the sentences and interventions themselves, which are less dependent on structure (McAra 2010, 2023). For example, Restorative Justice-based Family Group Conferencing, traditionally popular amongst Indigenous cultures (e.g. in New Zealand – Bredewold and Tonkens 2021), lends itself to non-judicial decision-making structures but can be easily integrated within court-based structures through statutory sentences with restorative elements (e.g. Referral Orders in England and Wales – Crawford and Newburn 2003).

The 'punitive turn' across Western youth justice systems

From the 1990s onwards, westernised youth justice generally moved away from welfare principles and towards more 'punitive' (i.e. punishment-focused) interpretations and applications of justice-based approaches. This move was illustrated by the proliferation of 'offending behaviour programmes' grounded in the explanatory evidence-base of Individual Positivism and ARFTs, and by the increasing systemic prominence of justice-based principles of proportionality and just deserts (Pratt and Eriksson 2012). Rapid globalisation, dramatic socio-economic transformations and increasing international and public insecurities (see Beck's 1992 'risk society' thesis[3]) combined to produce a growing penal populism – a political and social/public preference for more punitive forms of justice (Walsh and Fitzgerald 2022). This 'new punitive common sense' across criminal (adult) and youth justice systems emerged in the USA and was then exported internationally, illustrated by 'vertical expansion' such as burgeoning prison populations and 'horizontal expansion' through the proliferation and diversification of technologies of regulation, control and surveillance (Wacquant 2009: 1). In relation to youth justice specifically, the central strategic characteristics of the 'punitive turn' in youth justice were identified by Muncie (2008) as:

- Repenalisation: A move towards more punishment-focused justice responses with retributive, deterrent and custodial inclinations.
- Neo-liberalism: Placing less emphasis on social contexts, state protection and rehabilitation and more emphasis on prescriptions of individual, family and community responsibility (see also Dunkel 2014), active citizenship and governments governing at a distance.
- Responsibilisation: Allocating the primary responsibility for the prevention of youth offending to young people, families, communities and local authorities, rather than to the state.
- Adulterisation: The increasing treatment of young people who offend as though they are adults in terms of maturity, capability and responsibility.

Goldson (2014) expanded on this critique by outlining a 'dystopian vision' of 21st-century youth justice as constituted by contexts of dehumanising, undesirable and unpleasant youth justice systems and practices, contrasting starkly with the needs- and protection-focused welfare models that had characterised European youth justice for much of the 20th century (Bailleau and Cartuyvels 2002). The dystopian 'punitive turn' in westernised youth justice in the 21st century has been characterised by 'a decline in rehabilitative ideals, harsher prison conditions, more emotional and expressive forms of punishment emphasising shaming and degradation' (Snacken and Dumortier 2012: 2–3).

In focus: Justifying a 'punitive turn' in a context where 'nothing works'

The genesis of disillusionment with rehabilitation and the subsequent trajectory towards a 'punitive turn' across Western youth justice systems can be traced to around 40 years earlier and the findings of Martinson's

(1974) review of rehabilitative intervention programmes. The review concluded that there was a lack of evidence demonstrating the effectiveness of rehabilitative interventions, which led to the infamous assertion that 'nothing works' in reducing the reoffending of both adults and children. However, Martinson has been typically misrepresented here, because his alleged statement was actually posed as the question: 'Do all of the studies lead us irrevocably to the conclusion that nothing works?' (Martinson 1974: 48). Notwithstanding this misrepresentation, the 'collapse of the rehabilitative ideal' peaked during the 1970s as:

> virtually everyone came to forsake the rehabilitative ideal. Through an intersection of cataclysmic social events and strong intellectual currents, a social movement of sorts had risen up to purge systems of control of the insidious social welfare ideology that used the rhetoric of benevolence to mask the abuse of power.
>
> (Cullen 2013: 302)

Soon after this ostensible collapse of faith in rehabilitation, neo-liberal ideas began to influence and shape the social policy of westernised, anglophone (English-speaking) societies (Smith 2016). Into the 1990s, social and criminal justice policy became concerned less with issues of crime prevention and concentrated much more on concerns with public disorder and the increasingly pervasive labelling of so-called 'problematic' populations such as children and young people, most notably in the UK, Western Europe, the USA (Muncie 2021) and in Australia (Marsh and Melville 2019). Neo-liberal strategies of youth justice began to gain traction, marginalising the social contexts of crime and even the biological and psychological explanations of Individual Positivism (which at least embraced the possibility of treatment and rehabilitation), whilst privileging explanations focussed on assigning responsibility for the crime to individuals (as rational actors), families and communities (Dunkel 2014; Garland 2002). In other words, children and young people were 'responsibilised' by being held primarily responsible for their offending behaviour, regardless of their age, developmental capacity, social status or powerlessness relative to adults.

Developing youth justice models in the Western world: Five steps towards decontextualisation

1. **Welfare:** Contextualised welfare-based approaches to understand and respond to youth offending emphasise addressing unmet personal and social needs and well-being of young people who offend, encouraging

treatment and system change responses rather than formal justice and punishment.
2. **Justice:** This largely decontextualised approach to understanding and responding to youth offending emphasises legal rights, due process and accountability for crimes, whilst favouring formal justice and proportionality in sentencing and the deterrent aims of punishment in youth justice responses.
3. **Contemporary models:** Newer, hybrid models of youth justice have emerged in the 21st century (e.g. Neo-Correctionalism, Restorative Justice, Minimum Necessary Intervention), but all can be traced back to some extent to their welfare and justice predecessors.
4. **Systemic and structural contextual influences:** Contextualised (meso- and macro-level) systemic influences can shape constructions of youth justice interventions, including different system types (e.g. generic-specialised) and different sentencing structures (e.g. court-based-non-judicial).
5. **Punitive turn:** From the 1990s, Western youth justice systems and the interventions they privileged moved towards more punishment-based, controlling and managerial approaches characterised by strategies of repenalisation, neo-liberalism, responsibilisation and adulterisation.

The 'punitive turn': Constructing young people who offend as presenting risk

Since the 1990s, globalisation has precipitated sweeping socio-economic changes across westernised, anglophone societies and beyond, which increased political and public uncertainty, anxiety and concerns about a perceived 'youth crime problem' (e.g. in 21st century Australia – Walsh and Fitzgerald 2022; in China since the early 1980s – Jou, Chang and Hebenton 2014) and the associated 'risks' and 'threats' to the safety of populations (Case 2021). The growing need to predict, control and manage these perceived risks and threats (Beck 1992), often readily assigned to younger populations, became a priority for societal responses to globalised pressures and began to characterise the trajectory and evolution (arguably a reductionist 'devolution') of youth justice. The concept of 'risk' became a buzzword or shorthand for public insecurity and anxiety and was presented by politicians, the media and academics as denoting a threat or harm to be managed or mitigated. The growing perception of risk among the general public offered an ideal political vehicle to drive the social reconstruction of youth offending, lending itself neatly to representing young people as potential threats to themselves and others (see Case 2006; Goldson 2005). The approach was nothing new, however. The so-called 'respectable fears' of successive generations of adults had been manifested regularly in populist portrayals of the 'risks' and threats' presented by young people in society, a group often socially constructed as unpredictable, uncontrollable and unwelcome (Pearson 1983). Western governments expressed concerns regarding the perceived exponential rise in youth offending (especially by boys), deep-rooted failures of deterrent approaches, the escalating costs of youth custody and the urgent need for public protection (Kemshall, in Blyth et al. 2007).

The 1990s contexts of globalisation and the 'punitive turn' accelerated the return of the public's 'respectable fears' regarding crime, with the associated implication that the theoretical explanations provided by established criminological theories were no longer fit for purpose for either explaining youth offending or informing appropriate youth justice responses. Western governments throughout the 1990s challenged key stakeholders (typically academics and youth justice professionals) to provide an explanatory theory of youth offending that was valid (appropriate, relevant, accurate), straightforward and practical, with the tacit implication that it should also be politically acceptable, for example, inexpensive, straightforward to animate in practice and minimising of macro-level political and socio-structural influences. Consequently, Western governments wanted politically palatable explanations of and practical responses to youth offending that focused predominantly on individual-level dynamic factors amenable to change (Andrews and Bonta 2010), for example, through offending behaviour programmes. As a result, the context-dependent criminogenic influence of broader structural and systemic factors such as unemployment, poverty, social disorganisation and economic recession, all far less amenable to change (e.g. economically, in the short term), were to be relatively neglected by youth justice.

Neo-correctionalist risk management

In the 1990s context of globalisation, a new way of thinking about and delivering youth justice entered a political sphere more concerned with pragmatism than principles or philosophies. The 'risk management' approach aligned neatly with the strategies of the 'punitive turn,' particularly neoliberal responsibilisation (Dunkel 2014) and managerialism (Muncie 2021), whilst introducing a new 'explanatory' strategy grounded in evidence from Artefactual Risk Factor theories (see Chapter 1). This strategy was 'neo-correctionalism' (with 'neo' indicating new and updated), which advocated for the use of youth justice responses to correct the psychosocial 'deficits' identified in the immediate lives/contexts of young people who offended (Cavadino and Dignan 2013). This strategy was quasi-Positivist in nature because it employed evidence from Artefactual Risk Factor theories (ARFTs) to identify and target the alleged predictors of offending, rather than the causes allegedly identified by theories of Individual Positivism (Case and Haines 2009). Neo-correctionalism in the youth justice field privileged technical risk assessment methodologies that were populated by the findings and conclusions of developmental ARFTs and associated Developmental Crime Prevention approaches (see later in this chapter). According to Day (2020: 1):

> the management of risk...has unified the field [of youth justice], provided significant impetus to attempts to implement evidence-based

practice, and generally resulted in a more professional and accountable approach to service delivery.

Neo-correctionalist risk management in Western youth justice systems has its origins in the conception of the aforementioned 'risk society' (the 'risk' in risk management) and in the increasing implementation of methods of 'actuarial justice' to manage responses to offending based on the individual's predicted risk of reoffending (the 'management' in risk management). Westernised criminal justice systems began to place more emphasis on the effective, efficient and economical management of 'problematic' and 'high risk' youth populations and resources in the late 20th century, especially the 'new technologies to identify and classify risk' (Feeley and Simon 1992: 454–455). These techniques were categorised as 'actuarial,' in that they applied mathematical and statistical modelling to the assessment and management of risk. Actuarial risk management technologies such as risk assessment/prediction instruments mobilised new approaches to the management and control of young people, for example, through categorising them into sub-groups based on shared characteristics and shared levels of quantified 'risk' that could be targeted by the intervention (Porteous, in Thom et al. 2007).

Actuarial justice and risk management prompted a shift away from clinical or subjective judgements based on ideology or the expertise of youth justice professionals, which were implicitly seen as either inconsistently applied or flawed. Viewed positively, actuarial justice presents a constructive way of standardising and raising the level of effectiveness of youth justice systems and practices. Proponents of risk management and its associated methodology of risk assessment have argued that techniques of actuarial justice render decision-making more accurate and consistent by grounding decisions in a rigorously empirical framework based on data from a potentially wide range of information sources (e.g. Baker 2005; Grove and Meehl 1996). Critics have characterised actuarial justice as one element of a broader, politically motivated managerialist exercise intent on exerting increasing levels of centralised control over youth justice systems and the political management and manipulation of 'youth' as a social problem (Smith 2016). Undoubtedly, however, the rise to prominence of actuarial risk management approaches across Western youth justice systems was evidence-based and theoretically and empirically underpinned by the concurrent explosion in the popularity of Developmental ARFTs, which were proliferating in their identification of the (typically psychosocial) criminogenic influences in childhood and youth that allegedly predict/increase the risk of offending in later life (see Chapter one). As a result, it has been observed that 'risk-factor and prediction paradigms have taken hold of Criminology, especially for those interested in crime prevention and crime control policies' (Laub and Sampson 2003: 289).

The risk factor prevention paradigm: Linking explanation to response

Risk management as the dominant strategy across Western youth justice systems has been mobilised by the 'Risk Factor Prevention Paradigm' (Hawkins and Catalano 1992; see also O'Mahony 2007), which sets out a clear, common sense and practical approach to responding to youth offending through youth justice intervention:

> The basic idea ... is very simple: Identify the key risk factors for offending and implement prevention methods designed to counteract them. There is often a related attempt to identify key protective factors against offending and to implement prevention methods designed to enhance them.
>
> (Farrington, in Maguire, Morgan and Reiner 2007: 606)

The Risk Factor Prevention Paradigm (RFPP) was imported into youth justice from the fields of medicine and public health, where it is used to identify 'risk factors' that increase the likelihood of physical illnesses such as heart disease (e.g. high cholesterol diet, lack of exercise) and 'protective factors' that mediate against these illnesses (e.g. healthy, low-cholesterol diet, regular exercise). These risk and protective factors are then targeted by preventative interventions (e.g. health promotion) administered to 'high risk' or 'at risk' groups scoring highly in exposure to risk factors and low in exposure to protective factors. The major UK-based proponent of the RFPP, Professor David Farrington, has confidently (yet controversially) proclaimed that the paradigm:

> links explanation and prevention ... is easy to understand and to communicate...is readily accepted by policy makers, practitioners, and the general public ... [is] based on empirical research rather than theories [and] ... avoids difficult theoretical questions about which risk factors have causal effects.
>
> (Farrington 2000: 7)

In focus: Developmental crime prevention: Individualising youth crime prevention

The RFPP aligns with the Developmental Crime Prevention (DCP) model outlined by Crawford (1998) in his typology of crime prevention[4]). Crawford initially distinguished between 'Social Crime Prevention,' which views offending as the product of a range of interacting (criminogenic) influences impacting individuals to shape their criminal predispositions, and 'Situational Crime Prevention,' which presumes that offending is rational (chosen) and contextual (i.e. in relation to the immediate context/situation) and so can be reduced by making it more difficult to commit crimes (Crawford 1998: 18). According to Crawford, Social Crime Prevention is most commonly targeted at ameliorating both the underlying socio-economic causes of crime and offender motivation. He further distinguished between 'developmental' and 'community' models of Social Crime Prevention, with DCP targeting characteristics and behaviour that predispose individuals (particularly young people) to offend, whilst Community Crime Prevention (see Chapter 4) seeks to influence aspects of the social life of the community to reduce criminogenic influences on the individual. Consequently, DCP presents as most compatible with the RFPP, as both identify young people with developing criminal potential for secondary crime prevention (i.e. targeting groups/individuals who are 'at risk') and tertiary crime prevention (i.e. targeting identified offenders who are 'high risk'). Indeed, nearly 20 years later, the author acknowledged the insidious creep of risk-focused DCP approaches into Community Crime Prevention when suggesting that some 'community-based interventions ... have adopted a risk-focused approach' that effectively sees the community as an aggregate of 'individual risk profiles' (Crawford and Evans 2017: 808).

DCP approaches rarely focus on changing the material circumstances and contexts of potential offenders, instead prioritising individualising approaches such as early years interventions, parent training and behavioural programmes (Welsh and Tremblay 2021). Furthermore, despite its widespread acceptance across Western youth justice systems, the evidence-base for the hegemonic risk-focused form of DCP is worryingly underdeveloped and inconclusive, notably because 'the difficulty of establishing causes, not to mention the co-occurrence of risk factors, is a major impediment to understanding and replicating effective DCP' (Welsh, Zane and Rocque 2017: 147). Such overconfidence in an arguably flimsy, clearly reductionist evidence-base is perhaps unsurprising given the academic/empirical origins of DCP. For example, the Cambridge-Somerville Youth Study (Cabot 1940; Powers, Witmer and Allport 1951) was the earliest incarnation of a developmental approach to crime prevention, yet the evidence of its effectiveness is at best counterintuitive and at worst non-existent (see also Case and Haines 2009). Indeed, follow-ups of the Cambridge–Somerville sample have identified no significant positive effects from their exposure to the risk-based intervention in the study (i.e. a structured response targeting identified risk factors) and in some cases, even 'iatrogenic' (i.e. harmful, negative) effects such as reoffending due to the labelling and criminalisation associated with contact with the late formal youth justice systems (McCord 1978). These are certainly counter-intuitive conclusions from what has been heralded as the best-designed 20th-century longitudinal-experimental study of delinquency prevention (Tremblay et al., in Thornberry and Krohn 2003).

Since the mid-1990s, the RFPP has become a dominant model for conceptualising and delivering youth justice in the globalised Western world, particularly in the UK, Australasia and North America (Case 2022). The purported ability of the RFPP to effectively identify, target and then reduce risk in a clinical, evidence-based manner has offered a common sense, practical and readily understandable approach that has proved irresistible to some politicians, policymakers, practitioners and researchers seeking to ameliorate youth offending through youth justice responses. The paradigm has been especially attractive to professionals working in the contemporary neoliberal, modernising political climate/context that requires effective managerialism, audit focus, accountability, transparency, defensible practice and cost-effectiveness. The RFPP has provided stakeholders (e.g. governments, youth justice professionals) with a vehicle to administer actuarial justice by collecting quantitative, empirical data grounded in 'hegemonic' (dominant) developmental ARFTs and their related research evidence-bases (see Chapter 1), which can then drive evidence-based policy and practice (Stephenson et al. 2018; Bateman and Pitts 2005). Stakeholders have been particularly attracted to the paradigm's ability to identify a select group of individualised, psychosocial risk factors with a replicable statistical relationship to offending, which has encouraged Western governments to promote a risk-focused and correctional approach to operationalising evidence-based youth justice, with three commonly identified benefits:

1. Providing a rationale for distancing youth justice policy and practice from previously held beliefs about the causes and subsequent treatments of juvenile delinquency.
2. Offering a 'third way' alternative to traditional preoccupations with welfare or justice.
3. Implementing a mechanism for building a youth justice system capable of managing the youth 'problem.'

(France 2008: 3)

In summary, the RFPP has provided the youth justice sector with an evidenced framework (i.e. 'paradigm') and a 'foundational scientific body of knowledge' (Day 2020: 1) for governing the work of practitioners. The RFPP has proven highly attractive to youth justice policymakers, who have readily accepted the deterministic explanations and compelling evidence-bases of ARFTs as 'universal truths that are stable and reliable' (Smith 2016: 83) and have embraced the RFPP as offering 'clear, unambiguous guidance on how to solve a problem as complex as offending by children' (Smith 2016: 86). In a globalised era prioritising modernisation, managerialism, audit culture and quality assurance in the public sector, risk management through the RFPP has been employed as an 'effective,' defensible and transparent approach to constructing youth justice with an ostensibly robust empirical evidence-base (see Stephenson et al. 2018; Bateman and Pitts 2005). The explanations of ARFTs, animated in practice by the RFPP, have provided researchers, politicians, policymakers and practitioners with an expedient method of controlling and managing risk in an age where uncertainty and anxiety rule (Case 2022). The focus of this contemporary youth justice model, therefore, has been the practical prevention and reduction of exposure to risk factors and the risk of future offending, rather than prioritising punishment, any emphasis on welfare or justice principles or the protection of children's rights (see Chapter 4).

The RFPP as reductionist risk management: Psychosocial bias

The theoretical basis of the RFPP in developmental ARFTs, emphasising the criminogenic role of psychosocial risk factors, has also been criticised as individualising and decontextualising (Goddard and Myers 2017). As with theories of Individual Positivism (see Chapter 1), inherent developmental and psychosocial biases neglect the potentially criminogenic influence of broader socio-structural or contextual factors such as 'socio-economic status, local area … cultural, political or historical context' (Case 2007: 93). In other words, the RFPP is arguably a decontextualised approach because it measures and responds to certain purported 'determinants' of the development of youth offending, but practically ignores others. For example, it has been asserted that the RFPP 'embraces a 'myopic model' of rehabilitation that loses touch with the social roots of youth problems and focusses too heavily on improving internal thoughts and behaviors' (Goshe 2019: 559). Furthermore, the paradigm has been accused of supporting the neo-liberal strategy of responsibilising young people for reforming themselves whilst the influences of structural constraints and societal harms are overlooked (Gray and Smith 2024).

The RFPP as reductionist risk management: Lack of explanatory utility

The essential presumption that the RFPP identifies risk factors that provide a sound evidential basis for preventative interventions has been criticised for its lack of explanatory utility. Put simply, risk factors are no more than statistical correlates with and predictors of later offending behaviour; they are not causes of youth offending, despite often being treated as such in ecological discourse and youth justice policy and practice (Wikström and Treiber

2017). Even major proponents of the RFPP have admitted that 'While a great deal is known about risk factors for offending, less is known about causes, or about causal pathways or mechanisms. Ideally, intervention programme should target causes of offending' (Welsh and Farrington 2012: 62). To reiterate, correlation is not causation, and for explanatory purposes, 'statistical correlation explains nothing' (Bunge 2006: 123). Indeed, a cause is a factor bringing about an outcome (e.g. offending), whilst a predictor simply forecasts an outcome (Wikström, Treiber and Roman 2024) so it causes should be prioritised and targeted in youth justice interventions, rather than predictors (e.g. risk factors correlated with future offending). According to Wikström and Treiber (2017) in their ground-breaking 'Beyond Risk Factors' thesis, identifying causal factors can bring coherence to prevention/intervention practice that currently lacks strong guidance about what works (see later in this chapter) and, moreover, why it works, thus enhancing the efficiency and effectiveness of intervention practice.

Contextual challenge: Responding to risk 'in context'

Is it possible to argue that the hegemonic form of risk-based youth justice perpetuated by neo-correctionalism and the RFPP could be beneficial 'in context,' if the context is understood here as the relational and dynamic features of professional practices and interactions with young people in youth justice systems? For example, could an argument for practicality be made regarding the 'necessary reductionism' (see Case 2021) involved in converting risk to static, quantifiable, psychosocial factors, as opposed to pursuing overly complex constructions of no practical value or contextualised influences beyond the remit of practitioners? Could this necessary reductionism enable practitioners to design and implement pragmatic, evidence-based and targeted youth justice intervention activities? Conversely, does the oversimplified process of factorisation encourage professional stakeholders to artificially reduce the complexity and scope of 'risk' experiences and diminish young people's (contextualised) ability to negotiate them, which questions the ecological validity and practicality of resultant youth justice responses?

The RFPP as reductionist risk management: Factorisation and technicisation

The RFPP has oversimplified the complexity of youth offending and the criminogenic influences upon it by employing risk assessment methodologies to convert risk, a potentially complex construct into narrowly framed, quantifiable factors. This 'factorisation' process reduces potentially dynamic, multi-faceted and interacting experiences, characteristics, individual meanings/constructions, circumstances and behaviours into crude, potentially meaningless statistics that wash away the quality and validity of the outcomes measured. This reductionism has been compounded by the associated developmental and psychosocial biases that have simultaneously individualised and decontextualised explanations of and responses to youth offending.

The reductionist decontextualisation of youth justice through the RFPP has been exacerbated by the 'technicisation' inherent to the approach (Pitts 2003). Arguments that risk management processes have provided practitioners with structured and reliable evidence to support their decision-making and intervention planning (Baker 2005) have been countered by accusations that the RFPP collects data and evidence in overly technical, rigid and impersonal ways that have decontextualised explanations of youth offending and the youth justice responses to it (Myers, Goddard and Davidtz 2021; Haines and Case 2008). Notably, the RFPP has relied on factorising criminogenic influences through risk assessment instruments that are populated by mechanical, bureaucratic, tick-box processes. These overly technical procedures can deprofessionalise practitioners, depriving them of the ability to fully employ their expertise, knowledge and discretion to deliver nuanced assessment and intervention processes in relational and dynamic practice contexts (Souhami 2007). Technicisation compounds and is compounded by the adult-centrism of the RFPP, wherein the completion of risk assessment instruments and related decision-making and intervention planning are typically adult-led. Consequently, young people's constructions (e.g. perspectives, voices, meanings, realities) and the influence of the contexts they experience are often marginalised and neglected in youth justice processes, even though these young people may have the best understanding and 'lived experience' of the (risk factor) influences on their offending behaviour. As a result, the constructions and contexts of young people's lives are relatively ignored when explaining youth offending, and so the youth justice interventions informed by risk assessments may be crucially limited in their validity, practicality and effectiveness. Put simply, oversimplifies complex and dynamic aspects of young people's lives into quantifiable, 'dynamic' and restricted groups of psychosocial 'risk factors' can never hope to represent the 'lived realities' of young people who offend (France 2008) or to encompass the full range of criminogenic influences in their lives, which may include psychosocial factors, but will also include 'needs, motives, knowledge, social deficits ... [and] social and physical contextual factors' (Ward 2020: 2).

In focus: The popularity of individualised youth justice intervention in the USA

Individualised youth justice intervention has become commonplace across juvenile justice systems in the USA. In particular, 'cognitive behavioural' approaches (i.e. changing the way that young people think in order to change their behaviour) are considered one of the most effective ways to intervene in the lives of young people in trouble with the law (Myers, Goddard and Davidtz 2021). Individual-level interventions administered in the relational context of a supportive environment can play a role in changing young people's thought patterns, reducing their aggression and increasing their resilience to life's stressors and so can be extremely effective in reducing reoffending (Cullen and Jonson 2017; Andrews and Bonta 2010). However, there are clear limits to exclusively or even predominantly addressing youth offending at the level of behavioural and cognitive change. Notably, such individualised approaches to youth justice intervention and the risk-based logics that accompany them (e.g. the use of risk assessment tools and reliance on the RFPP) are inherently decontextualised, often ignoring the relationships that young people have with significant adults and the broader social, ecological, cultural, economic and political contexts within which these relationships develop (Goddard and Myers 2017).

Risk assessment instruments determining the nature and dosage of individualised, corrective intervention that young people (allegedly) need following offending continue to be widely used in the United States, despite specific concerns of race, class and gender bias in their content, implementation, conclusions and resultant intervention (Myers, Goddard and Davidtz 2021; Sawyer and Wagner 2020) and general concerns regarding the soundness of their risk-based logics (Hannah-Moffat 2019; Werth 2019). Consequently, the focus of many youth justice intervention programmes in the USA is upon young people improving, reforming and rehabilitating themselves by changing their thoughts and behaviours (Cox 2021; Goshe 2015). This individualised focus has come at the expense of developing policies that view youth offending in a larger social and relational context, with the overarching goal of addressing inequalities, strengthening communities and improving lives (Myers, Goddard and Davidtz 2021). Rather than being one aspect of a rational, just and effective approach to combating youth offending, individual-level change programmes/interventions have become the beginning and end points in discussions of what a reformed juvenile justice system should look like (Myers, Goddard and Davidtz 2021). This is considered by critics as short-sighted and potentially harmful because broader social conditions and contexts can be influential in the long-term efficacy of rehabilitative youth justice interventions, particularly as they address the root causes of offending (Cox 2021), rather than seeking to equip young people to better understand their lived reality of those root causes. Therefore, it has been argued that broader structural, social and economic policy change should accompany and support individual-level change programmes/interventions in order to realise a fully contextualised youth justice (Myers, Goddard and Davidtz 2021).

Algorithmic Risk Assessment: The new kid on the block

Algorithmic Risk Assessment (ARA) has emerged as another 'new kid on the block' for generating empirical and explanatory evidence through risk assessment mechanisms and the use of algorithms[5] as a way of informing youth justice interventions. ARA is a new frontier for knowledge production in youth justice, conceiving human nature in a radically different way from the individual theories that have previously dominated evidence generation (see Chapter 1). ARA offers a non-theoretical, predictive understanding of youth offending that is entirely lacking any humanistic component, privileging surface knowledge over depth of understanding (Mehozay and Fisher 2018). ARA rejects exploring scientific, empirical foundations for explanations of youth offending, instead trusting computational algorithms to identify patterns in the data. As such, ARA ostensibly represents an evolution (although some would argue devolution) of risk assessment methodologies that move beyond actuarial logic (Werth 2019a). Algorithmic forms of risk assessment purport to increase the accuracy and efficiency of risk-based youth justice by offering complete precision, devoid of the subjective bias (partiality) of actuarial risk management/assessment due to collecting data (as explanatory 'evidence') from diverse sources, rather than gathering restricted psychosocial data specifically for the purposes of risk prediction (Fisher and Mehozay 2019).

Despite its fast-growing popularity across westernised youth justice systems in the past decade, ARA remains extremely limited in its ability to generate evidence to inform youth justice interventions, notably because of its deliberate lack of a research foundation. In ARA, 'explanations' of offending are situated within an evidential 'Black Box,' rendering it both impossible and unnecessary to explain how risk scores have been deduced (unlike in actuarial assessment), and so reducing (to the point of elimination) any consideration of the aetiology of offending by young people (Hannah-Moffat 2018; Pasquale 2015). Through ARA, there is a greatly reduced (if any) necessity for empirical research in youth justice or any requirement to collect contextualised (or even humanised) research evidence relating to human beings, demographic groups or social situations (Fisher and Mehozay 2019; Pasquale 2015). ARA and the practice of decision-making that it informs are not intended to be empirically defensible or 'evidence-based' (Hannah-Moffat 2018). Consequently, ARA signifies a move away from generating research 'evidence' to inform practice in youth justice, yet simultaneously signifies a potential exacerbation of the overly technical, prescribed, non-reflective and deliberately decontextualised 'understandings' and decision-making engendered by actuarial risk assessment.

Furthermore, although ARA allegedly circumvents the pitfalls of partiality inherent to actuarial methods (e.g. due to its explicit lack of a pre-formed evidence-base), it has been asserted that 'it actually smuggles in all sorts of biases, assumptions, and drivers of inequality' (Brayne 2020). For example, it is possible that ARA suffers from 'layers of bias' (Eckhouse et al. 2019), illustrated by its tendency to disproportionately and artefactually identify black and minority ethnic groups as posing a higher risk (of reoffending, of harming others) by implicitly privileging psychosocial risk domains/factors during assessment, which these groups are more likely to be exposed to and disadvantaged by. Accordingly, the identification of minority groups as 'high risk' through ARA can compound existing socio-structural biases and disadvantages and also compound their existing over-representation in youth justice systems (Van Eijk 2020). As such, ARA could function as or be manipulated into a 'Trojan Horse' for risk-based reductionism in the youth justice field by dehumanising and decontextualising 'evidence' of criminogenic influences, with potentially deleterious effects on the recipients of youth justice interventions.

Adverse childhood experiences: A Trojan Horse for risk management?

The Adverse Childhood Experiences (ACEs) movement is one of the fastest-growing empirical research evidence-bases shaping contemporary youth justice (Gray, Jump and Smithson 2023). In Western youth justice systems, increasing prominence is being assigned to utilising ACEs research evidence as explanatory, for example, in England and Wales (YJB 2021) and in the USA (Division of Violence Prevention 2019). The rapidly expanding ACEs evidence-base is developmental, conceptualising traumatic experiences in childhood (e.g. psychological, physical and sexual abuse, physical and emotional neglect, household dysfunction, mental illness, substance abuse, divorce) as predictive of harmful behaviours and negative outcomes for young people in later life, including offending, aggression, imprisonment, psychiatric disorders, school exclusion, substance use and poverty (Jackson et al. 2023; McCartan 2020; MoJ and Welsh Government 2019). Accordingly, employing an ACEs lens has significant potential to instruct more contextualised explanations of and responses to youth offending through its focus on 'what has happened to' young people who offend and in what contexts this has happened, rather than privileging reductionist individualising and responsibilising explanations focussed on 'what they have done' (Gray, Jump and Smithson 2023). A logical practice corollary has been advocacy for integrated, multi-systemic responses to youth offending that utilise ACEs as their central explanatory mechanism by prioritising young people's health, well-being, psychology and behaviour (Taylor 2019). The common sense, practical nature of the ACEs evidence-base has proven readily amenable to application in the youth justice field. This ostensible utility, for example, in relation to young people with 'multiple complex needs' (a growing cohort within youth justice systems internationally – Wigzell, Paterson-Young and Bateman 2024), has encouraged widespread acceptance across the youth justice policymaking and practitioner communities.

Notwithstanding its burgeoning popularity, there is a research, policy and practice reality (arguably an immediate danger) that ACEs are unhelpfully conflated with and constructed as psychosocial risk factors. ACEs exposure is frequently measured quantitatively using a cumulative risk approach that involves totalling the number of adversities experienced by a child in order to evaluate and predict their 'risk' of negative outcomes (McCartan 2020; see also Case 2022). Consequently, this approach to constructing explanations of and responses to youth offending has significant potential to become a reductionist 'Trojan Horse' for actuarial, risk-based youth justice (i.e. risk management) due to its overriding reliance on employing the risk lens to identify, conceptualise, measure and target individualised criminogenic influences. For example, when examining the use of ACEs in youth justice interventions, researchers have employed the category of 'Risk Factors' to conclude that 'there are factors, warning signs and issues that can alert us to potentially problematic behavior' (McCartan 2020: 5). Additionally, ACEs are being increasingly measured in actuarial ways, with young people rated above a certain cumulative threshold of ACEs considered to be at higher 'risk' of negative outcomes and thus meriting more intensive intervention (i.e. akin to the risk-based 'Scaled Approach[6]' assessment-intervention framework in the YJS of England and Wales). Consequently, the emerging research evidence-base for ACEs-focused youth justice requires close scrutiny. There is a distinct danger across youth justice systems in the globalised Western world that ACEs will be uncritically adopted by governments and policymakers as psychosocial, decontextualised 'quick fixes' to more complex social issues (Fond, Haydon and Kendall-Taylor 2015) or worse still, as an over-simplistic and stigmatising proxy for continued reliance on explaining youth offending using psychosocial risk factors (Lacey and Minnis 2020). Both quick-fix and risk proxy understandings portray the ACEs evidence-base as a potential Trojan Horse for continued reductionism in youth justice.

In the context of this imminent danger of reconstructing ACEs as risk factors, there has been an inordinate degree of imputation from policymakers, service providers and academic stakeholders internationally (e.g. McCartan 2020; Taylor 2019; Justice Analytical Services 2018) regarding the causal, deterministic and predictive influence of ACEs on negative behaviours and outcomes in later life, particularly the uncritical attribution of aggregated/population risk levels to individuals (Lacey and Minnis 2020). This imputed causality and predictive validity serve as the rationale for retrospective practitioner assessments of ACEs, often leading to a quantified ACEs 'score' to guide intervention (i.e. the 'factorisation' of ACEs). However, the ACEs evidence-base is insufficiently developed to offer conclusive evidence of the predictive validity of ACEs themselves or explanations of their relationship with youth offending (Jackson et al. 2023), reflective of the conceptual and empirical ambiguity demonstrated by ARFTs and its body of related research (Case 2022). Despite this ongoing evidential ambiguity and partiality (e.g. psychosocial bias), the nascent ACEs evidence-base has benefited from an unjustified (non-evidenced) degree of policy pre-emption and support in youth justice systems. In England and Wales, for example, the 'Strategic Plan of the Youth Justice Board[7]' (YJB 2021) committed to rolling out explicit, 'trauma-informed'[8] responses to ACEs exposure, yet in the absence of sustained and convincing evaluation results of the efficacy of such an approach. This pre-emptive faith and support is reminiscent of the 'policy-based evidence' agenda of the UK Labour Government that introduced the Crime and Disorder Act 1998 (Goldson and Hughes 2010), where a self-fulfilling evidence-base was generated to validate preferred policy through post-hoc research and consultation with practice (e.g. validation of the 'Scaled Approach' to assessment and intervention using problematic and inconsistent evaluation results (Sutherland 2009; see also Haines and Case 2012). Therefore, there is an imminent danger that governments and policymakers internationally may (continue to) co-opt, repurpose, distort and exploit the ACEs agenda across youth justice systems in the service of continued risk reliance.

Risk management: Five steps towards decontextualised youth justice

1. **Punitivity:** Risk management came to dominate Western youth justice in the context of the 1990s 'punitive turn' and the associated rise to the popularity of actuarial, neo-correctionalist, evidence-based strategies, practices and technologies.
2. **Practicality:** Risk management arguably employs a strategy of necessary reductionism to enable practitioner-friendly, pragmatic, transparent, evidence-based youth justice approaches that link simplified (not overly complex) explanations of youth offending to youth justice responses.
3. **Impracticality:** Reductionist strategies inherent to risk management could render its interventions impractical and lacking in cogent and comprehensive evidence because the potential criminogenic influences are subjected to over-simplification (e.g. through factorisation), individualisation (e.g. through reliance on ARFTs) and decontextualisation (e.g. through psychosocial bias).
4. **Invalidity:** Risk management privileges the risk-based DCP approach to practical and 'effective' youth justice intervention, especially the RFPP, yet its associated evidence base is reductionist, partial, decontextualised and of dubious quality.
5. **Partiality:** Contemporary ARA and ACEs movements present as potential Trojan Horses for perpetuating the reductionist biases of actuarial risk management due to the partial, decontextualised ways in which they have been constructed in practice and due to the partial, decontextualised understandings of youth offending that they produce.

From 'nothing works' to 'What Works' as effective youth justice

The 'What Works' framework for evaluating what constitutes 'effective' criminal and youth justice intervention gained significant momentum in the

USA and UK in the 1990s, offering hope against the backdrop of the 'nothing works' collapse of faith in rehabilitation (see earlier in this chapter). The 'What Works' framework seeks to reduce reoffending through evidence-based treatment programmes 'rooted in criminological knowledge' (e.g. the explanations of Individual Positivism) and evaluated using 'rigorous science' (Cullen 2005: 1). The introduction of this approach in the 1990s chimed with the emerging neo-liberal, risk-based strategies that were increasingly influencing the direction of youth justice policy during this period. The genesis of 'What Works' dominance lies in a single, hugely influential study by Lawrence Sherman and colleagues in the USA at the end of the 20th century: 'Preventing Crime: What Works, What Doesn't, What's Promising.'

From its initial rise to prominence in the seminal Sherman et al. study, the 'What Works' framework for evaluating youth justice intervention effectiveness has been highly synergistic with the evidence-based RFPP, prioritising interventions that target criminogenic 'risk factors' using experimental and quasi-experimental methods of delivering youth justice. The 'What Works' framework has proven attractive to politicians in Western societies, not least because the Sherman review presented simple, quick, evidence-based, off-the-shelf solutions to the complex 'problem' of youth offending (Astbury 2018). As the framework had already demonstrated effectiveness in the field of health and medicine (Stephenson and Allen 2018), the translation of 'What Works' into youth justice appeared clear-cut – the impact of different interventions with different children in different contexts could be successfully measured through experimentation, RCTs and meta-analysis (Ward and Maruna 2007).

In focus: 'Preventing Crime: What Works, What Doesn't, What's Promising'

In 1996, the US Congress commissioned a comprehensive 'meta-evaluation' (i.e. a large evaluation of multiple other evaluations) of the effectiveness of crime prevention programmes across the USA. The resultant 'Preventing Crime: What Works, What Doesn't, What's Promising' review (Sherman et al. 1998) was required to prioritise programmes using 'rigorous and scientifically recognized standards and methodologies' and to give special emphasis to 'factors that relate to juvenile crime ... including "risk factors" in the community, schools, and family.' Sherman et al. (1998) utilised the 'Scientific Methods Scale' or 'SMS' (Cook and Campbell 1979) to assess the methodological quality of individual crime prevention evaluations according to three methodological criteria: control over 'extraneous' (i.e. external, unmeasured) variables that might influence the relationship between intervention and outcome, measurement error and statistical power to detect the effects of a programme (see also Hope 2005). The SMS consists of five levels of analysis, which escalate in rigour and detail (see Holloway, Bennett and Farrington 2005: 5):

1. Correlation between prevention programme and measure of crime at one point in time;
2. Measures of crime before and after the programme, with no control condition;
3. Measures of crime before and after the programme in experimental and control conditions;
4. Measures of crime before and after the programme in multiple experimental and control conditions, controlling for other variables that may influence crime (e.g. by matching, prediction scores, or statistical controls);
5. Random assignment to programme and control conditions – the 'Randomised Controlled Trial' (RCT).

According to Sherman et al. (1998), a risk-focused intervention exemplified 'What Works,' 'effective' youth justice if it was 'reasonably certain' that it prevents crime or reduces risk factors in the social context in which it was evaluated. The intervention must also have findings that are generalisable to similar settings in other places and times, in addition to at least two successful evaluations at level three or above. Programmes were labelled 'what's promising' if their ability to reduce crime or exposure to risk factors was too low to support generalisable conclusions, but there was still an empirical basis for predicting that further research could support such conclusions and they had at least one successful evaluation at level three of the SMS. Programmes were classified 'what doesn't work' if they could not be measured as reducing crime and reducing risk according to the SMS.

Notwithstanding its popularity across Western youth justice systems, the 'What Works' evidence of 'effectiveness' in relation to youth justice interventions could be accused of reductionism due to its privileging of a narrow range of (typically risk-based) evidence and rigid, experimental measures of intervention 'quality' based on the explicit randomised allocation of young people into control and treatment/experimental groups in order to evaluate whether an intervention 'works.' This was exemplified in England and Wales following the Crime and Disorder Act 1998 when youth justice staff were directed by the Youth Justice Board (YJB) to shape their work using a series of evidence-based 'Key Elements of Effective Practice' (KEEPs), which allegedly provided 'the essential elements of practice with all children at all stages of the YJS' (YJB 2003: 6). It was clear, however, that the KEEPs would be heavily reductionist, privileging findings from ARFTs (Smith 2016) within an implicit 'hierarchy of evidence' that placed experimental methods at its peak (Boaz and Ashley 2003: 6). Accordingly, the YJB placed an explicit expectation on commissioned KEEP authors to conduct systematic reviews of evidence using the SMS guidelines (Prior and Mason 2010), which elevated RCTs as their gold standard and championed the 'What Works' framework (France and Utting 2005). These reductionist partialities (biases) rendered 'certain research questions … "unaskable" because they cannot be addressed using experimental methods' (Prior and Mason 2010: 219); thus negating any potential for the production of 'inconvenient evidence' (Goldson and Muncie 2021); concurrently deprofessionalising youth justice staff by prescribing strict adherence to the 'risk' lens (Turnbull and Spence 2011).

'What Works': Perpetuating partiality

There are potentially significant limitations associated with the 'evidence' of youth justice intervention 'effectiveness' produced through the 'What Works' framework; limitations which conspire to perpetuate a weak, partial evidence-base with which to support practice. These limitations present most clearly in two key areas: The partiality (incompleteness) of explanations due to the intrinsic reductionism of 'What Works' evaluation methods and the partiality (bias towards evidence generated through the RFPP) of the most common methodological approaches adopted. The 'What Works' framework is designed to prioritise experimental research and is most commonly aligned with risk-based approaches, so it encourages the design, delivery and subsequent evaluation of methodologically reductionist interventions (Sutton et al. 2022; Tompson et al. 2020). Indeed, the Sherman et al. review privileged the experimental reduction of measurement errors and the use of 'statistical power to detect meaningful differences' between groups in experimental conditions (Sherman et al. 1998: 2–18), whilst minimising important contextual features that may be explanatory and that are most likely to be identified in qualitative research. This narrow, restricted, decontextualised approach to evaluating the 'effectiveness' of youth justice interventions illustrates how psychosocial 'causes' have been elevated atop an evidential hierarchy largely because their developmental and psychosocial origins align better with the scientific, experimental standards required by the hegemonic 'What Works' evaluation framework (Sutton et al. 2022). Priority status has been given to research that is devoid of the important contextual elements that are often only illustrated in qualitative research. This limitation is even acknowledged in the authors' comments regarding their 'What's Unknown' intervention category:

> This category includes major variations on program content, social setting, and other conditions which limit the generalisability of programs

> coded as working or not ... programs with unknown effects should not be judged deficient ... because a program has not been evaluated properly does not mean that it is failing to achieve its goals.
>
> (Sherman et al. 1998: 2–21)

The influence of reductionist, decontextualised, risk-based and experimental partialities of the 'What Works' framework is further evidenced in Sherman et al.'s acknowledgement that the SMS underpinning the framework is too restrictive and inflexible to adequately evaluate research on intervention programmes. The authors concluded that, on reflection, they would have raised the cut-off point for the scientific threshold and acknowledged that excluding 'moderately rigorous studies would waste a great deal of information that could be useful for policymaking' (Sherman et al. 1998: 2). This damning conclusion regarding the partiality (incompleteness) of the 'What Works' evidence-base was reinforced by Hough (2010: 13) when asserting that:

> The most consistent finding to emerge from ['What Works'] programmes for reducing reoffending is that insufficient research has been conducted of high enough quality to say much with any confidence. The second most consistent finding ... is that knowledge about what works is inconsistent and incomplete.
>
> (Hough 2010: 13)

Consequently, the reductionist and decontextualised nature of the 'What Works' evaluation framework raises critical concerns over its capacity to provide youth justice policymakers and practitioners with a clear, replicable, valid and truly contextualised guide for populating and delivering 'effective' preventative interventions (Astbury 2018; Wikström and Treiber 2017). Put simply, the decontextualised evaluation methods privileged by the 'What Works' framework 'ignore the emergent nature of the social world. People's agency, the factors that could make a difference are ignored or, at best, turned from rich relational accounts into variables, things to be empirically recorded' (Emmel et al. 2018: 4).

The proliferation of 'What Works': Five steps towards decontextualised youth justice

1. **Practicality:** The 'What Works' evaluation framework has been championed as an evidence-based, experimental and robust means of evaluating the 'effectiveness' of youth justice interventions and, as such, it offers a practical tool for intervention design.
2. **Pragmatism:** The framework is aligned with and characterised by neoliberal, neo-correctionalist, developmental and risk-based strategies for constructing and responding to youth offending.

3. **Explanatory partiality:** The 'What Works' approach perpetuates reductionism, partiality and decontextualisation by privileging developmental and individualising understandings of youth offending grounded in Individual Positivism and ARFTs.
4. **Responsive partiality:** The 'What Works' evaluation framework perpetuates reductionism, partiality and decontextualisation by privileging experimentalism, quantification and psychosocial bias at the expense of qualitative and contextualised interventions.
5. **Perpetuating decontextualisation:** 'What Works' marginalises the targeting of socio-structural and relational criminogenic influences (e.g. those present in macro- and meso-level contexts), the integration of qualitative personal experiences and constructions and alternative, non-risk approaches to intervention in its hierarchy of evidence.

Summarising the problem of decontextualised youth justice

This chapter has critically reviewed the variety of formal intervention responses to identified youth offending that come together in the social construction of 'youth justice.' These responses have been reflected in the laws, policies, strategies, cultures, theories and principles that inform and shape court sentences and professional practice (e.g. intervention design and delivery) with young people in westernised youth justice 'systems.' An overview of the trajectory of youth justice models, rationales and principles across Western society identified a long-standing battle for supremacy in the construction of youth justice between the competing priorities of welfare (underpinned by context-dependent, broader social explanations) and justice (underpinned by decontextualised, individualising explanations). It has been asserted that this perennial 'welfare versus justice debate' (Smith 2005) has been superseded since the 1990s by a 'punitive turn' in youth justice towards neo-liberal and neo-correctionalist strategies that individualise explanations of youth offending and adulterise and responsibilise young people when they offend, to the neglect of examining criminogenic influences in broader, non-individualised contexts. These modernising strategies have constructed, explained and responded to youth offending in decontextualised ways, prioritising actuarial risk management objectives and practice shaped by the RFPP, a technical, pragmatic, evidence-based approach grounded in individualising ARFTs and DCP approaches.

Thereafter, Algorithmic Risk Assessment was introduced as possibly the most (deliberately and explicitly) decontextualised approach to youth justice thus far, based on its reliance upon dehumanised/deindividualised and biased/discriminatory computational algorithms to predict and respond to youth offending. This 'context' of actuarial risk management and its animation through the RFPP and ARA has been compounded by the nascent Adverse Childhood Experiences movement, which was critically evaluated as

Table 2.1 Summarising the extent and nature of contextualisation in dominant youth justice responses to youth offending

Response category	*Criminogenic influences targeted*	*Approach*	*Psychosocial bias?*	*Contextual influence?*
Welfare Model	Unmet personal and social needs and well-being in a detrimental social context	Informal processes, treatment, support, indeterminate sentences	No	Yes – young people are seen as products of their environments and social contexts
Justice Model	Agency and psychosocial factors	Formal justice, punishment, determinate sentencing, due process, deterrence	Yes	Limited – constructed as immediate situational and immediate social
Punitive Turn	Agency and psychosocial factors	Repenalisation, neo-liberalism, responsibilisation, adulteration	Yes	No
Neo-Correctionalism/ Risk Management	Psychosocial risk factors, Adverse Childhood Experiences	Developmental Crime Prevention, Risk Factor Prevention Paradigm, risk assessment (including algorithmic)	Yes	Limited – constructed as immediate situational and immediate social
'What Works'	Psychosocial risk factors	Scientific Methods Scale, Developmental Crime Prevention	Yes	No

having the potential to provide contextualised explanations and responses to youth offending, yet also running a significant risk (ironically) of being constructed and animated as a Trojan Horse for reductionist, decontextualised risk-based youth justice.

The chapter ended with a critical discussion of the burgeoning 'What Works' evidence-based framework for evaluating the 'effectiveness' of youth justice interventions in Western youth justice systems. This evaluation framework has been promoted as a potentially practical and pragmatic basis for enabling practitioners to shape and deliver effective youth justice interventions in the real-world contexts they inhabit. However, it has also been criticised for promoting reductionist and decontextualised understandings of youth justice effectiveness through its experimental methodology and its privileging of quantitative evidence generated by and favourable to risk-based, individualised and psychosocial interventions shaped by the RFPP.

By way of a chapter summary, Table 2.1 below summarises the extent and nature of the (de)contextualisation discernible within the youth justice models, strategies and interventions reviewed thus far.

Notes

1 Youth justice systems are constituted by structures, laws, policies, strategies, practices, theories, principles, organisations and professional individuals. These elements interact with and inform youth justice decision-making and the design and delivery of youth justice responses in the form of the interventions and programmes used to pursue systemic sentencing, prevention, diversion and treatment objectives (Case 2021).

2 For example, there is growing evidence-base illustrating the local mediation and moderation of centralised government policy prescriptions and recommendations regarding youth justice (Case 2024).

3 In the early 1990s, there was a growing view that the Western world was becoming a 'risk society' – a world full of social, economic, political and physical risks resulting from rapid, widespread social changes, increasing processes of globalisation (e.g. the diversification and spread of technology) and socio-economic uncertainty.

4 Crawford elaborated on the Brantingham and Faust (1976) framework of 'primary,' 'secondary' and 'tertiary' prevention. Primary prevention manages and modifies the 'criminogenic conditions in the physical and social environment' (1976: 284); secondary prevention identifies and intervenes to reduce the likelihood of individuals or groups going on to offend; tertiary prevention is concerned with reducing the likelihood of reoffending.

5 Finite sequences of well-defined, computer-implementable instructions and data patterns.

6 An assessment-intervention framework dictates that young people subject to court disposals should have their level of intervention (frequency, intensity and nature) matched/scaled to their assessed risk level: low risk/standard intervention, medium/enhanced, high/intensive (YJB 2010).

7 The Youth Justice Board for England and Wales is a non-departmental public body with the dual responsibilities of advising the UK Government on youth justice policy development and guiding youth justice practitioners in the effective execution and delivery of these policies in practice.

8 It should be noted that trauma-informed practice can have a much broader lens than indicated by the current dominance of the psychosocial, risk-focused ACEs agenda, particularly the acknowledgement that children who offend are likely to have experienced greater levels of trauma, which need to be addressed when working with them (Lacey and Minnis 2020). This traumatic background does not have to be quantified or conceptualised in deterministic and predictive ways as it is within ACEs research and practice.

3 Explaining youth offending 'in context'

The opening thematic chapter critically explored the problem of decontextualised explanations of youth offending, arguing that the dominant theories across the Western world in the 20th and 21st centuries have been reductionist. It was shown that hegemonic aetiological/explanatory theories of youth offending have all situated the causes of youth offending within the individual, thus reducing and minimising potentially complex, constructed and contextualised explanations of criminogenic influence to a narrow, partial focus on over-simplified, psychosocial and decontextualised 'factors' operating in linear, deterministic ways. This 'explanatory reductionism' has been privileged at the expense of examining a broader range of macro-level economic, political, socio-structural, cultural and demographic influences that may contribute to explanations of and responses to youth offending. Criminological explanations of youth offending in the Western world have further neglected detailed consideration of the macro-level, socio-cultural and disciplinary biases of ethnocentrism, androcentrism, class-centrism and adult-centrism that have shaped the contexts in which these aetiological theories have been constructed, popularised and animated through youth justice interventions (see Chapter 2). Additionally, meso-level criminogenic influences have been marginalised, both in explanatory theories and in their associated responses, including the role of relationships/interactions (e.g. with immediate situational influences, with youth justice professionals, organisations and systems) and individual constructions of personal experiences. The opening chapters (1 and 2) concluded that in order to understand youth offending with sufficient complexity, completeness and validity, ongoing explanatory and responsive reductionism through partiality and decontextualisation must be acknowledged, unpacked, evaluated and ultimately addressed by seeking to understand youth offending 'in context.'

The third thematic chapter follows logically from the opening chapter by beginning this necessary journey towards explaining youth offending 'in context.' It explores the academic, political and professional contexts within which 'alternative' (e.g. non-individualising, non-risk-based) contextualised understandings of youth offending have been generated and applied. It will be asserted that these contextualised explanatory theories address and improve upon the theoretical, methodological and ethical limitations of their

DOI: 10.4324/9781003498100-4

predecessors, offering explanatory 'expansionism' to counteract traditional explanatory 'reductionism.' In summary, therefore, this third chapter provides an exploration of the contextualised criminogenic and criminalising influences situated at different levels of the social system (e.g. macro, meso, micro), including the influences upon how youth offending is constructed and reconstructed in different places at different times. The chapter is structured by four categories of aetiological/explanatory theory that each incorporate contextual considerations to varying degrees:

- 'Sociological Positivism' pursues explanatory foci that are sociological, socio-structural and socio-systemic, so situating criminogenic influences external to the individual.
- 'Quasi-Contextualised Risk Factor Theory' incorporates contextual considerations of the interactions between agency/choice, psychosocial risk factors, structural context, in/formal social controls, critical life events and young people's constructions of their exposure to risk as shaping pathways into/out of crime.
- 'Critical Criminology' has produced theories arguing that 'crime' is the social construction of powerful groups exercising unequal power relationships and typically disadvantaging less powerful groups. These critical theories challenge the Classical-Positivist explanatory 'orthodoxy' in the Western world and its construction of 'crime' and the 'problem' of youth offending.
- 'Left Realism' is a theory developed to challenge the perceived 'left idealism' of Critical Criminology (e.g. blaming the powerful) and the pathologising claims of 'Right Realism,' which assert that rational choice and moral poverty (e.g. blaming the powerless) encourage offending. Left Realists believe that it is mistaken to neglect the harmful behaviour of the powerless (e.g. young people) because the public's greatest fears of crime focus on street crime (perpetrated by relatively powerless groups), so this issue must be addressed in explanatory and responsive terms.

Sociological positivism

This opening section provides a critical exposition of alternative aetiological theories of (typically youth) offending that locate criminogenic influence within contexts that are immediate social (e.g. neighbourhood, peer group) or more broadly socio-structural (e.g. environment, poverty, unemployment). The focus will be on theories of Sociological Positivism that were developed in the late 19th century and early to mid-20th century to challenge Individual Positivism: early sociological theories, Concentric Zone Theory, Strain Theory, Subcultural Theory and Differential Association Theory.

Sociological positivism: The early years

A branch of the criminological theory emerged within Sociology in the early 20th century to explicitly challenge the explanatory limitations of Individual Positivism, whilst retaining a Positivist commitment to identifying the causes of crime through scientific methods. 'Sociological Positivism' extended the narrow focus of Individual Positivism (see Chapter 1) by considering the deterministic criminogenic influence of immediate social factors (e.g. community, neighbourhood, peer group) and structural factors (e.g. environment, poverty), all of which are external to the individual, as opposed to a narrow focus on the internal biological and psychological factors privileged by Individual Positivism when explaining (youth) offending.

The earliest theories of Sociological Positivism of offending appeared in the 1830s and 1840s and were not limited to explaining *youth* offending. French statistician Guerry and Belgian mathematician Quételet analysed official crime statistics within specific geographic areas and both identified statistical differences in crime levels in relation to gender, occupation, religion and age, along with broader socio-structural differences concerning the social, political and economic structures in particular societies. These differences indicated that offending may not be simply the product of individual motivations but instead may be an interaction between influences at various levels of the social system, both internal and external to the individual. This new focus was furthered by Italian criminologist Ferri (1895), who argued that offending was most appropriately explained and responded to by targeting a range of factors: Individual (e.g. age, gender, psychological variables), physical/environmental (e.g. race, geography, temperature) and social (e.g. population, religion, culture). Subsequently, in the early 20th century, sociologist Durkheim established his 'functionalist' perspective, which he utilised to argue that the social construction of 'offending' is a necessary tool for establishing moral, social and legal norms and boundaries. This perspective also viewed offending as a consequence of society's focus on competitive individualism and a highly structured division of labour. Durkheim argued that unless society regulates and restricts individual aspirations, a state of 'anomie' or 'normlessness' (i.e. the absence of social norms to guide and regulate behaviour) will occur, leading to a context of social disorganisation from which crime and disorder can result (Durkheim 1895/1964). Theorising of offending as an everyday behaviour within certain local areas prompted a new academic emphasis on exploring sociological factors as criminogenic. The early theoretical emphasis on sociological foci as potential explanations for offending behaviour was subsequently elaborated by three main strands of Sociological Positivism: Concentric Zone Theory, Strain Theory and Subcultural Theory.

Sociological positivism: Concentric zone theory

A group of sociologists working at Chicago University in the 1920s and 1930s, collectively known as the 'Chicago School,' innovated a Sociological

Positivist theory of crime by analysing the characteristics, social changes and distribution of people across Chicago, USA (Park and Burgess 1925; see also Benai 2019). The Chicago School researchers established that urban areas have much higher rates of recorded crime than rural areas, leading them to conclude that there is something criminogenic about certain places and spaces (e.g. immediate environment, local areas, neighbourhoods, communities). To illustrate their 'Concentric Zone Theory,' Park and Burgess (1925) divided the city of Chicago into five concentric 'zones' or areas of increasing size with a common centre: 1) Central business district; 2) transition from business to residences – the 'zone of transition'; 3) zone of independent workers' homes (working-class homes); 4) zone of better residences (middle-class homes); and 5) commuter's zone (suburbs). The 'zone of transition' was identified as having by far the highest rates of adult and youth offending. This was explained by identifying several criminogenic social characteristics that differentiated it from other areas in the city, notably social disorganisation animated by the regular displacement of residents, undesirable living facilities and being a deteriorating and transient neighbourhood, thus lacking social control of its residents. Shaw observed that:

> In this state of social disorganization, community resistance is low. Delinquency and criminal patterns arise and are transmitted socially just as any other cultural and social pattern is transmitted.
>
> (Shaw 1930: 205)

The researchers explained adult and youth offending as the product of neighbourhood factors resulting from environmental and cultural determinism, rather than from biological and psychological determinism (Case et al. 2021; see also Benai 2019). However, the theory downplayed the influence of broader structural factors (e.g. poverty, overcrowding) and foregrounded the immediate social influence of space and place (similar to the Rational-Contextual theories discussed in Chapter 1), thus constructing context as more immediate and static than relational and dynamic. Furthermore, in explanatory terms, Concentric Zone Theory has been criticised for advocating contradictory notions of crime causation. On the one hand, the theory explains offending as predetermined by social disorganisation (i.e. offenders as 'predetermined actors'), but it also assigns an element of free will to offending (i.e. offenders as 'rational actors') – explanations that have been viewed as theoretically incompatible (Hopkins-Burke 2016). Later studies from the Chicago School (see Hardyns and Pauwels 2017) employed research methods that incorporated more consideration of the lives, circumstances and perspectives of individuals in different communities (e.g. their ethnographies and life histories). This enabled Concentric Zone Theory to move away from strictly Positivist, deterministic explanations and towards multi-factor explanations of offending in criminal neighbourhoods as resulting from individual motivations, psychosocial influences and meso-level social interactions.

Sociological positivism: Strain theory

Durkheim's early 20th-century concepts of 'anomie' and competitive individualism as criminogenic (see earlier in this chapter) motivated a new theory of Sociological Positivism known as 'Strain Theory' (Merton 1938; see also Agnew 2011), which explained offending as a response to the socio-structural strains and pressures (e.g. to succeed, to gain wealth, to achieve recognised status) faced by individuals. Merton theorised that 'strain' results when there is a disparity between socio-cultural *goals* defining success and status and the institutionalised *means* available to the individual to achieve those goals. Thus, strain is criminogenic. Strain Theory provided a culturally specific explanation of crime, focussing on the 'American dream' of boundless/unlimited opportunity for all, which encourages individual aspirations (goals) that are often blocked by socio-structural restrictions and limited means, especially for young people. Therefore, (American) society encourages individuals to develop unrealistic, unachievable aspirations and expectations, which leads to strain, which then can lead to crime in order to alleviate the strain. According to Merton (1938), when an individual's goals cannot be realised because they are infeasible based on that individual's capabilities and means, then any of five adaptations occurs:

- Conformity: The acceptance of goals and means (the most common adaptation).
- Innovation: The value of attaining goals is accepted and acted upon irrespective of the impropriety, immorality or illegality of the means used to pursue them.
- Ritualism: Individual goals are abandoned in favour of adherence to institutionalised means.
- Retreatism: The individual rejects cultural goals and institutionalised means.
- Rebellion: The individual rejects cultural goals and institutionalised means, with the intention of altering the social structure.

Subsequently, Agnew (2011) validated Merton's conclusion that failure to achieve goals through conventional means could be criminogenic, but also proposed an expanded list of 'strains' that he claimed were directly related to youth crime/juvenile delinquency. These strains were akin to psychosocial risk factors and included masculine status, parental rejection, erratic and harsh discipline, child abuse and neglect, negative school experiences, unemployment or work with low pay and prestige, unpleasant tasks, little autonomy and limited opportunities for the future. Agnew (2011) also identified specific strains more closely related to socio-structural risk factors, such as youth homelessness, criminal victimisation and discrimination based on race, status and ethnicity.

In summary, Strain Theory explains (youth) offending as the result of individual adaptations to the criminogenic strain caused by a mismatch between an individual's goals and means, along with associated strains experienced in psychosocial and socio-structural domains of life, all of which can be viewed as negative life experiences. Critics of Strain Theory (e.g. Froggio 2007) have pointed to its reductionist and highly culturally specific empirical evidence-base (e.g. founded in a very limited number of studies, predominantly conducted in the USA) and the theory's inability to explain the complexity of the relationship between strain and delinquency.

Sociological positivism: Subcultural theory

The principles of Strain Theory were extended across the 1950s and 1960s by different forms of 'Subcultural Theory' developed in the USA, each of which focused on explaining offending by 'delinquent' young people (Agnew and Kaufman 2017). The seminal Subcultural Theory of Cohen (1955) emerged from his research into delinquent working-class boys and gang culture in Chicago. Cohen identified a series of working-class adaptations (see also Strain Theory) that these groups of boys would make to adhere to dominant middle-class social norms and values. However, whilst Strain Theory did not explicitly explore the forms of adaptation that led to irrational (criminal) behaviours that were not a means to an end (e.g. minor theft, petty vandalism), Cohen's Subcultural Theory did just this through its concepts of 'status frustration' and 'reaction formation.' Status frustration was the label that Cohen gave to the phenomenon whereby the subcultural group (gang) operated collectively by using specialised vocabulary, developing internal beliefs (e.g. norms) of their own and promoting unique ways of dressing and behaving (e.g. committing a crime), all of which demonstrated their frustration at their own inability to attain conventional goals. Status frustration was seen as a reaction formation, whereby the group inverted dominant middle-class values in order to offer them a collective solution to restricted opportunities. Cohen (1955: 28) observed that 'the delinquent conduct is right by the standards of his subculture precisely because it is wrong by the norms of the larger culture.'

A different form of Subcultural Theory was developed by Edwin Sutherland to explain the criminogenic influences of peer group membership and neighbourhood disadvantage on youth offending. Sutherland's 'Differential Association Theory' (Sutherland 1947; Sutherland and Cressey 1960) emphasised the role of psychological learning (see chapter one), but within social contexts (e.g. of neighbourhood disadvantage). He theorised that youth offending and attitudes favourable to it are learnt in interaction with other young people in intimate social groups, not necessarily young people who commit a crime, but certainly those who do not consistently support the law or established social norms. However, Differential Association Theory has been unable to explain why certain young people choose (not) to associate with others who approve of crime or to evidence of the precise nature of the associations that can lead to different types of crime.

In response to criticisms that his explanation was reductionist and deterministic, Sutherland (with Cressey 1960) revised his theory to argue that offending can occur when young people's associations with group attitudes favourable to crime are early, frequent and intense.

There has been much subsequent support for the role of differential association in the learning of youth offending (e.g. Rutter and Giller 1983), most notably for its broader explanatory model linking psychological learning with socio-structural (sub-cultural) elements to produce a more integrated theory of youth offending. For example, around the time that Differential Association Theory was being revised, a related Subcultural Theory was offered by Cloward and Ohlin (1960) to explain how working-class delinquents in subcultural groups pursue high-status goals by aspiring to meet their own working-class criteria and values, rather than seeking to attain middle-class values (which Cohen had argued). Cloward and Ohlin's (1960) version of Subcultural Theory combined anomie/strain with Differential Association Theory to explain why working-class individuals (typically boys) preferred certain adaptations over others, in particular, due to the differential availability of legitimate/illegitimate means to gain material and social status. Their conclusion was that criminal subcultures develop in working-class neighbourhoods where successful criminals become visible to young people and associate with them, providing a criminal success model of status and achievement based on working-class criteria.

Theories of Sociological Positivism have explained youth offending by arguing that young working-class males living in neighbourhood contexts with certain criminogenic characteristics (e.g. anomie, disorganisation, social deprivation, poor facilities, few social controls) are more likely to offend. The implication is that the neighbourhood context can be criminogenic and that young people in these contexts are more likely to experience strain and/or join subcultures, both of which may encourage them to offend. A critical overview of theories of Sociological Positivism highlights five crucial explanatory elements indicative of tentative, yet underdeveloped, contextualisation.

Evaluating sociological positivism: Tentative contextualisation 'take five'

1. **Broader determinism:** Youth offending is viewed as the structurally and culturally determined product of broader contextual pressures and influences external to the individual young person, rather than a product of choice or individualised, internal biological or psychological factors.
2. **Ignoring the 'centrisms':** Theories of Sociological Positivism remain relatively reductionist and partial (e.g. ethnocentric, androcentric, class-centric, adult-centric). In particular, they have privileged the study of offending by white, working-class males (typically youths/adolescents), constructing these groups as more likely to be criminal and restricting their explanatory utility by marginalising the criminality of ethnic minority groups, the middle-class or females.

3. **Limited explanatory utility and scope:** A reductionist by-product of ignoring the contextualised 'centrisms' is limited explanatory utility and scope. Consequently, associated evidence-based youth justice responses 'informed' by these theories may be of limited validity and applicability to young people as a broader group, whilst potentially perpetuating the criminalisation of the groups targeted by dominant explanations of youth offending (e.g. working-class boys).
4. **Decontextualisation:** Relative neglect of qualitative methodologies and meso-level, relational influences, combined with restricted constructions of context as immediate and static, risks decontextualising explanations of Sociological Positivism such that they lack ecological validity and applicability to the real lives/lived experiences of young people.
5. **Social construction:** Explanatory decontextualisation in Sociological Positivism is further promoted by the failure to acknowledge 'crime' and 'youth offending' as dynamic, contested and contingent social constructions by powerful institutions, groups and individuals in different societies. Assuming consensus in the definition of 'youth offending' in this way can neglect the exploration of the criminogenic influences associated with its construction, such as systemic influences and individual subjective experiences.

Contextual challenge: Is 'centrism' justified when explaining youth offending?

It is clear that the socio-historical construction of explanations of youth offending has been shaped and distorted by 'centrisms,' with theories typically created in the Western world by white, middle-class men, based on their study of the behaviour of white, working-class boys. But are these centrisms indicative of theoretical and methodological bias or reflective of the reality of who offends in society? Are they a mixture of both? Moreover:

- Do Western societies prioritise explanations of youth offending that apply to white, working-class boys (and adult men) because they do actually commit the majority of crimes? This would be a Realist view (see later in this chapter).
- Are androcentric and class-centric foci (e.g. in Strain and Subcultural theories – Brownfield 2018) products of uncritical assumptions that working-class males commit the most crime, which leads to the targeting of research, theory, policy and criminal justice practices (e.g. police activity) on this group to the exclusion of others? If so, then this bias constructs a 'self-fulfilling prophecy' – a belief/prediction that causes itself to come true as a direct result of the new behaviour it creates.

Should proponents of Strain and Subcultural explanations rethink their theories to ensure that youth subcultures are not benchmarked by Anglo/

American cultural identities, but instead refer to youths whose behaviours are oppositional to mainstream culture, regardless of the society they come from? (Nwalozie 2015).

Quasi-contextualised risk factor theory

A group of contemporary risk-based explanations have begun to incorporate considerations of the social construction of youth offending and the role of contextualised criminogenic influences, whilst remaining predominantly artefactual (hence 'quasi' contextualised). Two main groups of 'Quasi-Contextualised Risk Factor Theory' have come to the fore in contemporary explanations of youth offending: 'Age-Graded Life Course Theory' examining interactions between psychosocial risk factors, structural context, in/formal social controls and critical life events and 'Constructivist Pathways Theory' exploring how young people construct, make meaning of, negotiate and resist exposure to risk, shaping pathways into or out of crime and emphasising interactions and relationships between agency and structure (e.g. power relations and dynamics).

Age-graded life course theory: Crime in the making

Following an extensive process of reanalysis of data from two associated studies, 'Unraveling Juvenile Delinquency' (Glueck and Glueck 1930) and '500 Criminal Careers' (Glueck and Glueck 1950), Sampson and Laub constructed an Age-Graded Life Course Theory (AGLCT), which they called the 'Age-Graded Theory of Informal Social Control.' Set out in the highly recommended text 'Crime in the Making' (Sampson and Laub 1993), their tripartite explanatory theory posited that:

- Structural context (e.g. social class, ethnicity, gender, poverty, broken home, household overcrowding, parental employment), mediated by informal social controls in the family and school, explains delinquency in childhood and adolescence.
- Continuity in antisocial behaviour from childhood to adulthood is evident in a variety of life domains.
- Informal social bonds to family and employment in adulthood explain changes in criminality over the lifespan, despite early childhood propensities.

(Sampson and Laub 1993: 7)

According to this AGLCT, a young person's behaviour, whether prosocial or antisocial, is met with a range of formal and informal responses (e.g. official sanction, parental discipline, approval/disapproval of peers). The nature of these responses interacts with existing psychosocial and socio-structural risk factors to shape the young person's future behaviour. For example, official sanctions for offending may diminish educational or vocational opportunities by incarcerating the young person and thus removing them from school. Conversely, official sanctions may set the young person on a prosocial pathway by rendering a neglected education compulsory. In this way, the interaction between risk/protective factors and formal/informal responses to behaviour can form either vicious or virtuous circles. Sampson and Laub added individual agency into their theory, asserting that risk/protective factors and formal/informal responses to behaviour are not seen as wholly deterministic of future behaviour, but as providing the context that shapes the decisions young people make about how to behave (Sampson and Laub 1993).

Sampson and Laub made a particularly important contribution to explaining youth offending by identifying life events that interrupt the supposedly predetermined criminal career path, thereby challenging the previously held belief that risk factor influence was stable over the life course. They identified the possibility that offending trajectories could *change* during times of transition and significant periods (dynamic contexts) in an individual's life (e.g. moving or leaving school, gaining or losing employment, getting married or separated). Thus, social contexts, transitions and/or exposure to short-term (often abrupt) critical life events can promote offending or desistance from offending. Where this occurred, a substantive change in an individual's offending trajectory could result, which the authors labelled a 'turning point.' Although Sampson and Laub (1993) acknowledge the importance of early childhood experiences in influencing later problem behaviours, they rejected reductionist developmental determinism and the oversimplification of risk factor influence. Instead, they argued that an individual's behaviour is shaped by exposure to psychosocial and socio-structural risk factors and the critical life events they experience throughout the life course. In this way, Sampson and Laub's AGLCT moved ARFTs forward from a narrow over-reliance on quantitative, developmental and deterministic understandings of the impact of early life risk factors (see France and Homel 2007) and towards constructivist explanations of the individual's ability to actively influence their trajectories and pathways into and out of crime.

Despite its explanatory expansionism, however, Sampson and Laub's 'Age-Graded Theory of Informal Social Control' does not represent a complete break from traditional developmental ARFTs. The authors demonstrated that young people's propensity to offend is largely linked to psychosocial risk factors and that the influence of these factors can be stable over the life course, with offending usually increasing during adolescence and slowly falling away in adulthood. In reaching their conclusions, however, Sampson and Laub were inevitably wedded to re-analysing the Gluecks' original, narrow set of simplified, quantified psychosocial risk factors as criminogenic influences identified in childhood using a staunchly developmental approach. These constraints placed limits on the scope and range of Sampson and Laub's conclusions (see Case and Haines 2009). For example, there remain unexamined and unresolved tensions between the deterministic influence of early life risk factors and the possibilities for varied outcomes resulting from the impact and influence of dynamic, contextualised social processes and the impact of immediate social circumstances/contexts (Bottoms and McClintock 1973; see also Case and Haines 2009). Indeed, intuitively, the elements of Sampson and Laub's theory examining the impact and importance of contemporary 'factors' and social processes seem more able to capture the realities and dynamism of social life than the less fluid, more developmentally deterministic, psychosocial and artefactual elements of the Gluecks' research. Furthermore, it remains unclear whether risk factors and life events are substantively different concepts in this theory and, if so, how they differ. It also remains unclear how and to what extent early life risk factors, current risk factors and life events influence behaviour and how they combine to influence behaviour over the life course. Therefore, whilst Sampson and Laub's analysis clearly calls into question notions of developmental determinism, their theory of vicious and virtuous circles between risk/protective factors and offending outcomes ultimately lacks clarity regarding its key concepts, is restricted by pre-determined lists of psychosocial risk factors and is hypothetical in its explanations of the impact of risk factors, social processes and individual agency on future behaviour (Case and Haines 2009).

In recognition of their original theoretical and analytical limitations, Sampson and Laub re-evaluated and revised their Age-Graded Theory of Informal Social Control a decade later in a text entitled 'Shared Beginnings, Divergent Lives' (Laub and Sampson 2003; see also Laub, Sampson and Sweeten 2017). In follow-up research, Laub and Sampson conducted detailed life history interviews with 52 men from the original delinquent group studied by the Gluecks, supplemented by analyses of the criminal histories and death records of all 500 men who formed part of the original sample. This qualitative, narrative life history approach evolved ARFTs (even more than Crime in the Making already had) from their traditional emphasis on quantitative, variable-based methods towards a focus on the life stories of the individual, in an attempt to obtain richer, more comprehensive data to illuminate why some people persist with and others desist from crime across their whole life course (Laub and Sampson 2003). Although this research was not focused on young people, Laub and Sampson were addressing a crucial contradiction within the developmental approach of the Gluecks and others – that childhood risk factors apparently determine offending in later life, yet young people also seem to grow out of crime.

'Shared Beginnings, Divergent Lives' identified four main self-reported 'transitions' in the lives of the delinquent sample that functioned as contexts containing turning points promoting desistance from offending in adulthood: marriage, joining the military, attending reform school and moving to a more prosperous neighbourhood. Interviewees reported that each of these transitions offered them the opportunity to change the direction of their lives, to receive supervision, monitoring and social support, to bring change and structure to their routine activities and to transform their identity (Laub and Sampson 2003). Therefore, desistance from an offending career was dependent on two central developments in the life of sample members: 'knifing off' from their immediate environment and obtaining 'structured role stability' across life domains (e.g. marriage, work, community). Knifing off enabled the desisters to transform their identities into a more positive form and to access social support. Structured role stability enabled the young men to have structure, certainty and support related to their routine activities. In contrast, frequent and persistent offenders or those who desisted from offending at a much later age appeared to lack these supportive structures and relationships throughout their life course. They reported that a lack of informal social control and support structures rendered them unable to forge attachments to significant others and that the general lack of structure in their lives exposed them to more criminogenic situations on a routine basis.

Laub and Sampson concluded that their original theory had failed to examine the progression or 'pathways' of change in behaviour over the life course, particularly in relation to desistance from offending. Consequently, using life history data, Laub and Sampson developed an integrated life course theory to account for the respective roles and impacts of risk factors in adulthood (as opposed to just in childhood and adolescence), individual agency, situational factors, routine activities, culture and historical context. They drew on constructivist understandings of risk to explore the 'inner logic of lives' (Laub and Sampson 2003: 8). By studying individuals through adulthood using qualitative research methods and by focussing on individual agency, situational factors and cultural and historical contexts, Laub and Sampson claimed to be 'reconsidering the risk-factor paradigm' (Laub and Sampson 2003: 289) and enabling a richer, more holistic understanding of persistence and desistance in offending careers. In explaining their findings, Laub and Sampson rejected the deterministic view of developmental forms of ARFTs that the life course is 'an unwinding, an unfolding, or an unrolling of what is fundamentally 'already there'' (Sampson and Laub, in Farrington 2005: 178). They also rejected the 'structural determinism of turning points in the life course' by arguing that 'desistance is best viewed as a process realized over time, not a single event' (2003: 278). The authors therefore extrapolated their original Age-Graded Theory of Informal Social Control to include 'the idea of situated choice as central to an understanding of crime from childhood through old age' (2003: 293).

Critical evaluation of 'Shared Beginnings, Divergent Lives,' however, indicates that the revised theory does not offer enough substance or detail to sufficiently address the question of whether the human agency and young people's ability to construct their offending/desistance pathways undermine the view that youth offending is developmentally determined. Crucially, due to its emphasis on desistance in adulthood, the revised theory does not explore why young people offend (Case 2021). Additionally, there is only a tentative and limited understanding of the precise role of agency and its interaction with risk factors and risk processes in different domains of life, in different contexts and at different ages (Case and Haines 2009). For example, Laub and Sampson suggest that changes in social and situational circumstances (e.g. contact with official agencies, increased informal social support, chance) can prompt changes in behaviour, notably desistance from offending, yet they offer only limited explanatory understanding of how these social circumstances may promote processes of change.

Age-graded life course theory: The Edinburgh study of youth transitions and crime

Beginning in 1998, the prospective longitudinal 'Edinburgh Study of Youth Transitions and Crime,' commonly known as 'The Edinburgh Study,' was 'not concerned with early childhood influences, but with [criminogenic] transitions and personal transformations during adolescence and adulthood' (Smith and McVie 2003: 169–70). The rationale for this later life focus was that dominant (developmental) ARFTs to that point had consistently demonstrated the predictive ability of psychosocial risk factors experienced in childhood (see Chapter one), but with limited focus on criminogenic influences in adolescence or on socio-structural and contextual influences. Therefore, the key aim of the Edinburgh Study was to integrate 'explanations [of youth offending] at the level of the individual and local community' (Smith and McVie 2003: 169). This theoretical integration was central to the study, which explored individual development (aligned with ARFTs – see Chapter one), interactions between psychosocial, neighbourhood and socio-structural risk factors (aligned with Ecological Theory – see Chapter one), young people's interactions with formal and informal agencies of control (aligned with AGLCT) and how young people negotiated their pathways into and out of offending (aligned with Constructivist Pathways Theory – see next section).

The Edinburgh Study examined the lives of a cohort of 4,317 young people aged between 11½ and 12½ years who entered secondary school in Autumn 1998. Data was collected about these young people from multiple sources and using multiple methods: Pastoral teacher questionnaire (1999 only), parent/carer survey (2001 only), official records (e.g. social work, police, Children's Hearings, schools, Scottish Criminal Records Office), neighbourhood information (e.g. police recorded crime, youth population statistics, rates of unemployment, overcrowding, renting and single-parent households) and a community survey of Edinburgh residents (2001 only). The main data collection methods employed *with* the young people themselves were:

- Questionnaires measuring the prevalence and frequency of self-reported offending and a set of 'explanatory factors' seen as increasing the 'risk' of offending – identified following extensive consultation with researchers in the UK, USA and New Zealand (Smith et al. 2001).

- Interviews followed up the questionnaires by measuring a range of more specific issues, including reasons for involvement in, and desistance from, offending.

The so-called 'explanatory factors' in the questionnaire related to the typical (micro-level) psychosocial domains privileged by ARFTs and related research, whilst the researchers were also interested in exploring the potential (meso-level) criminogenic influences of system contact (e.g. with police, courts, youth justice staff). The Edinburgh Study identified a series of allegedly causal and explanatory risk factors for youth offending in the psychosocial domains examined (McAra and McVie 2022), notably:

- Individual and Family: Impulsivity (Smith 2006), poor parental supervision and parent-child conflict (Smith et al. 2001), parenting style and family functioning, parental consistency, parent–child conflict and excessive punishment (Smith 2006).
- School: Attitudes to school, relationships with teachers, school-based misbehaviour (Smith et al. 2001) and attachment to school, which suggested that 'there is a role for schools in preventing the development of delinquent behaviour' (Smith 2006: 4).
- Neighbourhood: Neighbourhood deprivation, including high unemployment, dense local authority housing, dissatisfaction with the neighbourhood and living in a disorderly neighbourhood (Smith 2006).
- Peers and Lifestyle: Gang membership (Bradshaw and Smith 2005), contact with the police and local criminal justice agencies (Smith 2006; McAra and McVie 2007, 2022).
- System contact: The authors concluded that 'repeated and more intensive forms of contact with agencies of youth justice may be damaging to young people in the long-term' (McAra and McVie 2007: 333) due to labelling creating a master status of 'offender' for them. This, in turn, can exacerbate the criminogenic influence of socio-structural factors already outside of the young person's control, such as family structure, social deprivation and gender discrimination (McAra and McVie 2007, 2022).

The Edinburgh Study was an ambitious project that aimed to develop a more comprehensive, integrated 'explanatory model' of how risk factors for youth offending interact with a broader set of meso- and macro-level contextualised influences than had been explored by more restricted ARFTs. For example, the integrated approach adopted moved beyond typical ecological considerations of neighbourhood 'collective efficacy,' community functioning and neighbourhood socio-economic status (Wikström and Loeber 2000) to explore the criminogenic influence of broader socio-structural factors (e.g. gender, family structure, social deprivation) and the deleterious/harmful impact of contact with youth justice agencies. However, whilst the Edinburgh Study's focus on socio-structural influences and the influence of system contact was a welcome challenge to the reductionist, psychosocial and decontextualised biases of ARFTs, it still retained a predominantly psychosocial, factorised and thus largely reductionist construction of 'risk' in line with the limitations of much previous developmental ARFTs. It is also debatable as to whether the various explanatory strands hang together in a coherent and consistent integrated explanatory model of youth offending (Case 2021), particularly one intent on reducing/factorising complex risk measures and fitting diverse theoretical explanations into a developmental, risk-based, predictive paradigm. Consequently, it is difficult to evaluate whether the Edinburgh Study actually represents an integrated theoretical evolution of ARFTs or whether it is merely a collection of loosely connected theories and approaches examining different aspects of risk within a methodology that remains devoutly developmental and deterministic in orientation (Case and Haines 2009). The diverse, disparate theoretical foci have, to an extent, robbed the research of a clear and coherent theoretical identity and have had their central tenets over-simplified by a somewhat reductionist approach to measurement and analysis, which has limited the definitiveness with which conclusions can be supported.

In summary, AGLCT explanations of youth offending have gained increasing prominence since the early 1990s through a new breed of Quasi-Contextualised Risk Factor Theory incorporating more detailed considerations of the social construction of youth offending and the role of contextualised, systemic (meso-level) and socio-structural (macro-level) criminogenic influences within their explanations of youth offending. However, AGLCT has remained wedded (to a degree) to explanatory and methodological reductionism by (at worst) focussing on the established, partial and decontextualised psychosocial risk factors of ARFTs and (at best) extending this explanatory focus by considering their interactions with contextual influences such as social-structural context, in/formal social controls, system contact and critical life events. Therefore, this continued faith in the central importance of developmental, deterministic and decontextualised explanations of ARFTs renders AGLCT only 'quasi' (partly) contextualised.

Evaluating age-graded life course theory: Five steps towards quasi-contextualised explanations of youth offending

1. **Integrating interactional criminogenic influences**: AGLCT explains youth offending is a product of interactions between psychosocial risk factors, structural context, formal social controls (e.g. official punishment), informal social controls (e.g. parental disapproval) and critical life events (Sampson and Laub 1993).
2. **Integrating the role of social construction**: AGLCT pursues a richer, more complex understanding of stability and change in youth offending trajectories as resulting from individuals' constructions and their interactions with risk factors, structural contexts and social controls.

3. **Integrating stability and change in contexts experienced across the life course:** Interactions at different life stages shape continuity/stability and change in offending pathways for young people, which can lead to transitions and turning points into and out of youth offending, including 'knifing off' from a criminogenic environment and obtaining 'structured role stability' from marriage, work or moving neighbourhood (Laub and Sampson 2003).
4. **Integrating socio-structural, contextualised criminogenic influences:** The Edinburgh Study evidenced the criminogenic influence of socio-structural, contextualised risk factors through a multi-faceted measure of 'neighbourhood deprivation.'
5. **Integrating systemic, contextualised criminogenic influences:** The Edinburgh Study evidenced the criminogenic influence of young people's contexts, interactions and relationships with official systems, agencies and processes of youth justice (McAra and McVie 2007).

Constructivist pathways theory: Explaining risk in socio-structural context

Understanding youth offending through a 'Constructivist Pathways' lens focusses on how young people are able to actively experience, negotiate and, therefore, construct their own pathways into and out of offending. The Constructivist Pathways perspective examines how young people's ability to negotiate and construct their responses to risk factors can be mediated by socio-structural contexts they inhabit and experience, such as neighbourhood socio-economic status, poverty, unemployment, localised cultural influences and political influence (France and Homel 2007, 2013). According to Elder, Kirkpatrick Johnson and Crosnoe (2004: 7), Constructivist Pathways Theory evolves ARFTs and AGLCT by focussing on 'social pathways, their developmental effects, and their relation to personal and social-historical conditions' (see also Tisdall et al. 2023). Young people are seen as active agents in their own lives and as active constructors and interpreters of risk factors and risk processes (see Case and Haines 2009). However, their agency, opportunities, choices and ability to negotiate and resist risk are also limited, constrained and bounded by contextual and structural factors outside of their control (France and Homel 2007).

Constructivist pathways theory: Pathways into and out of crime

In the early 21st century, a partnership of longitudinal studies sponsored by the Economic and Social Research Council (ESRC) focused on how young people are able to negotiate and make meaning of their 'pathways into and out of crime' (e.g. how they negotiate and construct their exposure to risk factors) and how social processes and demographic characteristics operating in different contexts can mediate the influence and experience of risk factors (Hine 2005; see also France and Homel 2013; Kemshall, Marsland and Boeck 2013). The 'Pathways Into and Out of Crime' partnership sought to improve understanding of youth offending in contextualised ways by moving research away from the developmental determinism of ARFTs and towards a deeper consideration of how young people interpret and choose to respond to risk in their current lives and how their ability to negotiate risk is affected by others. The partnership projects were:

- 'Risk and resilience in children who are offending, excluded from school or have behaviour problems': An investigation of the 'factors that enhance or reduce risk,' critical turning points and pathways into and out of crime for first-time offenders working with Youth Offending Teams (YOTs), young people permanently excluded from school and young people with statements of special educational needs (Hine et al. 2007). The study methodology consisted of interviews with young people and key professionals.
- 'Risk, protection and resilience in urban Black and Asian culture': A project utilising video stimuli created by young people and focus group discussions with researchers to examine young people's experiences, constructions and negotiations of risk in their area and 'the combination of risk and protective factors which can lead to resilience or susceptibility' in Black and Asian young people (see Haw, in France and Homel 2007).
- 'Risk, protection and resilience in the family life of children and young people with a parent in prison': An exploration of the factors, experiences and processes related to risk, protection and resilience for children with a parent in prison, using questionnaires, pre- and post-release interviews with imprisoned parents and interviews with children and young people (Walker and McCarthy, in Preston 2005).
- 'Young people, social capital and the negotiation of risk': A study of the influence of social and material resources (social capital) on perceptions, experiences and negotiations of risk, decision-making (risk choices) and risk-taking behaviour by young people from secondary schools, YOTs and community groups (see Kemshall et al. 2013; Boeck, Fleming and Kemshall 2006). The study has employed survey questionnaires, interviews and focus groups with young people.
- 'Risk, protection and substance misuse amongst young offenders': an examination of the relationship between substance use and offending, using structured questionnaires, with a particular focus on the 'relationships between substance misuse, offending and personal and social risk factors' (Hammersley, Marsland and Reid 2003).

Taken together, the 'Pathways Into and Out of Crime' partnership projects utilised qualitative methodologies (with strong quantitative elements in certain projects) to engage with so-called 'hard-to-reach' and minoritised groups of young people. The studies aimed to explain the complex mechanisms that link 'risk' with youth offending (see France and Homel 2007), challenging the reductionist and decontextualised way in which ARFTs framed the risk 'problem' (see Webster 2007). Thus, the partnership studies rejected explanations of youth offending based on linear interpretations of causality and the deterministic nature of early life experiences (e.g. explanations promoted by ARFTs), preferring to examine the young person as a 'social actor' who experiences, feels, perceives, constructs and makes meaning of their lives, including their exposure to risk factors. In this way, young people were seen to have a reflective and reactive relationship with their social and physical environment (contexts), rather than being passive and helpless recipients or 'victims' of exposure to the inevitably criminogenic effects of childhood risk factors.

When synthesising findings from across the studies, Hine (2006) concluded that:

- *Context* can be important in determining whether a factor is associated with risk or protection and circumstances assumed to signify risk (e.g. school exclusion) may actually be protective.
- Young people's *responses to risk* can depend on community context, peer group, family context (e.g. relationships with family) and their relationship with professionals.
- *Resilience* to risk factors and negative influences can be promoted by family and peers.
- '*Risk stagnation*' can occur when young people are unable or unwilling to remove themselves from their current situation due to feelings of hopelessness and fatalism.

According to Hine (2006), the studies demonstrated that for young people, there are substantial differences between the reality of their everyday experiences and the explanations of youth offending that 'inform' youth justice policy and interventions. Collectively, the studies understood 'risk' as an interactive and dynamic process that is complex, multi-faceted and contextualised.

Constructivist pathways theory: The Teesside studies

A group of constructivist and contextualised studies of youth offending from researchers at Teesside University came to prominence at the same time as the ESRC Pathways partnership studies. Each of these studies took a biographical approach to examine how young people construct and deal with risk in their daily lives and how socio-structural context could be criminogenic (MacDonald and Shildrick 2018). 'The Teesside Studies' adopted a constructivist perspective to study how young people experience risk in different socio-structural contexts and how their resultant perceptions, decisions and constructions affect their transitions into adulthood. In 'Snakes and Ladders: Young People, Transitions and Social Exclusion' (Johnston et al. 2000), interviews were conducted with a cohort of 98 young people aged between 15 and 25 years old from the same neighbourhood, social class and ethnic background about their transitions into adulthood. In 'Disconnected Youth? Growing Up in Britain's Poorest Neighbourhoods' (McDonald and Marsh 2005), interviews were conducted with 88 young people aged between 15 and 25 years old living in socially disadvantaged neighbourhoods in order to examine the relative merits of underclass theories (see also the discussion of Right Realism later in this chapter) and how ideas of social exclusion connected to the 'lived realities' of these young people. The initial Teesside studies were followed up by 'Poor Transitions: Young Adults and Social Exclusion,' which set out to examine where youth transitions had led members of the original two samples once they reached adulthood. It is this final study that has had the most explicit focus on examining the influence of risk on young people's offending pathways.

'Poor Transitions: Young Adults and Social Exclusion' was a qualitative, retrospective longitudinal study of socio-structural and contextual criminogenic influences such as neighbourhood destabilisation and socio-economic deprivation (Webster, Macdonald and Simpson 2006). In 'Poor Transitions,' Webster, MacDonald and Simpson (2006) took issue with the plethora of 'backward looking' developmental and deterministic ARFTs that had strongly linked negative experiences in early life to later offending. Following a series of retrospective biographical interviews with young people aged between 16 and 25 years old, the researchers observed and concluded that risk factors experienced in teenage years and early adulthood were indeed influential on offending behaviour but had been interpreted deterministically in previous theories without any exploration of their potential interrelationships with other risk factors, notably socio-structural risk factors. The study concluded that young people faced 'a myriad of risks scarcely recognised in risk and prediction studies' which inextricably linked biography, place and social structure (Webster, MacDonald and Simpson 2006: 15). Moreover, it was concluded that young people experienced transitions in their lives that were fluid, unpredictable and chaotic, implicating the inextricable and complex relationships between biography, place and social structure. Therefore, young people's exposure to risk factors and their ability to resist them were influenced by accelerated socio-economic contexts of change, which destabilised neighbourhoods and precipitated unpredictable life events (see MacDonald 2013).

Evaluating constructivist pathways theory

The 'Pathways Into and Out of Crime' partnership and the 'Teesside Studies' challenged the inherent determinism, psychosocial bias and decontextualisation of ARFTs by utilising a constructivist and contextualised lens to examine how young people negotiate their environments and the contexts they experience (MacDonald and Shildrick 2018; France and Homel 2013; see also Case and Haines 2009). Accordingly, Constructivist

Pathways Theory has enabled detailed exploration of the 'chaotic, complex, relative, contextual' relationships between risk factors and offending across diverse cultures, social contexts and political settings (see Ungar 2004), emphasising individual agency and the structural limitations placed upon it. Furthermore, the Positivist, deterministic search for globally applicable causal and predictive risk factors has been rejected as androcentric, ethnocentric, over-generalised and unable to accommodate the plurality of meanings that young people negotiate in their constructions of self. The theories enabled the identification of three levels of constructivist explanation of youth offending, which increase in the degree to which they integrate considerations of construction and context (Kemshall et al. 2006, in France and Homel 2007):

- Weak constructivism: Focusses on young people's agency and immediate situational context in which risk decisions are made, examining the interaction between a young person's propensity to respond to situational temptations and the social mechanisms that influence their routines and decision-making processes (see also Rational-Contextual theories in Chapter 1).
- Moderate constructivism: Sees pathways into and out of offending as negotiated processes dependent on continuing interactions between agency (individual choice and decision-making) and structure (e.g. power relations and cultural processes within a society), which can determine the contexts and opportunity routes within which decisions to offend are made.
- Strong constructivism: Emphasises the pivotal role of social structure and cultural understandings of risk, rather than the individual's risk decisions, and challenges the traditional reductionist translation of social risks (e.g. unemployment) into individual deficits (e.g. lack of skill or effort). Strong constructivism, therefore, views risk as a historical, social and political product.

Constructivist Pathways Theory has evolved the methodologies and foci of ARFTs by examining how young people's narratives, biographies and meso-level relationships with significant adults are mediated by macro-level socio-structural context, thus exploring influences beyond (yet often interacting with) micro-level psychosocial risk factors. The theory sees young people as social actors participating in the construction of their own childhoods and how adults respond to these dynamic constructions (Tisdall et al. 2023). There has been an accompanying focus on how young people's agency can be bounded and mediated by socio-structural and contextual influences such as social class, gender, race and social exclusion (see Furlong and Cartmel 2006) and social power relations that influence their access to social capital, social networks and opportunities (Boeck, Fleming and Kemshall 2006).

Constructivist pathways theory: Five steps to contextualised explanations of youth offending

1. **Acknowledging explanatory complexity:** Constructivist Pathways Theory acknowledges the complexities and difficulties of young people's lives and has attempted to understand how they make meaning of risk and being 'at risk' (France and Homel 2007), directly challenging quantitative, statistical 'artefactual' approaches to understanding youth offending (see Kemshall et al. 2007). The research that underpins Constructivist Pathways Theory has analysed the influence of structural, political and cultural contexts on young people's current behaviour and current exposure to risk factors (France and Homel 2007);
2. **Challenging established reductionist explanations:** The theory illustrates an alleged 'qualitative consensus' amongst criminologists seeking to explain youth offending (Webster 2007) that has pitted itself against deterministic ARFTs and has emphasised choice, contingency and contextual-correctness over statistical-correctness. In particular, the theory challenges the bold claim from ARFTs of a supposed tight causal fit between risk factors and offending (see Macdonald, in France and Homel 2007) and the view of young people as behaving in a 'mechanistic and dehumanized fashion abstracted from day-to-day lives and contexts' (Lawy 2002: 408);
3. **Reductionist determinism:** Notwithstanding its challenge to reductionist explanations, Constructivist Pathways Theory could be accused of making insufficient attempts to escape the pull of Individual Positivism and ARFTs towards explanatory reductionism, particularly the over-simplification (through factorisation) of criminogenic influences, a process that can reduce the complexity and diversity of young people's lives to uniform actuarial descriptions (Nagin and Tremblay 2005). Therefore, there is a sense that the espoused developmental determinism of psychosocial risk factors has been taken for granted and serves as the normative touchstone from which the theory has evolved;
4. **Reductionist partiality:** Despite constructivism, contextualisation and prioritisation of inclusive, qualitative methodologies, Constructivist Pathways Theory has (arguably) privileged developmental and deterministic understandings of how psychosocial risk factors influence youth offending, rather than starting afresh with an inductive investigation of which risk factors young people perceive as influential in their lives and how these risks may operate within dynamic, fluid and relational processes and contexts. Despite a desire to understand risk factors in non-developmental ways (e.g. as actively constructed by young people in their current lives), the methods adopted remain wedded (at least partly) to the developmental, deficit-based explanations mobilised by factorised risks;
5. **Contextualised construction:** Constructivist Pathways Theory provides a less simplistic, more qualitative, interpretive, appreciative and

ethnographic perspective of youth offending. It asserts that risk is experienced, constructed, resisted and negotiated by young people in specific social contexts through meso-level interactions with significant others and their environment, recognising the broader impacts of social context, relations of power, opportunity/constraint and institutional factors on youth offending (Macdonald and Marsh 2005). This introduces the consideration of the neglected roles of (bounded) agency and structure, moving explanations of youth offending away from their reductionist psychosocial biases by incorporating more examination of subjectivity, power and socio-political influence (France and Homel 2007), thus 'giving appropriate attention to socio-structural factors, social processes and social context' (Kemshall et al. 2006).

Critical criminology

As discussed in Chapter 1, there has been a general consensus within Western Criminology regarding Positivism's central explanatory ideas about youth offending. Indeed, Positivism's notions of objectivity, quantification, determinism and biopsychosocial causality continue to shape explanations and youth justice intervention responses to youth offending, most notably in the form of including (quasi-Positivist) ARFT explanations focused on the predictive validity of psychosocial 'risk factors' (see Chapter 1). The privileging of the methodologies and explanations of Positivism when explaining youth offending reflects the contemporary dominance of Psychology across the social sciences more generally and across Criminology (particularly in the USA) specifically in the 20th century and into the 21st century. In response, a school of critical criminological thought has developed since the 1950s that is more sociological in nature, with the central aim of mounting a strong challenge to biopsychosocial, developmental Positivist and quasi-Positivist theories (DeKeseredy 2021). According to 'Critical Criminology,' the 'hubris of positivism' (Goldson and Hughes 2010) has effectively 'closed down' the criminological imagination (Young 2011), for example, through overreliance on reductionist methodologies and explanatory frameworks. Theories of Critical Criminology invert the central historical tenets of Positivism: That the definition of crime is agreed upon in society (consensus); that the scientific method is neutral and value-free (objectivity), that the causes of crime are predetermined (determinism), and that the key causal explanations for crime are primarily located in individual and immediate social contexts (i.e. psychosocial bias). Consequently, the evolution of theories of Critical Criminology has led to theoretical explanations that are more attentive to the social construction of 'youth offending' and to the potentially criminogenic nature of meso- and macro-level influences.

Critical Criminology argues that 'crime' is not an objective fact but rather a contextualised social construction that is the dynamic, contingent and contested product of social processes and interactions between institutions and stakeholders in particular societies at particular times (Ugwudike 2025; DeKeseredy 2021). Crucially, Critical Criminology asserts that certain groups in society have the power to decide how 'offending' and 'offenders' are defined, explained and responded to through formal youth justice intervention. For example, white populations, the middle class, males and adults have tended to dominate the key stakeholder groups in society (e.g. academics, politicians, policymakers, practitioners, media) that produce knowledge and make and enforce social norms and laws through processes that typically benefit them (e.g. in terms of avoiding prosecution and criminalisation), yet can hinder less powerful groups such as young people (e.g. due to disproportionate systemic attention and targeting). In other words, the power to criminalise behaviours and to shape the definitions of, explanations of and responses to (youth) offending sits with a select few.

Critical Criminology theories are especially relevant for the purposes of this book because a significant and vociferous body of critical *youth* criminologists[1] has emerged (largely in the UK, Australasia and Canada) to challenge the androcentric, ethnocentric, class-centric, adult-centric status quo in youth justice. With these arguments in mind, this section explores the main critical criminological theories of (youth) offending, starting with 'Labelling Theory,' which essentially bridges the gap between Sociological Positivism and the critical movement. This discussion is followed by an examination of the most prominent theories identified under the banner of 'Critical Criminology': Marxist Criminology, the 'New Criminology' and Gendered perspectives (Feminist and Masculinity theories). Finally, there is a discussion of the 'Realist' theories that have been developed since the 1980s as a direct challenge to the perceived 'left idealism' of Critical Criminology, whilst retaining some of its core critical principles.

Critical criminology: Labelling theory

As discussed, in the 1950s and 1960s, a set of criminological perspectives began to gain momentum in the USA as a challenge to the 'prevailing Positivist orthodoxy' and its psychosocial, deterministic and reductionist bases (Case et al. 2021). A group of critical sociologists began to explore the potential role of power in shaping definitions of youth offending, with a particular focus on who has the power to criminalise individuals and behaviours, in other words, to decide who and what is considered 'criminal' and how society should respond to it. This led to explanations that those in power undertake processes of 'criminalisation' by assigning labels to people and behaviours (e.g. through creating laws) and acting on these labels (e.g. by targeting certain groups) in order to make them 'criminal' – a self-fulfilling prophecy. In other words, the power to construct youth offending and youth justice functions as a criminogenic influence. This hypothesis led critical sociologists to explore how individuals in society (typically young people) may react to being labelled as criminals. Consequently, the dual foci of 'Labelling

Theory' were process and reaction, moving away from the biopsychosocial bases of Individual and early Sociological Positivism and towards a greater appreciation of the systemic (criminogenic) influence of structures, processes and agents of criminalisation on youth offending.

Labelling theory: Dramatization of evil

Labelling Theory can be traced back to Tannenbaum's (1938) 'dramatization of evil' hypothesis. Focussing exclusively on young males as the archetypal 'offender,' Tannenbaum believed that only a small proportion of those young males who offend are actually identified and caught, namely working-class males living in working-class neighbourhoods. He argued that once they are caught, they are labelled as an 'offender' and may be labelled as 'evil' by their community and wider society. This label can prompt the young person to define themselves as evil, marginalising them from their usual social groups and encouraging specialised treatment and punishment as youth justice responses. The young person's redefinition of their own identity in line with their offender and evil labels encourages further offending (i.e. is criminogenic), thus dramatising (exaggerating, deepening) their 'evil' behaviour, with the 'offender' label becoming a self-fulfilling prophecy.

The 'dramatization of evil' hypothesis was extended by Edwin Lemert (1951) in his book 'Social Pathology,' wherein he distinguished between two forms of deviance:

- Primary deviance: Temporary, inadvertent and often hidden behaviour, causing no long-term damage to the 'offender' because it does not create a social reaction, or if it does, one that is not particularly strong or stigmatising. Consequently, primary deviance does not lead to an individual becoming labelled or viewing themselves as an offender if they are labelled.
- Secondary deviance: A criminalising process causing the individual (young person) to see themselves as an 'offender' due to the social reaction to their original offending. This social reaction is sufficiently strong to create a label that has a negative psychological impact on the individual's self-identity. The young person internalises the label and subsequently acts in a more deviant way (i.e. a self-fulfilling prophecy) because they now see themselves as a deviant/offender or as part of a group that is viewed as deviant/offending. Therefore, that offender label has a transformative effect on self-perception and identity.

Labelling theory: Criminalisation

Labelling Theory was elaborated in explanatory terms by Howard Becker (1963) through a focus on the criminalisation processes conducted by significant, powerful individuals (e.g. politicians, criminal justice professionals) who construct and enforce criminal labels and categories, rather than the reactions of recipients to these labels (typically young people). According to Becker, no behaviour is inherently criminal and a behaviour only becomes criminal when a label is conferred upon it:

> Social groups create deviance by making the rules whose infraction constitutes deviance, and by applying those rules to particular people and labelling them as outsiders. From this point of view ... the deviant is one to whom the label has been successfully applied; deviant behaviour is behaviour that people so label.
>
> (Becker 1963: 4)

Becker's central explanatory theory was that criminal laws and social rules are made (constructed) by people in power, such as middle-class adults (typically white men) and enforced upon those without power, such as working-class young people (typically boys). He contended that some laws/rules may be cynically designed to keep the less powerful in their place, whilst others may be genuinely intended to benefit the powerless (see also Case 2021). However, such laws/rules may have inadvertent or unforeseen negative consequences, such as the creation (through labelling) of new groups of 'outsiders,' such as the wave of youth subcultures that emerged across the 1950–1990 era. These newly created groups infringed the new laws/rules and created their own replacements, which prompted the creation of new formal agencies of social control to enforce these new laws/rules (e.g. criminal justice organisations). Becker's thesis concludes that ultimately the new laws/rules, the new social control agencies and the 'deviant' social role start to permeate the collective consciousness and become taken for granted by society, thus creating new stereotypes and labels such as 'youth offender' and 'juvenile delinquent' (see also Case et al. 2021).

Labelling theory: Criminogenic stigma

In recent years, Deakin, Fox and Matos (2020) have extended the explanatory scope of Labelling Theory by arguing that labelling young people as 'risky' and as 'offenders' produces and reproduces negative labels and stereotypes that drive disadvantage and trigger multifaceted processes of 'stigma' (see Link and Phelan 2001). The authors defined stigma as 'the situation of the individual who is disqualified from full social acceptance' as a result of any attribute or 'undesirable difference' that is 'deeply discrediting' (after Goffman 1990: 9). Drawing on case study data from four European countries, Deakin, Fox and Matos (2020) found that young people's reactions and responses to being labelled and stigmatised existed on a continuum, ranging from apathy and withdrawal to active resistance in the form of transgressive behaviours and actions that explicitly challenge social norms. They concluded that young people's responses to the labelling and discrimination attached to criminalised identities often serve to both amplify and reproduce the stigma they experience, resulting in reduced life chances and limited opportunities for self-development. Deakin et al. theorised the criminogenic influence of interconnected processes of stigmatisation, notably:

- Labelling: Young people being labelled as 'problematic,' 'risky,' 'criminal';
- Stereotyping: Applying negative attributes and expectations;
- Separation: Exclusion from peers and opportunities;
- Status loss: Due to exclusion and the lowering of expectations;
- Discrimination: Harsher treatment, reduced opportunities.

This led the authors to discuss the context within which this 'cycle of stigma' exists. They asserted that stigma exists where the 'stigmatiser' wields power over the stigmatised group (young people) and enacts this through policies and practices that reproduce and embed elements of stigma, which then creates (constructs) stigmatising identities for those young people who contravene these norms. They argued that the youth justice (and other official) responses that result tend to perpetuate elements of the stigmatisation process, namely separation, status loss and discrimination, without consideration of the contextual factors experienced by young people, such as their experiences of socio-economic deprivation, neglect, abuse, bereavement, growing up in local authority care, or a range of other ACEs.

Evaluating labelling theory

Labelling Theory provided a much-needed challenge and counter-view to the mainstream, orthodox Classical-Positivist explanations of (youth) offending, which arguably lacked a degree of validity due to their neglect of both systemic influences on the creation of offending and subjective influences that can influence an individual's reaction to their treatment by society. As such, Labelling Theory provided a highly innovative and arguably valid set of perspectives on youth offending when it was introduced into Criminology. However, critics have accused Labelling Theory of paying insufficient attention to explaining *why* specific behaviours are labelled and stigmatised, whilst others are not, and why certain individuals are criminalised and not others – beyond generalised notions of power differences (Hopkins-Burke 2016; Muncie 2021). Arguably, Labelling Theory has been too focused on the criminogenic influence of small-scale, meso-level interactions (e.g. between two people) rather than broader interactions between (individuals within) larger social groups and institutions. There has also been a lack of specific explanation around why and how individuals internalise labels and become (secondary) deviants. Labelling explanations are also somewhat idealistic, arguing that youth offending is largely constructed/created and exaggerated through the application of labels, rather than existing as a real phenomenon or problem (see the discussion of Left Realism later in this chapter). Such idealism deprives the explanations of a degree of ecological validity and practical utility for informing youth justice responses in the real world, beyond support for 'minimum necessary intervention' (Lemert 1972; McAra and McVie 2015) approaches that can avoid stigmatising interventions and marking out 'offenders' for 'special' treatment.

Critical criminology: Marxist criminology

The origins of Critical Criminology can be traced back to the second half of the 19th century when philosopher, sociologist and economist Karl Marx created his famous theory to explain behaviour in modern capitalist societies (Marx 1867, in Muncie 2021). Marx argued that the capitalist economic system creates a distinct mode of production of goods and services that is controlled by the ruling class (the 'bourgeoisie') because they own the means of production, whilst the majority of the wealth-creating work is done by the working class (the 'proletariat'), who own little. The ruling class employ the working class, who sell their labour for a wage and are exploited because they need money to buy the goods that they themselves have produced. This unequal power relationship creates conflict between the classes that may need to be resolved through the rule of law. However, the powerful ruling class controls the processes of law-making and law enforcement, so any laws are likely to reflect their own economic interests and not those of the working class. The Marxist criminologist Willem Bonger (1916, in Muncie 2021) applied Marx's theory to the explanation of offending. Bonger's 'Marxist Criminology' explained that the social, political and economic structures of capitalist society can create crime and the social reactions to it, so capitalism is criminogenic. He outlined six propositions that encapsulated his Marxist theory of crime (Bonger 1916, in Muncie 2021: 128):

1. Immorality and criminality are socio-historically constructed variables;
2. The criminal law exists to protect the interests of the powerful;
3. Capitalism is driven by coercion and exploitation, not cooperation and consensus;
4. Capitalism encourages greed and the pursuit of pleasure, which makes both classes more prone to crime and weakens their sense of responsibility towards one another;
5. Poverty can prompt crime by creating a desperate need for food and other necessities;
6. Crime can occur when there is a perceived opportunity to gain an advantage through illegal means or when opportunities for pleasure are restricted by a biased legal system.

Bonger argued that both powerful and powerless groups commit crime through greed and opportunity but noted that explanatory theories in

Criminology were class-centric, ignoring middle-class offending and the 'crimes of the powerful,' which can actually cause greater harm than everyday crimes (see also Sutherland 1940). Therefore, Marxist Criminology provided a socio-economic explanation of crime by examining differential power relations between the ruling class and the working class in capitalist societies, centred on control of the means of production of goods and services (see Lea 2014; Chambliss 1975; see also DeKeseredy 2021).

Contextual challenge: Explaining offending by young people from ethnic minority groups through processes of 'racialisation' (Webster, in Case 2021)

Power-led processes can result in 'institutional racialisation' and ethnic inequalities operating at three contextual levels (micro, meso, macro), producing ethnically disparate welfare outcomes and ethnic inequalities in education (attainment), policing (stop-and-search practices) and levels of offending (disproportionality):

- Micro-level racialisation is framed by the influence of familial socialisation and shared cultural values among young people in various ethnic, classed and gendered groups, and influenced significantly by neighbourhood environmental conditions;
- Meso-level racialisation involves individual decision-making in institutions (e.g. school, youth justice, care, welfare) which are, in turn, influenced by socio-economic disadvantage; neighbourhood composition and effects; political, media and popular discourses; political incorporation and power; and institutional processes and practices. Finally, institutional racialisation recognises cumulative disadvantage experienced across interrelated welfare experiences (housing, education, employment etc), produced through institutions' routine operations;
- Macro-level racialisation considers structural forces beyond individual decision-making and institutional practices and processes. Structural determinants of material conditions provide the frame through which institutional processes/practices at the meso-level are enacted. Globalising forces change the economy, social relations and structure, transnational politics and crucially, the unequal distribution of resources.

(Webster, in Case 2021)

Applying these theoretical and conceptual analyses to explain the relationship between ethnicity and offending (see Webster, in Case 2021) points to various dimensions, including change and continuity in the experiences of successive generations of young people from ethnic minority groups. For example, there is broad agreement that child poverty has significantly increased over the last decade, particularly among children from ethnic minorities, and yet the adverse influence of concentrated, long-term poverty on children's behaviour is well-known. At a micro-level, familial socialisation under conditions of persistent or recurrent poverty induces extreme stress among children and parents. At a macro-level, often marginalised and disadvantaged, young people from ethnic minority groups have faced a series of cumulative crises/disruptions in their transitions to adulthood as they adopted new identities and adapted to economic and social change (see Webster 2018). Thus, youth transitions to adulthood are marked by increased precariousness and vulnerability visited on marginalised young people by socio-economic crises.

Critical criminology: 'The New Criminology'

The origins of Critical Criminology in the UK can be traced back to the National Deviancy Conference of 1968 at York University. The conference was founded by the forefather of modern Critical Criminology, Jock Young, along with other noted critical criminologists such as Stan Cohen, Mary McIntosh, Ian Taylor, Paul Walton, Paul Rock and David Downes. The group was described as 'naughty schoolboys' by the venerable Positivist Sir Leon Radzinowicz, with the implication that they were intent on causing trouble within Criminology through their challenge to the Positivist 'orthodoxy.' In a sense, they were because these sociologists-cum-criminologists wanted to shake up a criminological explanation by considering why society perceived some acts to be deviant and why it reacted to deviance in the way that it did; in addition to exploring the subjective experiences and opinions of the powerless 'deviant.' Accordingly, in 1973, three of the criminologists at the heart of the National Deviancy Conference, Taylor, Walton and Young, published a 'manifesto' for Critical Criminology entitled 'The New Criminology' (Taylor, Walton and Young 1973), which integrated elements of Labelling Theory, Marxist Criminology and Interactionism[2] to create what was claimed as a 'fully social theory of deviance.' The New Criminology put forward seven incremental elements required to explain deviance/youth offending in a fully social and contextualised way:

1. The wider origins of this deviant act: placing offending in its wider socio-structural context neighbourhood socio-economic characteristics, unemployment and poverty levels);
2. The immediate origins of the deviant act: explaining the different 'events, experiences and structural developments that precipitate the deviant act' in the wider socio-structural context;
3. The deviant act: explaining the relationship between the behaviour and its causes (e.g. status frustration);
4. The immediate origins of social reaction: how significant others such as family, peers and police respond to the deviance;
5. The wider origins of deviant reaction: the reaction in terms of who holds the power and sets the rules;

6. The outcome of the social reaction on the deviant's further action: the labelling process;
7. The nature of the deviant process as a whole: the relationship between elements 1–6 in forming a 'fully social theory of deviance.'

(Taylor, Walton and Young 1973)

In 1998, Walton and Young updated their original theory in 'The New Criminology Revisited' (see also Taylor, Walton and Young 2013), which added more detailed consideration of feminist arguments (see next section) and re-evaluated their original position 25 years later in the context of contemporary criminological theories. The New Criminology remains committed to the anti-Positivist belief that individuals who commit crimes do not necessarily need to be corrected (through treatment or punishment), but rather that appropriate youth justice responses should pursue broader socio-structural changes to address youth offending, such as the redistribution of wealth and power in society. Responses should target the power differentials that encourage labelling and social reactions to a crime that are disproportionately visited upon powerless, socially disadvantaged groups such as the working-class boys who have become the focus of socially constructed definitions and explanations of youth offending.

Critical criminology: Gendered theories

'The New Criminology Revisited' reflected how the explanatory scope of Critical Criminology had expanded since the 1970s to encompass a more detailed examination of gendered issues, particularly through integrating tenets from feminist theories. Prominent feminist criminologists such as Carol Smart and Pat Carlen have attacked the androcentric nature of Criminology and its historically 'patriarchal' (i.e. male-controlled) focus on the behaviours and activities of males as offenders, victims, criminal justice professionals, academics, politicians etc, whilst criminological studies of females have tended to view them as weak or corrupt creatures unable to control their actions. Female criminality has been largely constructed in terms of biology and sexuality (e.g. Lombroso's theorising). A number of different feminist perspectives have emerged (e.g. liberal, radical, black, lesbian) to explore and explain the lives of women in society, and as such, feminism can be seen as a divided movement, which some groups of women (e.g. the socially excluded, black, poorly educated) feel does not speak for them or promote their interests (see Smart 1990; see also Case et al. 2021). Indeed, some feminist theorists even reject the term 'Feminist Criminology,' viewing it as reductionist and androcentric in its apparent need to comply with simplistic, 'malestream' (i.e. mainstream, androcentric) perspectives on crime (Ugwudike 2025). Others assert that Feminist Criminology, with its attendant qualitative, appreciative methods of research and analysis, is much needed in order to reflect and explore the neglected lives of females (including female offenders) and the exploitation of male power to criminalise (e.g. Sharpe 2015).

Despite being a somewhat fractured set of theories, the different forms of Feminist (criminological) Theory cohere around a focus on disparities in power and unequal relations in society. Consequently, they critique the patriarchal, androcentric nature of orthodox Criminology, viewing it as 'malestream' and 'gender blind,' neglecting and downgrading the behaviours, experiences and needs of women and girls (see Smart 1990). In 'Women, Crime and Criminology,' Smart (1990) not only criticised orthodox Positivist Criminology but also theories of Interactionism Labelling and Critical Criminology (e.g. The New Criminology) for not fully considering female criminality or victimisation. Smart's work has prompted a new wave of studies by feminist academics (see Ugwudike 2025 for a detailed review). More recently, Feminist Criminology has turned its attention towards youth justice issues by exploring the extent and nature of the differential treatment of girls who offend within youth justice systems. I discussed these developments with Dr. Gilly Sharp (in Case 2021), who has researched and published extensively on youth offending and youth justice issues as they relate to girls (Sharpe 2015, 2011; Sharpe and Gelsthorpe 2015). The interview is provided in full in appendix one.

These developments in feminist explanations of youth offending and how youth justice is applied to girls reflect broader developments in gendered theory as it relates to women, men and sexuality. The popularity, quality and necessity of feminist theories of offending have encouraged Critical Criminology to expand its explanatory focus to incorporate gendered issues more broadly. This development has contributed to the emergence of 'masculinities' as a key issue for explaining offending by men and boys. The culturally informed scholarship of academics such as Messerschmidt (2017) and Connell (2005) has further informed criminological thinking in this area by identifying a hegemonic form of masculinity in the identities of Western males, especially those who offend, which is characterised by personality and behavioural traits including competitiveness, toughness, aggression, power and competence. I discussed the issue of masculinities and youth offending with Dr. Eric Baumgartner (in Case 2021), author of 'And Then There Were the Men – Masculinity and the Youth Justice System in England and Wales' (Baumgartner 2012). The interview is provided in full in appendix two.

Evaluating critical criminology

In the second half of the 20th century, Critical Criminology emerged as a challenge to the Positivist orthodoxy in Criminology by conceptualizing offending as a social construct, by examining who has the power to criminalise behaviours and individuals (the 'victimised actor' – Hopkins-Burke 2019) and by examining the processes through which this criminalisation occurs. Initially, Marxist Criminology argued that capitalism is criminogenic, with the powerful ruling class controlling the means of production in society and the powerless working class selling their labour and consuming what is produced. This disparity, it was argued, resulted in socio-economic power differentials that precipitated crime through greed, strain and poverty (see also Strain Theory). Subsequently, the New Criminology integrated Labelling Theory, Marxist Criminology and Interactionism into a 'fully social theory of deviance,' which focused on the wider and immediate origins of the offence, the social reaction to it and the outcomes of this (criminogenic) social reaction. Neither Marxist Criminology nor the New Criminology specifically examined youth offending. However, both theories constituted an important step towards a more detailed and valid explanation of youth offending because young people are disproportionately likely to be victims of the criminogenic socio-economic power differentials of Marxist Criminology and the stigmatising social reactions of the New Criminology. As Critical Criminology developed, critical gendered perspectives of crime were initiated by feminist theorists, who addressed the neglect of females and girls in explanations and responses to crime. Subsequently, gendered masculinity theory has focussed on the influence of hegemonic masculine identity on explaining youth offending and the differential youth justice responses to offending committed by boys.

In summary, Critical Criminology subverts the need for responses to youth offending to correct 'deficits' in an individual, instead providing power-based explanations that recommend broader, contextualised socio-structural and economic changes such as the redistribution of wealth and power and changing the contexts within and processes by which marginalised, powerless groups such as working-class boys are criminalised. These critical theories have offered a necessary alternative explanatory perspective to counter the hegemony of Positivism (notably Individual Positivism), which (traditionally) has taken the definition of 'crime' for granted and focussed on individual deficit as its central explanatory mechanism. However, Critical Criminology is not without its own critics, notably from the Realist camp (see next section), who portray its explanations as idealistic, unrealistic and as failing to engage with the 'real' extent, nature, causes and impacts of crime as committed and experienced by powerless groups.

Critical criminology: Towards contextualised explanations of youth offending in five bold steps

1. **Incorporating meso-level explanations:** Labelling Theory argues that youth offending is the product of a 'criminal' label being placed on individuals and behaviours by powerful social groups. By approaching offending as a 'social construction,' Labelling Theory offered the first 'critical' theoretical explanations of youth offending by constructing young people who offend as often labelled, stigmatised and powerless groups in social contexts.

2. **Youth offending as reaction and process:** Labelling Theory focussed on the young person's reaction to being labelled criminal, which can lead to them committing a further crime (i.e. is criminogenic). It prioritised the social processes by which powerful individuals and organisations create and enforce criminal labels that then create 'outsiders' in society and the need for agencies of social control, which ultimately creates more crime (i.e. is a self-fulfilling prophecy).
3. **Power as a criminogenic influence:** Marxist Criminology argued that the unequal socio-economic power relations caused by capitalism are criminogenic, whilst the 'New Criminology' expanded this thesis by integrating concepts from Labelling Theory and Interactionism into a 'fully social theory of deviance.'
4. **Youth offending as a social construction:** Theories of Critical Criminology emerged as a direct challenge to Positivism's hegemony by examining the socially constructed nature of offending as created through socio-structural inequalities and processes of criminalisation enacted by powerful social groups, rather than assuming 'offending' to be an agreed social fact resulting from individual deficits.
5. **Gendered theory:** Critical Criminology and its associated explanations of youth offending have challenged androcentric biases by adapting broader feminist theories to explore differential explanations of and responses to offending by girls and by adapting theories of masculinity to enable the examination of offending behaviour by boys.

Left realism

Critical Criminology has been subject to criticism regarding its explanatory bases and the consequent limitations that these place on recommendations for realistic, pragmatic policies and practices to address crime. In particular, the view that individuals who offend are somehow victims of labelling and criminalisation by powerful groups (the 'victimised actor' model – Hopkins-Burke 2019) has been criticised as overly romantic and as unrealistic 'left idealism' by a new wave of 'Realist' theories. Realists do not view offending as a social construction that results from criminalisation processes led by the powerful, nor necessarily as the political expression of class conflict and status frustration on the part of the powerless (e.g. young working-class males). Instead, Realists view offending as a real phenomenon that takes place in the real world and is committed and experienced by (young) people who are members of so-called powerless social groups such as the working class, females, ethnic minorities and notably, young people. A body of 'Left Realism' has been developed to challenge the 'left idealism' of Critical Criminology (e.g. blaming the powerful) and the pathologising notions of Right Realism (see Chapter 1 and below), with its emphasis on rational choice and moral poverty (e.g. blaming the powerless).

Contextual challenge: Right realism's deliberate explanatory decontextualisation

'Right Realism' is a Neo-Classical explanatory theory of crime (see Chapter 1) that has reimagined Classicism in the late 20th century by re-emphasising the criminogenic role of rational choice, low morality and lack of self-control. As such, Right Realism favours Biological Positivist explanations of offending (Herrnstein and Murray 1994), which has encouraged the perception that there is a feral, feckless and moral 'underclass' among the working class who are disproportionately responsible for crime (Murray 1990). Right Realists have advocated that the individual is the source of crime and that social causes are of no significance (i.e. explicitly decontextualising explanations of youth offending). James Q. Wilson (1975) alleged that previous criminological theorising had been dominated by ideology and conjecture as opposed to empirical evidence, and so the 'facts' of crime were being ignored. Crime was seen as a moral issue, with a view that appropriate levels of blame and responsibility should be assigned to individuals when responding to crime. The central thesis, therefore, was that some individuals are criminal by nature and have an innate disposition to offend. In short, 'Wicked people exist. Nothing avails except to set them apart from innocent people' (Wilson 1975: 235). In 'The Emerging British Underclass,' Murray (1990) identified a criminal 'underclass' subculture within the working class who suffer from a 'moral poverty' that compounds their economic poverty. This group is allegedly characterised by violent, feckless males (often young adults) and similarly immoral and feckless females who may be less violent, but are prone to teenage pregnancy and substance use. Their supposed widespread immorality and irresponsibility perpetuate high illegitimacy rates and low levels of participation in the workforce, along with high levels of offending. In Murray's view, the 'underclass' has to be given the tools to help itself (e.g. socio-economic incentives) to take individual responsibility for its plight and to engender a collective moral and social responsibility among the group. An obvious criticism of this view is that the theory is both reductionist and inflammatory, 'pathologising' (i.e. representing as flawed, ill) individuals who suffer most from the deeply entrenched socio-economic disadvantage that can limit their life choices (e.g. young people), thus further stigmatising, disadvantaging and criminalising (Barry 2006).

Left Realists believe that it is mistaken to neglect the harmful behaviour of the powerless because the public's greatest fears of crime focus on street crime (perpetrated by powerless groups), so this issue must be addressed in explanatory and response (policy) terms (DeKeseredy and Schwartz 2018; Lea 2016). They are sceptical of Critical Criminology's idealistic view of offending as the political expression of victimised actors and of the consequent unrealistic, impractical recommendations for youth justice responses based on limited intervention at the individual level. Accordingly, Left Realism has been developed to reflect the reality of crime in origins, nature and impact, which involves a rejection of tendencies 'to romanticise crime or to pathologise it, to analyse solely from the point of view of the administration of crime or the criminal actor, to underestimate crime or exaggerate it' (Young 1986: 21). Consequently, Left Realism has been inclined towards integrating explanations from Sociological Positivism, notably the socio-structural elements of Strain and Subcultural theories. The central mechanism for Left Realism's explanations of (youth) offending has been 'relative deprivation,' the individual's perception and experience of being deprived of what they feel entitled to when comparing themselves to other individuals in the modern, competitive society (Lea and Young 1984). In this way, relative deprivation is a subjective perception, whereas 'absolute deprivation' is a measurable fact based on statistical ratings of levels of poverty, income, unemployment, etc. According to Jock Young (2007: 488), a former proponent of Critical Criminology who subsequently 'jumped ship' to Left Realism, in certain conditions, relative deprivation is 'a major cause of crime,' particularly when people experience levels of unfairness in their allocation of resources and utilise individualistic means to attempt to right this condition. It is a reaction to the experience of injustice. Left Realists have illustrated their theoretical explanation through the 'Square of Crime' (see Figure 3.1 below), which depicts the (potentially criminogenic), dynamic, contextualised interactions between the 'offender,' the State (e.g. the Criminal Justice System for adults, youth justice systems, local crime prevention partnerships), the public and the victim.

As with all explanatory theories, inevitably, Left Realism has been subject to a series of criticisms and has provided appropriately 'realistic' responses to each of these.

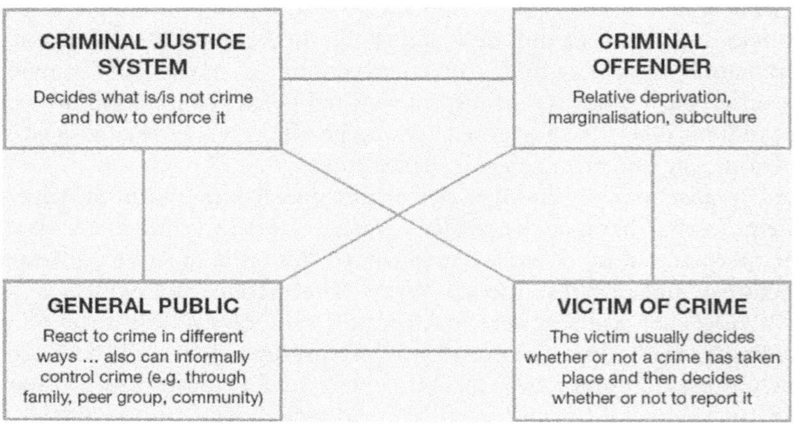

Figure 3.1 Left Realism's 'Square of Crime.'

Evaluating left realism: Criticising the critic in five easy steps

1. **Requisite realism:** Left Realism views youth offending as a real phenomenon with real effects on victims and communities (including the working class); effects that must be addressed through realistic, practical policies, integrating theories of Labelling, Strain, Control and Critical Criminology in order to explain crime as the product of relative deprivation and interactions between offender, state, public and victim in a dynamic, contextualised 'Square of Crime.'
2. **Constructing crime:** Criticisms of Left Realism's uncritical reliance on State definitions of what constitutes 'crime' and 'offending' have been countered by arguing that their priority was to challenge Right Realism and to offer practical policies for responding to youth offending in the real world. Therefore, Left Realism argues that it should work with the same definitions of offending as Right Realism (Lea 2016).
3. **Explanatory utility:** Criticisms that Left Realism has abandoned the explanatory gains of Critical Criminology by neglecting the crimes of the powerful are refuted in a similar fashion, arguing that the primary focus has been on the lived realities of excluded, powerless groups in order to challenge right-wing recommendations for the deterrence and punishment of these groups (Ugwudike 2025).
4. **Explanatory confusion:** Left Realism has been accused of offering a theoretically contradictory integration of Social Control, Labelling, Strain and Critical Criminology theories of crime. The response has been that Left Realism seeks to develop understanding of crime, the processes of criminalisation and techniques of crime control in rapidly changing times. This urgent, practical and realistic set of objectives should not be encumbered by unnecessary concerns about resolving appropriate theoretical contradictions and should always be seen as a work in progress (Mooney 2021).
5. **Limited evidence-base:** The weak empirical evidence-base of Left Realism (especially when compared to Positivism), generated largely through limited localised victim surveys, has been criticised. Left Realists accept this limitation but argue that local victim surveys address the dark figure of crime and so target the real, hidden crime problems in communities which require realistic solutions (see Case et al. 2021).

Addressing the problem of decontextualised explanations of youth offending

The theories explored in this chapter have offered alternative, more contextualised explanations of youth offending compared to traditionally dominant individualising and decontextualised theories (i.e. Classicism, Individual Positivism, ARFTs). Whilst these alternative theories have evidenced a clear chronological evolution in explanatory breadth and depth, some have remained reductionist (to a degree), tending to pursue Positivist

Table 3.1 Summarising the extent and nature of contextualisation in contemporary explanatory theories of youth offending

Explanatory category	*Theory*	*Criminogenic influences*	*Psychosocial bias?*	*Contextual influence?*
Sociological Positivism	Concentric Zone	Neighbourhood disorganisation, lack of social control	Limited (individual motivations)	Limited – immediate neighbourhood/ community focus
	Strain	Socio-structural strains and pressures		Yes – socio-structural, cultural, relational
	Subcultural/ Differential Association	Peer interactions in social contexts	Limited (psychological learning)	
Quasi-Contextualised Risk Factor: Age-Graded Life Course	Age-Graded Theory of Informal Social Control	Structural context mediated by informal social controls (family, school), agency and situation	Limited (focus on Gluecks' psychosocial risk factors)	Yes – socio-structural, historical, cultural, relational
	Edinburgh Study	Explanatory psychosocial and socio-structural factors, meso-level system contact	Yes (privileges psychosocial risk factors)	
Quasi-Contextualised Risk Factor: Constructivist Pathway	Pathways Into and Out of Crime	Psychosocial risk factors mediated by context		Yes – relational, viewed as constructed
	Teesside Studies	Psychosocial risk factors mediated by context		Yes – socio-structural, historical, cultural, relational, viewed as constructed
Critical Criminology	Labelling	Dramatization of evil, power-led processes of criminalisation, stigma	No	Yes – socio-structural, relational
	Marxist	Poverty, greed, power-led processes of criminalisation	No	Yes – socio-structural, socio-economic, relational

	New Criminology	Socio-structural context, status frustration, societal reaction, labelling	No	Yes – socio-structural, socio-economic, relational
	Gendered and Racialised	Unequal societal power relations, peer influence, victimisation, masculinities, racialisation	No	Yes – socio-structural, relational, viewed as constructed
Realism	Left Realism	Interaction between youth justice systems (decision-making), offenders (influenced by relative deprivation, marginalisation, subcultures), general public (reactions), victims (decision-making)	No	

understandings of youth offending (e.g. Sociological Positivism) or quasi-Positivist, developmental/life course understandings (e.g. AGLCT) that privilege the deterministic, predictive influence of psychosocial 'risk factors' on later offending. Other alternative contextualised theories (e.g. Constructivist Pathways Theory, Critical Criminology, Left Realism) have incorporated an additional focus on meso-level systemic and macro-level socio-structural contextual influences that can be criminogenic in their own right and which can interact with psychosocial risk factors in criminogenic ways. For example, contemporary constructivist variants of ARFTs have incorporated ideas from Critical Criminology, such as considering the effects of labelling processes, criminogenic social interactions and young people's reactions to their exposure to risk. Constructivist Pathways Theory has extended the explanatory utility of contemporary understandings still further by considering the young person's capacity to construct, negotiate and resist their experiences of 'risk' (e.g. constructed as factors and processes) and how these constructions may shape their pathways/trajectories into and out of offending over the life course. Therefore, Constructivist Pathways Theory has evolved to challenge the reductionism of Individual Positivism and ARFTs, a challenge initiated by Sociological Positivism and AGLCT.

This explanatory challenge of Constructivist Pathways Theory has run parallel to that of Critical Criminology, which has directly challenged the Positivist hegemony by focussing on the socially constructed nature of youth offending and the neglected criminogenic and contextualised influences of socio-structural inequalities and processes of criminalisation enacted by powerful groups against relatively powerless groups. Importantly, Critical Criminology has asserted that young people and certain sub-groups of young people (e.g. ethnic minorities, those of lower working class/socio-economic status) are disproportionately likely to be criminalised, typically in contexts characterised by unequal power relations (e.g. in youth justice systems). Equally important, however, is the critique from Left Realism, which has criticised Critical Criminology as romanticising and under-estimating the realities of youth offending and its real-world impacts on victims and communities in real-world contexts.

By way of a chapter summary, Table 3.1 below summarises the extent and nature of the contextualisation discernible within the 'in context' explanatory theories of youth offending reviewed.

Notes

1 This cadre of critics includes academics such as Barry Goldson, John Muncie, Roger Smith, John Pitts, Tim Bateman, Jo Phoenix, Gilly Sharp, Kevin Haines, Tim Goddard, Diana Johns and myself.

2 A meso-level sociological perspective argues that meaning is produced through social interactions between individuals.

4 Responding to youth offending 'in context'

Chapter 2 examined the problem of decontextualised youth justice by focussing on the interventions that have most typically been used in practice to animate the laws, policies, strategies, cultures, theories and principles of youth justice 'systems.' Critical review of the socio-historical construction of youth justice in the Western world identified a longstanding battle for dominance between the competing priorities of context-dependent welfare-based responses linked to social explanations of youth offending and decontextualised justice-based responses linked to individualising explanations of youth offending. It was shown that this perennial 'welfare versus justice debate' (Smith 2005) was supplanted in the 1990s by the 'punitive turn' in youth justice, characterised by neo-liberal and neo-correctionalist strategies mobilised by actuarial risk management using the Risk Factor Prevention Paradigm (RFPP). Like the Artefactual Risk Factor Theories (ARFTs) and Developmental Crime Prevention that underpin it, the RFPP was criticised as reductionist due to its individualisation, decontextualisation and oversimplification of criminogenic influences as predominantly psychosocial, deterministic and amenable to simplistic measurement and factorisation. The associated 'What Works' framework for evaluating the 'effectiveness' of youth justice interventions was subject to equivalent criticisms in this chapter due to its promotion of reductionist, individualised and decontextualised understandings of 'effectiveness' through privileging experimental methodologies and quantitative evidence generated to inform and validate predominantly risk-based youth justice interventions.

This final thematic chapter explores a series of contemporary contextualised youth justice intervention responses to youth offending that provide a degree of 'expansionism' to directly challenge the reductionism of decontextualised youth justice in the Western world. The chapter reiterates and further explores the growing complexity and hybridity of approaches to constructing youth justice in contemporary westernised youth justice systems. Critical discussion then moves to emerging forms of contextualised intervention responses to youth offending prior to and/or during young people's contact with formal youth justice systems. Firstly, there is an exploration of the application and 'effectiveness' of 'Social Crime Prevention' in the form of 'Community Crime Prevention,' a model addressing the social causes of

DOI: 10.4324/9781003498100-5

crime and so requiring youth justice interventions to focus on the social contexts within which individuals offend, rather than trying to treat or correct individualised symptoms. Secondly, there is discussion of the contextualised 'Realist Synthesis' approach to designing, administering and evaluating 'effective' crime prevention programmes by situating them 'in a much wider context related to change processes of individual children' (Stephenson and Allen 2018: 69) and by unpacking 'what works for whom, in what circumstances, in what respects, and how?' (Pawson 2013). Thirdly, there is a critical review of 'Child-Friendly Justice,' a progressive and expansionist approach to conceptualising and delivering youth justice that is explicitly situated within a children's rights context and advocates for bespoke structural and systemic intervention contexts to be constructed for young people who offend, notably welfare-based and prevention-focused minimum necessary intervention delivered in youth justice systems that are distinct from adult criminal justice systems. Finally, the principle, strategy and model of 'Child First' justice are evaluated as an expansionist challenge to reductionist youth justice. It will be demonstrated that Child First is mobilised by principles or 'tenets' promoting contextualised evidence-based understandings of and responses to youth offending that consider a range of meso-level (e.g. relational, interpersonal, procedural) and macro-level (e.g. cultural, structural, systemic) contextual influences on youth offending and on the effectiveness of youth justice responses. The chapter concludes by emphasising how contextualised methodologies and perspectives enable stakeholders (academics, policymakers, practitioners, etc.) to better articulate and conceptualise the criminogenic influences in young people's lives and the ways in which youth justice interventions can be expected to work. In other words, contextualised forms of intervention move youth justice policy, practice and academia towards better understandings of, and responses to, youth offending 'in context.'

The increasing complexity of Western youth justice

In the 21st century, there has been an increasing complexity and hybridity in youth justice approaches globally (Case 2021). Whilst remaining largely faithful to key elements of the historically dominant welfare and justice approaches (see Chapter 2), the construction and execution of the rationales, principles and models of youth justice internationally have become exponentially diverse, integrated, multi-faceted, complex and contextualised (see Cavadino and Dignan 2013), such that:

> Discourses of child protection, restoration, punishment, public protection, responsibility, justice, rehabilitation, welfare, retribution, diversion, human rights, and so on, intersect and circulate in a perpetually uneasy and contradictory motion.
>
> (Goldson and Muncie 2021: vii)

In this context of increasing hybridity and complexity, at least three alternative contemporary 'models' of youth justice have emerged to challenge and expand upon welfare- and justice-based models (Hazel 2008; see also McAra 2023; Dunkel 2014; see also Chapter 2):

- **Neo-liberalism:** Promotes freedom of choice (agency) and embraces principles that support self-actualisation (Smith and Gray 2024). This model/strategy prioritises individual, family and community responsibility over the social contexts of crime, the negative effects of poverty and structural disadvantage on young people in the YJS, as well as state protection/intervention as responses to these harms (Gray and Smith 2024; Garland 2002), so it is largely decontextualised (see also Chapter 2). Neo-liberalism is driven by strategies of 'neo-liberal responsibilisation' (Muncie 2021, 2008), whereby governments assign primary responsibility to individuals/families/communities for causing and responding to youth offending, rather than the State taking primary responsibility, and 'neo-correctionalism' (Cavadino and Dignan 2013), whereby youth justice strategies and practices focus on the correction of perceived deficiencies (e.g. 'risk factors') located in the individual. Neo-liberalism has been animated by neo-correctionalism and has been evidenced most clearly in the 21st-century youth justice systems of England and Wales, the Netherlands, Canada and certain states of the USA (see the detailed discussion in Chapter 2).
- **Restorative Justice:** Views young people as calculating, rational individuals who should be compelled to take responsibility for their actions (i.e. neo-liberal responsibilisation), acknowledge the harms that they have caused by offending, repair the damage and attempt to restore the broken links between them, their victim and the community (McAra 2010, 2023). Whilst certain, more contextualised forms of Restorative Justice have sought to acknowledge (at least in limited ways) that young people who offend can be shaped by their community and cultural contexts (Zehr and Mika 2003, 1998), the emphasis of restorative justice is often decontextualised, focussing on individual accountability, reparation, reintegration and mediation for victims (Cavadino and Dignan 2013). Restorative Justice approaches with young people (e.g. Family Group Conferencing, Victim-Offender Mediation) have been evidenced most clearly in the 21st-century youth justice systems of Australia and New Zealand, predominantly used with young people from Indigenous cultures (Richards 2017; Cunneen and Goldson 2015), Belgium and Canada (Arnull and Fox 2016) and Northern Ireland (Payne, Yong and Hobson 2022).
- **Minimum Necessary Intervention/Diversion:** Challenges the responsibilisation and increasing 'interventionism' (increasing and excessive use of intervention) encouraged by Neo-liberalism (Cavadino and Dignan 2013) by advocating for Minimal Necessary Intervention and Diversion

responses to youth offending. These responses minimise the criminogenic influence (e.g. labelling, stigmatisation, criminalisation) of macro-level youth justice systems (McAra and McVie 2007, 2022) and the meso-level contexts underpinning them (e.g. practitioner-young person relationships). Minimum Necessary Intervention has been evidenced most clearly in the 21st-century youth justice systems of Germany (diversion-based), Scotland (welfare-based), the revised out-of-court system in England and Wales (YJB 2021) and the ambiguous diversion-punishment hybrid system in Denmark (Henriksen, Bengtsson and Henriksen 2024). It has also been evidenced in the juvenile justice system of China (Jou, Chang and Hebenton 2014), where the principles of 'dual protection' and 'adopt leniency and waive severity' seek to minimise the use of punishment in combination with other effective measures to control and prevent youth crime and to reintegrate young people into society (Ye 2013).

It has been argued that constructing and evidencing a broader range of youth justice models and rationales to supplement the more traditional Welfare and Justice approaches can encourage contextualised youth justice by enhancing understandings of the 'myriad principles' that shape youth justice policy in the Western world and that produce youth justice systems with 'complex architectural phenomena ... with a multiplicity of processes, procedures and programmes' (McAra 2010: 287). In particular, drawing on a wider range of youth justice models can enable a much-needed nuanced analysis of specific youth justice contexts (e.g. cross-national, national, local); however, in order to be sensitive to the precise, multi-faceted, complex and contextualised nature of how youth justice (and its associated intervention approaches) is constructed within and between nations (Goldson and Briggs 2021; McAra 2010). For example, increasing regional and local mediation and moderation of centralised (e.g. national) youth justice philosophies, strategies, objectives and practices can be discerned internationally, often shaped by and within socio-historic, political, economic, cultural, judicial and organisational contexts and resulting in hybridised models of youth justice and approaches to youth justice intervention (Goldson and Briggs 2021; Bateman 2020). It is to these increasingly contextualised approaches to youth justice intervention that we now turn.

Social crime prevention: Contextualised youth justice prevention

When typologising crime prevention approaches, Crawford (1998) situated Developmental Crime Prevention (DCP) within the broader model of 'Social Crime Prevention,' which views offending as the product of a range of interacting (criminogenic) influences impacting on individuals by shaping their criminal predispositions (see also Sutton et al. 2022). He contrasted Social Crime Prevention with 'Situational Crime Prevention,' which presumes that offending is rational (chosen) and contextual (i.e. founded in immediate context/situation) and so can be prevented by making it more difficult to commit crimes (Crawford 1998: 18). According to Crawford, Social Crime Prevention most commonly targets two sets of criminogenic influences: Offender motivation (micro-level) and the underlying socio-economic causes of crime (macro-level). He further distinguished between 'Developmental' and 'Community' models of Social Crime Prevention, with DCP targeting micro-level characteristics and behaviour which are believed to predispose individuals, particularly young people, to offend (see Chapter two), whilst 'Community Crime Prevention' seeks to influence aspects of the social life of the community to reduce criminogenic influences on the individual. Consequently, Community Crime Prevention offers a more context-sensitive approach to understanding and responding to macro-level criminogenic influences in the lives of young people in order that youth justice intervention may prevent and reduce youth offending.

Community crime prevention with young people

The Community Crime Prevention (CCP) form of Social Crime Prevention focusses on managing and modifying the 'criminogenic conditions in the physical and social environment' (Brantingham and Faust 1976: 284) through 'interventions designed to change social conditions influencing offending in residential communities' (Tonry and Farrington 1995: 3). Consequently, CCP aims to identify broader social and community/neighbourhood-based (contextualised) criminogenic influences, rather than exclusively focussing on influences situated within individuals. The concept of CCP has turned crime prevention on its head by exploring the impact of the community on the behaviour of individuals, rather than prioritising how individuals affect their communities (Lewis and Salem 2017). The 'effectiveness' of CCP with young people was tentatively addressed in the UK at the end of the 20th century in the 'Reducing Reoffending' review of 'What Works' initiatives conducted for the UK Government (Goldblatt and Lewis 1998). The commissioned author of the review's CCP chapter, Tim Hope, hypothesised that effective CCP should seek to target two interrelated dimensions of social systems: Horizontal social relationships between people and groups and vertical relationships connecting local institutions to wider society. The most common CCP programmes across the UK at that time were categorised by Hope as:

- 'Community Organisation' such as local institutions (e.g. schools, churches) provide effective socialisation and positive role models;
- 'Community Defence' through environmental design and defensible space measures (e.g. Neighbourhood Watch);
- 'Order-Maintenance' by controlling physical disorder (litter, vandalism, graffiti) and antisocial behaviour;
- 'Community Development' through rebuilding the social, physical and economic fabric of neighbourhoods;

- 'Structural Change' through economic development and employment, education, health provision and the delivery of welfare, benefits and other social services;
- 'Risk-Based Programmes' target individual risk factors in community members, particularly young people, thus achieving community change by changing young people, not by the community changing them.

(Hope 1998: 56–57)

Hope's review highlighted that CCP programmes and interventions in the UK were overwhelmingly risk-focused and faithful to the RFPP (see also Chapter two), tending to target a single, specific community-based risk factor: Poverty. The common rationale for this seemingly reductionist focus was that impoverished neighbourhoods compound socio-economic disadvantage, which in turn exacerbates social/community disorganisation (e.g. gangs, vandalism, availability of drugs) and a lack of informal social control (e.g. residents willing and able to supervise and discipline other residents). These socially disadvantaged contexts allegedly encourage the accumulation of multiple social problems for young people, including offending, substance use, teenage pregnancy, school failure and unemployment, hence their prioritisation within preventative interventions (Hope, in Goldblatt and Lewis 1998). The review concluded by advocating that CCPs be targeted at high-crime neighbourhoods/communities and that Comprehensive Community Initiatives (CCIs) be put in place to tackle the multiple, interrelated social problems that can produce crime and a host of other negative outcomes. However, the author warned of the 'major methodological and practical difficulties in evaluating the effectiveness of community-based prevention programmes' and emphasised that 'very few crime prevention CCIs have been evaluated with any great degree of any scientific rigour' (Hope 1998: 57).

A subsequent review of youth-focused CCIs was produced in the UK, entitled 'Promising prevention: A review of promising and effective approaches to preventing offending by young people' (Archer, Skinns and Longstaff 2002). The report authors identified two apparently polarised forms of 'promising' community-based programmes:

- Community-based mentoring projects: A reductionist, RFPP-based approach providing positive adult role models to enhance the protective factors of trust, respect and informal social control, whilst tackling risk factors such as low school achievement, friends involved in problem behaviour, alienation and lack of social commitment;
- Community policing: A broader, more contextualised approach promoting informal social control and tackling community disorganisation through improved communication and more effective partnerships between communities and the police.

Despite highlighting both approaches as 'promising,' Archer et al. (2002) concurred with Farrington's (1996) bleak assessment that there had been a lack of methodologically rigorous evaluations of the effects of CCP on young people. The report reinforced previous review conclusions that youth crime prevention interventions in the community tended to target risk factors relating to young people's individual circumstances (see also Farrington 1996), rather than community-level influences on the young person. This prompted Archer et al. (2002) to recommend 'holistic and joined-up approaches' (e.g. CCIs) as offering the most promising avenues of CCP with young people (see also France and Crow 2005; ARCS 2008).

Evaluating CCP as 'effective' with young people

To this day, CCP remains notable by its absence from and under-representation in influential 'scientific' reviews of crime prevention projects with young people since their introduction at the end of the 20th century (Sutton et al. 2022; Emmel et al. 2021; Tompson et al. 2020; Thornton et al. 2019). A major reason for the longstanding paucity of evaluations of CCP programmes has been the continued dominance of the Scientific Methods Scale or 'SMS' that underpins the 'What Works' framework for evaluating intervention effectiveness (see Chapter 2). The SMS has proven poorly suited to measuring the complexities of CCP, especially given the longer-term outcomes, complex and multi-faceted, open-ended nature of such problem-solving interventions and their related 'theories of change' (Emmel et al. 2018). This concept refers to providing a comprehensive description and illustration of how and why a desired change is expected to happen in a particular context, for example, by using a specific intervention (Center for Theory of Change 2024). Interestingly, Noble and Hodgson (2016: 4) cautioned that 'what makes theory of change complicated or challenging are the social problems we are looking to address and the context in which you are working,' offering further indication of the invalidity of decontextualised SMS evaluation of CCP interventions. Put simply, the SMS-based 'What Works' approach to evaluating youth crime prevention programmes is largely unsuited to the valid and context-sensitive evaluation of CCP interventions (e.g. CCIs) for a number of reductionist reasons including:

- Complexity of CCIs: There are numerous contextualised social, political, financial and geographic circumstances, events, resources and individuals located outside of the local community that can have a direct influence on the success of CCIs, but which cannot be controlled or influenced by CCIs (e.g. economic recession influencing levels of poverty and unemployment). In addition, CCIs are community-specific and responsive to changes in neighbourhood dynamics over time. As such, community-based interventions are inherently flexible, dynamic, context-specific and often difficult to monitor and evaluate using experimental methodologies such as the SMS.
- Reductionist 'Black Box' understandings: The 'What Works' framework employs an experimental methodology to physically and statistically

manipulate (control) aspects of young people's environment in order to identify constant and predictable 'causal' relationships between interventions and outcomes. However, this focus on interventions (inputs) and reductions in youth offending (outputs) has neglected to examine mechanisms/processes of change (whether conceptualised as causal, predictive or simply influential) that can intervene between inputs and outputs and has neglected the potential influence of context upon intervention implementation and outcomes (see Pawson and Tilley 2004; Edwards and Hughes 2009). Instead, the 'What Works' framework makes assumptions as to what is going on in the 'Black Box' between inputs and outputs (Johnson et al. 2015) and 'bleaches out' the complexities of context by treating them as variables to be controlled (ARCS 2008). This reductionist approach renders it almost impossible to understand *how* a particular intervention generates positive impacts or, as Pawson and Tilley (1998) put it, 'what works for whom and in what circumstances?' (see Realist Synthesis discussion – this chapter).

- Evidential partiality (bias): The SMS and 'What Works' evaluation framework impose artificial restrictions on the type of evidence of intervention effectiveness that can be considered robust and high-quality, leading to an under-emphasis of more complex programmes/interventions that are difficult to evaluate, particularly those of CCP (Hope 1998; 2009), hence the under-representation of CCP interventions in reviews of 'successful' crime prevention evaluations. According to Maruna et al. (2008: 52) in their review of SMS-based evaluations, 'By the criteria used in this report, there are no community-based programs of "proven effectiveness" by scientific standards to show with reasonable certainty that they 'work' in certain kinds of settings.'
- Decontextualisation of 'community': Employing 'What Works' criteria to evaluate CCP programmes inevitably decontextualises the central concept/construct of 'community' under investigation. The framework's random allocation of communities to interventions flattens out their influence in order to 'eliminate their special features from the explanatory equation so that we are left to examine the unadulterated impact of the "program" on outcomes. Communities are reduced to the status of a confounding variable' (Pawson and Tilley 1998: 81). Therefore, CCP programmes are less able to conform to the artificial restrictions of the SMS approach and, as such, may be wrongly evaluated as having a poor quality research design.
- Lack of ecological validity: In a rebuttal to the continued advocacy of experimental 'What Works' approaches by Sherman, Hope (2009: 279) pointed out that 'unfavourable inferences could be drawn simply on the basis of comparing foolish/flawed efforts at experimentation in community settings with experiments in settings more amenable to manipulation and control of human subjects.' For example, CCP programmes are likely to suffer from what is known as 'Type II error,' the inaccurate

conclusion that the programme has no positive effects when it actually does. Hope (2005, 2009) warned in the strongest terms that the 'inappropriate application of SMS criteria' to CCP programme evaluations has the potential to 'seriously mislead policymakers' into rejecting effective programmes, simply because they do not conform to a restricted and inappropriate notion of 'evidence.' Pawson and Tilley (2004: 83) equated the experimental evaluation of CCP programmes to 'aiming an unwieldy hammer at an inappropriate sack of nuts.'

In summary, youth justice interventions that target social criminogenic influences and are predominantly situated in non-experimental, community contexts do not sit well with SMS-based, 'What Works' methods of evaluating intervention effectiveness (Ward 2020; Stephenson et al. 2018). This renders these evaluation methods of restricted ecological validity and largely unsuitable for assessing the effectiveness of youth justice interventions in real-world contexts[1]. As a result, Social Crime Prevention in its CCP form remains an undervalued and underutilised approach to understanding and implementing youth justice intervention in contextualised ways.

Five context-related lessons from community crime prevention

1. **Contextualised youth crime prevention:** Social Crime Prevention, animated through CCP (and related CCIs), challenges the reductionist and individualising nature of DCP (see Chapter 2) by offering an explicitly social and contextualised approach to understanding and preventing youth offending.
2. **Primary crime prevention:** CCP further challenges the micro-level, individualisation of youth offending explanations (see Chapter 1) and youth justice responses explanations (see Chapter two) by seeking to modify 'criminogenic conditions in the physical and social environment.'
3. **Macro-level intervention:** CCP promotes macro-level understandings of and responses to youth offending through 'interventions designed to change the social conditions influencing offending in residential communities.'
4. **Risk-based partiality:** Bias towards risk-based explanations and associated risk-focused interventions in the implementation, review and evaluation of CCP has restricted its effective utilisation and evaluation as representing macro-level intervention and contextualised youth justice.
5. **Problematic evaluation:** CCP is largely incompatible with the SMS-based 'What Works' evaluation framework due to the marginalisation of qualitative data in the dominant, experimentally biased and reductionist 'hierarchy of evidence' that underpins the framework, leading to difficulties in formally evaluating CCP as 'effective' in the youth justice field.

Realist synthesis: Evaluating contextualised youth justice intervention

Western youth justice systems in the 21st century have responded to the increasing pressures of globalisation for modernising, managerialist and accountable responses to youth offending by recommending that 'effective' youth justice interventions be 'evidence-based' explanations (see Chapter 2). The cultural shift towards 'evidence-based practice' has been seen as a positive step for the youth justice sector because it encourages moves away from discretionary, opaque and inconsistent practice towards the systematic and transparent integration of good practice lessons from research and evaluation (Stephenson et a. 2018; Wilcox 2003). However, youth justice interventions have been increasingly adjudged to be 'evidence-based' and 'effective' based on the experimental, SMS criteria of the 'What Works' evaluation framework (see Chapter 2), which privilege interventions targeting the psychosocial risk factors that allegedly predict reoffending. This narrow, restricted approach to evaluating youth justice interventions illustrates how psychosocial 'causes' have been elevated atop a 'hierarchy of evidence' (Boaz and Ashby 2003). For example, the gold standard Randomised Controlled Trial (RCT) cannot assess the mechanisms of change through which interventions give rise to outcomes, as these remain hidden in a 'Black Box' (Johnson et al. 2015), thus the impact of context is ignored (see previous section). Consequently, critics have characterised evidence-based practice in youth justice as perpetuating a reductionist, partial and narrow appreciation of what evidence is (Case 2022) and have thus lamented its evolution into an influential neoliberal managerial tool that is often founded in actuarial risk management, the RFPP and the 'What Works' framework (Stephenson and Allen 2018; see also Smith and Gray 2019).

In the past decade, there has been growing acknowledgement across the 'What Works' community (e.g. in UK-based 'What Works Centres') that methods traditionally deemed robust for evaluating the 'effectiveness' of preventative interventions should now be accompanied by a more systematic analysis of 'what is working, where and why?' (Tompson et al. 2020). Unfortunately, guidance for conducting these analyses often operationalises 'context' as the observable, static and temporally-fixed 'features' of a situation or population, rather than as the relational and dynamic (changeable) features that shape the mechanisms of change through which an intervention works (Greenhalgh and Manzano 2021; see also YJB 2016). As a result, practitioners are left with a partial understanding of *how and why* interventions may work for some young people, but not for others (Sutton et al. 2022; Stephenson and Allen 2018) and an incomplete evidence-base with which to inform the design and implementation of preventative interventions. Ultimately, therefore, the dominant evidence-base for 'effective' interventions in Western youth justice systems has been restricted and shaped by reductionist and partial hierarchies of evidence, which preclude review methodologies able to illustrate how contextual factors can shape the 'mechanisms' of change in preventative interventions and how, why and for whom these interventions work (Sutton et al. 2022).

Enter the contextualised approaches of the 'EMMIE' framework (Johnson et al. 2015) and the 'Realist Synthesis' approach (Pawson and Tilley 2004) for evaluating the 'effectiveness' of youth justice interventions. Both approaches are driven by collecting discrete data relating to the causes, effects and theories that underlie (youth justice) interventions, seeking to understand the 'mechanisms' that can initiate (youth) offending and the neglected intervention 'mechanisms' that can promote desistance from offending (Case et al. 2022) .

EMMIE: Effects, moderators, mechanisms, implementation and economics

The EMMIE approach was designed to bridge the gap between practitioners' need to understand an intervention's 'mediating causal processes ... characteristics of recipients, providers, and settings' (Lipsey and Wilson 1993: 1201) and the requirement to draw on evidence of effective practice from 'What Works' evaluations, which have tended to focus solely on effect sizes and their moderators (Johnson et al. 2015). EMMIE systematically examines the effects (E) of interventions, whilst also encouraging reviewers to look for evidence on the moderators (M), mechanisms (M), the nature of implementation (I) and the costs, or economics (E) of interventions (Thornton et al. 2019). In other words, EMMIE provides a framework to evaluate not just the effect of interventions but also the causal mechanisms through which the interventions work, the contextual features that shape the way interventions work and their impact and the practical implementation issues for policymakers. Additionally, the EMMIE framework enables an assessment of whether evaluations provide value for money. Use of this nuanced evaluation methodology, therefore, can allow researchers to identify the criminogenic influences (e.g. mechanisms of change) and contextual features (e.g. relational, dynamic, socio-structural) that shape how interventions 'work' and are 'effective.' The EMMIE framework (Thornton et al. 2019; Johnson et al. 2015) has become a key part of the evaluation and systematic review landscape in terms of understanding the crime reduction and crime prevention evidence-base, but as yet remains relatively under-explored in the context of youth justice interventions (Tompson et al. 2020; see also Sutton et al. 2022).

Realist synthesis: Contexts-mechanisms-outcomes of interventions

The Realist Synthesis approach examines the Context-Mechanisms-Outcomes (CMO) relationships that shape intervention 'effectiveness' – relationships between the Contexts in which interventions work, the Mechanisms (of change) through which they work and the Outcomes that these contexts and mechanisms produce (Pawson and Tilley 2004). The central unit of Realist Synthesis analysis is the 'programme theory' that underpins an intervention and explains how the intervention is designed to produce its intended outcomes. A key objective of Realist Synthesis, therefore, is to synthesise literature and evidence in order to identify, test and refine programme theories and to build explanations about how, why and in what circumstances preventative interventions work. Consequently, Realist Synthesis challenges the reductionism of the 'What Works' evaluation framework by situating interventions 'in a much wider context related to change processes of individual children' (Stephenson et al. 2018: 69). Crucially, Realist Synthesis asks the theory-driven question of 'what works for whom, in what circumstances, and how?' (Pawson and Tilley 2004). Whilst this approach has been advocated as a valuable methodology to synthesise evidence in crime prevention (Johnson et al. 2015), it remains largely untested and overlooked in the youth justice context (Sutton et al. 2022).

Understanding preventative intervention in youth justice

In order to address the paucity of Realist Synthesis evaluation of youth justice intervention, Case and colleagues utilised the methodology to evaluate prevention-focused interventions in youth justice systems internationally, with a particular focus on the YJS of England and Wales. They examined how criminogenic influences have been conceptualised/constructed in the most popular youth justice interventions and how these constructions impacted how the interventions were designed to work. The researchers then provided practical guidance and recommendations for identifying 'what works for whom, in what circumstances' (Pawson 2006) in relation to preventing youth offending (Case et al. 2022). The Realist Synthesis was conducted in two related phases:

- Phase one, 'Identification and analysis of programme theories': A three-stage process of thematic documentary analysis of legislation, policy publications and related literature, expert interviews with key policymakers, strategists, practitioners and academics, and systematic searches to identify programme theories underlying particular interventions identified. Phase one found that early 21st-century interventions to prevent youth offending in the Western world had been characterised by reductionist, punitive, offender-focused, managerial and interventionist approaches shaped by risk management and evaluated using 'What Works' criteria. However, since economic austerity impacted the globalised Western world (circa 2010 onwards), there has been a clear move away from risk-based policies and programme theories and evolution towards more 'Child-Friendly Justice' and 'Child First' policies and programme theories (see later in this chapter).
- Phase two, 'Theory testing and refinement': Analyses of two community disposals[2]: Referral Orders, a restorative justice-based community-based order most often used in the YJS of England and Wales by the courts, and the Intensive Supervision and Surveillance Programme, a preventative

disposal for persistent and serious offenders. Phase two demonstrated that these disposals were most effective in child-centric, promotional, prosocial contexts of positive relationships[3] between the young person and adult professional that were characterised by the young person's inclusion, engagement, meaningful participation and collaborative, non-hierarchical (i.e. power-led) dynamics. These meso-level contexts shaped mechanisms of change integral to positive, prosocial identity development driven by intrinsic motivation (i.e. internal belief, desire to change), feelings of trust, self-esteem/worth, being valued, being listened to and attachment/bonding (see also Axford et al. 2022). Conversely, interventions were less effective in negative, risk-led, adult- and system-centric contexts characterised by enforcement, control, managerialism, responsibilisation and criminalisation, with the young person feeling that youth justice is being done *to* them (see Chapter 2). These contexts gave rise to feelings of punishment and compliance, which encouraged young people's extrinsic motivation, illustrated by superficial, tokenistic, instrumental participation in interventions based on external rewards (e.g. completing an order) and disengagement (Case et al. 2022).

Findings highlighted that 'effective' youth justice interventions function within supportive and engaging contexts underpinned by positive relationships between the child and adult professionals (see also Case et al. 2022; Axford et al. 2022). Realist Synthesis was able to evidence that relationship-based practice and intervention design/implementation were able to promote prosocial identity development/positive outcomes by encouraging young people to feel trust/trusted, respected (not judged/punished), safe and secure and by addressing young people's needs, strengths, capacities and rights as mechanisms of change (Case et al. 2022). The researchers concluded that it was crucial to deliver youth justice intervention in contexts where young people feel positively challenged, feel a sense of enjoyment, satisfaction, purpose, achievement and contribution and become more aware of their own skills, attitudes and behaviour. Therefore, relational and dynamic features of intervention contexts function as the key mechanisms or 'active ingredients' of intervention effectiveness with young people (see also Center for Youth Impact 2017).

In summary, Realist Synthesis and its associated EMMIE framework challenge and extend the perceived limitations of the 'What Works' framework, moving beyond examining the effects of youth justice interventions and into the evaluation of the causal mechanisms through which interventions work, the contextual features that shape the way interventions work and their impact and the practical implementation issues for policymakers. Starting with the premise that interventions are never universally successful, Realist Synthesis can examine the ways in which interventions work and how the multiple outcomes they produce are shaped by the contexts in which they are implemented (Pawson 2013; see also Tompson et al. 2020). The implications of adopting a Realist Synthesis approach to intervention evaluation as a means of better understanding and responding to youth offending 'in context' are explored in more detail in Chapter 5.

Realist synthesis: Challenging reductionist youth justice intervention in five contextualised pieces

1. **Broader conceptions of intervention 'effectiveness'**: Realist Synthesis and EMMIE advocate for a more extensive, dynamic and contextualised understanding of youth justice intervention effectiveness to challenge the reductionist, static and decontextualised constructions of criminogenic influences and how interventions 'work' that are perpetuated by the dominant 'What Works' evaluation framework.
2. **Broader conceptions of evidence-based practice**: Realist approaches challenge and evolve the reductionist, partial and narrow conceptions of what constitutes the acceptable evidence of intervention 'effectiveness' to inform youth justice practice by requiring much closer consideration of qualitative and contextualised influences on a broader range of intervention outcomes.
3. **Contextualised evaluation framework**: Realist Synthesis adds much-needed contextual sensitivity to the 'What Works' approach by considering 'what works, for whom, in what circumstances?'
4. **Contextualised explanation**: The Realist Synthesis framework challenges the explanatory 'Black Box' of the 'What Works' framework by examining relationships between the Contexts in which youth offending and youth justice take place, the Mechanisms of change promoted by interventions and the outcomes of interventions, which can be broader than simple binary offending-desistance measures, that underpin an intervention's 'effectiveness.'
5. **Theories of Change**: The explicitly contextualised Contexts-Mechanisms-Outcomes lens of Realist Synthesis evaluation prioritises the identification of the programme theories and theories of change (e.g. containing mechanisms) that underpin how interventions are intended to be effective, rather than relying on a reductionist dismissal of the importance of the processes of change occurring between intervention inputs and behavioural outputs.

Child-friendly Justice in children's rights context

A movement of 'child-friendly' youth justice has developed since the 1990s to directly contrast with and challenge the punitive (retributivist) and practical/pragmatic (risk-based) nature of dominant youth justice movements of that time (see Chapter 2). 'Child-Friendly Justice' has emphasised the protection of young people who offend and rejected the necessity for punitive and neo-liberal responsibilising youth justice measures, reflecting the historical ambiguity and contradiction over whether to construct and respond to young people who offend as:

> vulnerable *becomings* in need of protection, help, guidance and support, or as undisciplined and dangerous *beings* necessitating correction, regulation, control and punishment.
>
> (Goldson and Muncie 2021: vii)

The Child-Friendly Justice approach (Goldson and Muncie 2021; see also Salford, Cairns and Marshall 2017) has been increasingly developed within children's rights contexts across youth justice systems internationally in the 21st century (Liefaard 2020); contexts that can be traced back to the inception of the 'United Nations Convention on the Rights of the Child' (UNCRC) in 1989. This influential children's rights instrument established a baseline for constructing children's rights and for implementing rights-compliant responses through 54 articles focused on the protection, provision and participation of children, with the 'child' defined as any young person below the age of 18 (UNICEF 1989). The UNCRC, which has now been ratified by every country in the world (except the USA), outlines the civil, political, economic, social and cultural rights of every child. These rights are considered to be 'universal,' in that they are available to all children, regardless of their ethnicity, gender, age, religion, ability or history of offending behaviour. When operationalising children's rights in the context of youth justice systems, the UNCRC makes explicit that the common and principal aim of youth justice should be to act in the best interests of the child, not to punish, correct or prevent. Implementation of the UNCRC in individual countries is monitored on a five-yearly basis by the Committee on the Rights of the Child (CRC). The most relevant youth justice provisions of the UNCRC are:

- Article 3 (best interests of the child) establishes the primacy of the best interests of the child in all decisions affecting them, notably in terms of budgets, policy and law-making.
- Article 4 (protection of rights) asserts that governments should respect, protect and fulfil children's rights.
- Article 12 (respect for the views of the child) sets out the right of children to express their views and have them taken into account on all matters affecting them, with children's participation appropriate to their level of maturity.
- Article 13 (freedom of expression) outlines the child's right to receive and share information that is not damaging to themselves or others.
- Article 17 (access to information) establishes that children have the right to information that is important to their health and well-being.
- Article 37 (custody as a last resort) stresses that the detention or imprisonment of a child shall be used only as a measure of last resort and for the shortest appropriate period of time.

- Article 40 (juvenile justice) provides that children who are accused of breaking the law have the right to legal help and fair treatment in a justice system that respects their rights.

Since their introduction, the youth justice-focused articles of the UNCRC have consolidated and been consolidated by specific guidelines in other international children's rights instruments from the United Nations General Assembly, notably:

- United Nations Standard Minimum Rules for the Administration of Juvenile Justice (United Nations General Assembly 1985): The 'Beijing Rules' provide guidance for the protection of the human rights of children and young people in the development of separate and specialist youth justice systems.
- United Nations Guidelines on the Prevention of Delinquency (United Nations General Assembly 1990a): The 'Riyadh Guidelines' emphasise that the prevention of juvenile delinquency should be prioritised by youth justice systems and should be pursued through progressive diversionary and other non-punitive measures (see also the earlier discussion of 'Minimum Necessary Intervention').
- United Nations Rules for the Protection of Juveniles Deprived of their Liberty (United Nations General Assembly 1990b): The 'Havana Rules' state that deprivation of liberty for a child who offends should be a disposition of 'last resort' and used only 'for the minimum necessary period.'

Several UNCRC principles were subsequently reflected in the 'European rules for juvenile offenders subject to sanctions or measures: Basic principles 2008' (Council of Europe 2008; see also Muncie and Goldson 2015), including the right to be respected, effective participation, minimum necessary intervention, deprivation of liberty as a last resort and non-discrimination. The children's rights context for youth justice that is encouraged by United Nations instruments has been consolidated by more recent, formally adopted Council of Europe guidelines for 'Child-Friendly Justice' (Council of Europe 2010). These guidelines state that any young person under the age of 18 years should be regarded as 'a child' and that youth justice systems internationally should prioritise children's rights to participation in criminal/youth justice proceedings, their best interests, dignity and protection from discrimination through adhering to the rule of law. These guidelines must apply to 'all ways in which children are likely to be, for whatever reason and in whatever capacity, brought into contact with … bodies and services involved in implementing criminal, civil or administrative law' (Council of Europe 2010: section I, paragraph 2).

The principles of the UNCRC are 'a vital first step for governments … [to] move towards child-centred and rights-compliance systems of youth and juvenile justice' (Muncie 2010: 201), specifically where they assert that children and young people in conflict with the law have a right to treatment that is age-appropriate, meets their needs and enhances the support of family relationships (Liefaard 2020). Additionally, the UNCRC principles of diversion and of detention as a last resort, which is key to the children's rights approach to youth justice, seek to minimise (the harm caused by) children's contact with the YJS (Kilkelly, in Case and Hazel 2023). According to the Committee on the Rights of the Child (CRC), the body of experts that monitors and reports on the implementation of the UNCRC in nation states, '[e]vidence shows that the prevalence of crime committed by children tends to decrease after the adoption of systems in line with these principles' (CRC 2019: para 3). The broader socio-political, conceptual and ethical context here is that the UNCRC and associated children's rights instruments establish a positive view of children and seek to promote and protect the place of children in society and the value and status of children as citizens (Haines and Case 2015). To this end, the UNCRC (through Article 4) creates binding legal obligations on states parties to take legislative, administrative and other measures to implement children's rights. These efforts have intensified in recent years, with a growing global momentum behind the approach to fully incorporate the UNCRC into domestic law, including in the area of youth justice (Kilkelly and Bergin 2021; Liefaard 2020).

Youth justice in a context of children's rights: Conflict, ambivalence and avoidance

As 'legally binding' as the UNCRC is, nation states regularly contravene its articles, and the CRC has no sanctioning powers to respond officially to these breaches, instead having to 'rely on persuasion and admonishment rather than enforcement' (Muncie 2010: 202). Indeed, critics have noted that children's rights conventions have created conflict and ambivalence when applied in the youth justice context, most notably through the introduction of tensions between welfare and justice imperatives (Put and Walgrave 2006). For example, McAra (2010) contends that in the Beijing Rules for the administration of juvenile justice, youth justice systems are presented with the simultaneous requirements to meet the needs of the child (a welfare principle), to protect their rights (a children's rights principle) and to meet/protect the needs of society (a justice objective). Further to this, the Beijing Rules require children's rights to be met through minimum necessary intervention (Dunkel 2014; Cavadino and Dignan 2013), prevention, diversion, community sentences and the use of custody as a last resort. However, any intervention must also be proportionate to the offence's seriousness (i.e. justice-based) and offender circumstances (i.e. welfare-inclined), including the use of care, protection, education and vocational training. Therefore, the Beijing Rules children's rights instrument requires that nation states and practitioners address a range of (potentially conflicting and contradictory) youth justice principles and rationales when responding to youth offending. Worse still, very limited guidance has been given regarding how to balance and reconcile these competing youth justice imperatives in a children's rights context (McAra 2010). The level of discretion that states enjoy in the implementation of UNCRC rights can play out in negative ways for children and young people in youth justice systems (Liefaard 2020). Particular examples include the broad range of sentencing mechanisms that are tolerated within the terms of the UNCRC, including detention, up to and including life imprisonment, as long as parole is permitted (Liefaard 2020: 294). More generally, discretion in the interpretation and application of the UNCRC in youth justice contexts permits nation states to pick and choose those provisions they consider most relevant or appealing. Against the ever-politicised context of youth justice, nation states can and do set the bar very low for those children deemed less worthy, especially those at the extreme end of the offending spectrum (Lynch and Liefaard 2020).

Analyses of CRC 'Concluding Observations' following national inspections have discovered a general lack of compliance with and implementation of UNCRC principles across youth justice systems globally, not limited to the Western world. Notably, there has been a widespread absence of 'sympathetic understanding' of UNCRC principles in youth justice approaches, typified by punitive practices such as 'torture, inhumane treatment, lack of separation from adults, police brutality, poor conditions in detention facilities, overcrowding, lack of rehabilitation ... and the improper use of the juvenile justice system to tackle other social problems' (Abramson, in Muncie 2010: 202). This criticism has been reinforced by successive CRC 'Concluding Observations' regarding the excessive systemic criminalisation and adulterisation of children who offend, combined with a punitive ethos of 'offender first, child second' (CRC 2008: 32). Following an analysis of UNCRC compliance in 15 Western European countries, Muncie (2010: 203) observed that 'most of these European states [except Norway] appear to have failed to recognize the centrality of such issues as distinctive needs, dignity, humane treatment and so on as core to the realization of children's rights.' Further afield in Australia, criminalised children have been afforded very few human rights, according to critical commentators (see Ogilvie et al. 2024; Forde 2021). Indeed Australia is the only democratic country in the world that does not have a federal Bill of Rights. Although some Australian states and territories have introduced Human Rights Acts, the protections they offer to criminalised children are much more limited than those recognised in international law (Walsh and Fitzgerald 2022; Forde 2021). This is especially true for Indigenous Aboriginal and Torres Strait Islander children, a situation (socio-political context) which scholars consider to be indicative of systemic discrimination and racism across Australian (State-based) youth justice systems (Walsh and Fitzgerald 2022; Cunneen 2020).

In summary, contemporary 'Child-Friendly Justice' embodies a positive, children's rights-based approach and ethos for working with young people who offend by protecting their universal, unconditional rights established under the UNCRC and Council of Europe rules. These conventions and instruments acknowledge a young offender's inherent status as a child, promote their best interests and actively reject punitive, negative youth justice approaches such as custody and excessive intervention (i.e. interventionism). However, despite the ostensible legally binding status of the UNCRC principles, international reviews and CRC inspections consistently identify a lack of compliance with and recognition of these principles across nation states, indicating that much work is still needed to realise the rhetoric of rights in real-world youth justice contexts internationally.

Child-friendly justice as political rhetoric, not contextual reality? Five contextualised arguments

1. **Contextualised justice:** Child-Friendly Justice promises a progressive and expansionist approach to conceptualising and delivering youth justice that is explicitly situated within a children's rights context.
2. **Structural and systemic contexts:** Child-Friendly, rights-based youth justice advocates argue that young people who offend should be responded to as children within bespoke structural and systemic contexts, notably in youth justice systems that are distinct from adult criminal justice systems.
3. **Structural and systemic processes: Rights-based** Child-Friendly, rights-based youth justice advocates for responding to young people (constructed as 'children') who offend through bespoke and principled child-centric processes that prioritise their best interests, prioritise prevention over punishment, emphasise minimum necessary intervention and use custody only as a last resort.
4. **Inconsistent implementation:** The youth justice requirements of the children's rights instruments that underpin Child-Friendly Justice have been complied with and applied inconsistently across the globe, resulting in numerous national and local youth justice contexts being characterised by punitive and inhumane treatment of children who offend.
5. **Inconsistent understanding:** Inconsistent compliance and implementation of international children's rights instruments have been underpinned by a lack of understanding of their youth justice requirements and a lack of clarity, guidance and training in relation to their effective implementation in policy and practice.

'Child First' youth justice

The principle of 'Child First' youth justice has its origins in the Welsh principle of 'Children First, Offenders Second,' which was created by Haines and Drakeford and set out in their ground-breaking text 'Young People and Youth Justice' (Haines and Drakeford 1998; see also Haines and Thomas 2023). Through 'Children First, Offenders Second' (CFOS), Haines and Drakeford argued that young people who offend and come into contact with youth justice systems should be viewed and treated (constructed) as 'children first,' prioritising their status as a child and their associated lack of capacity, development and power relative to adults over their status/label/identity as an 'offender.' Accordingly, CFOS challenged the perceived anti-child elements of the impending neo-liberal, modernising, managerialist, punitive and neo-correctionalist strategies of youth justice about to be introduced in England and Wales through the Crime and Disorder Act 1998; strategies that were predicted to:

- *Criminalise* young people[4] through the application of 'youth offender' labels (i.e. ignoring their 'child' status);
- Prioritise *offence- and offender-based* interventions;
- Assign too much *responsibility* to young people for causing and desisting from offending;
- *Breach children's rights* under the United Nations Convention on the Rights of the Child (UNCRC);
- Mobilise non-child-friendly strategies using *punitive (punishing) and risk-based* approaches to delivering youth justice.

(after Haines and Case 2015)

The CFOS principle became the foundation of the 'All Wales Youth Offending Strategy' (Welsh Assembly Government and YJB 2004), subsequently revised into the 'Children and Young People First' strategy (Welsh Government and YJB 2014), and underpinned the 'Youth Justice Blueprint for Wales' (MoJ and Welsh Government 2019). These strategic developments in the socio-political context of Wales were supported by a long-term body of academic research conducted with youth justice stakeholders, including 'children' (not constructed as 'young people' in this approach), parents, youth justice staff, police, schools, third sector organisations and national policymakers. This research and the evidence it produced evolved the CFOS principle into a practice model entitled 'Positive Youth Justice' (Haines and Case 2015), which itself was founded on identified, inter-related component principles for 'effective' youth justice practice:

- *Child-friendly, child-appropriate* treatment in accordance with 'child' status and capacities;
- *Promotion of positive behaviours and outcomes* for children (e.g. access to universal entitlements and rights);
- *Diversion* from the formal YJS, including Child-Friendly decision-making at all stages of the YJS;
- *Engagement and participation* of children in youth justice processes, such as in decision-making and intervention planning;
- *Responsibilising adult professionals* for ensuring that children in the YJS achieve positive outcomes and access support and guidance.

Throughout the policy-based and strategic development of CFOS in Wales, a succession of multi-agency interventions and programmes provided empirical evidence of the effectiveness of Positive Youth Justice and its component principles (see Case and Browning 2021). This evidence included reductions in negative behaviours by and negative outcomes for children, including the annual numbers of children receiving school exclusions, reporting substance use, offending, entering the YJS for the first time, re-offending and receiving custodial sentences (Haines and Case 2015). These research programmes also provided evidence that the CFOS-based Positive Youth Justice model enhanced positive behaviours and outcomes, for example, increasing annual numbers of children diverted from the formal YJS and into appropriate support services (Haines and Thomas 2023), improving children's perceptions that they can access their universal rights (Case et al 2005) and increasing children's engagement with positive, prosocial opportunities and services in their community (Case and Haines 2018).

From 'CFOS' to 'Child First'

> We see children first and offenders second. We make every effort to champion the needs of children wherever they are in the youth justice system and ensure we give them a voice; We strongly believe that children can and should be given every opportunity to make positive changes.
>
> (YJB 2021: 7)

In September 2015, a full-scale 'Review of the Youth Justice System in England and Wales' called for a re-orientated system of youth justice where 'we see the child first and the offender second' (Taylor 2016: 3). Following publication of the report, the author (Charlie Taylor) was appointed Chair of the YJB (serving from 2016–2020), during which time he oversaw a formal and deliberate organisational culture shift away from previous adherence to risk management criteria and towards embedding CFOS-based principles for youth justice throughout the YJB's organisational identity (Case 2024). These structural, cultural and systemic changes were accelerated by a concurrent macro-level context of significant philosophical, political and strategic developments nationally and internationally, which challenged the status quo of dominant neo-correctionalist, risk management thinking in youth justice systems across the Western world (Case and Browning 2021). These macro-level contextual changes were most evident in relation to:

- Socio-economic change: A socio-economic context of sweeping economic austerity internationally had begun to necessitate the enforced downsizing of vital children's support services. However, these socio-economic 'crises' actually motivated key stakeholders in youth justice contexts to develop new understandings of and responses to youth offending that were founded in more expansionist, yet also more context-specific and localised, evidence-bases (see hello) and that were potentially more innovative and cost-effective than previous approaches.

- Political dynamism: A socio-political context of governmental instability and insecurity resulting from significant, critical and often unpredictable national and international events (e.g. economic austerity, the global COVID pandemic, the influence of Brexit in the UK and across Europe) catalysed frequent changes in key stakeholder personnel in youth justice contexts and changes (often decreases) in the visibility and priority of youth justice as a central political issue (see Case 2024).
- Evidential evolution: New and evolving academic and empirical insights regarding successful and appropriate components of youth justice strategies and models of practice internationally (see also the start of this chapter), alongside emerging evidence-based critiques of the weaknesses and limitations of previous models and approaches (see also Chapter two), were expanding knowledge and understanding of the influences on youth offending and how best to respond to it through youth justice intervention (Baker for YJB 2014; see also Case and Browning 2021).
- Principled debates: The 'Principled Youth Justice' model argues that youth justice should address socio-economic inequalities, prioritise diversion from the formal YJS and promote child-appropriate justice (Harding and Becroft 2013). An associated 'Child-Friendly Justice' movement emerged (see earlier in this chapter) seeking to protect the rights, inherent child status and best interests of children once they had offended.

Faced with these dynamic, unpredictable and precarious socio-political, strategic and academic contexts, the YJB took ownership of the principle of CFOS by reconstructing it as 'Child First' (YJB 2018, 2024) and using the principle to reconstruct its own organisational identity and that of youth justice in England and Wales (Case and Hazel 2023). Child First was operationalised as a fusion of the central evidence-based tenets of the 'Positive Youth Justice' model for delivering youth justice in community contexts (Haines and Case 2015; see previous section) and the more recent 'Constructive Resettlement' approach for resettling young people in community contexts following custody (Hazel and Bateman 2020; YJB 2018). Constructive Resettlement provided a theory of change for how youth justice interventions can enhance effective support for children re-entering the community. The model was underpinned by its identified '5Cs' (Hazel and Bateman 2020), each of which had been evidenced to facilitate pro-social identity development. These principles advocated for youth justice interventions that were: 'Constructive' via strengths-based, future-focused, empowering approaches, 'Co-created' with the child, 'Customised' for the child, 'Consistent' through shared objectives and 'Co-ordinated' through multi-agency partnership (Hazel and Bateman 2020).

The YJB Strategic Plan 2021–2024 officially committed to Child First as the 'strategic approach and central guiding principle' for youth justice in England and Wales (YJB 2021: 3), dividing Child First into four inter-related 'tenets' (after Case and Browning 2021):

- See children as children: Prioritise the best interests of children, recognising their particular needs, capacities, rights and potential. All work is child-focused, developmentally informed, acknowledges structural barriers and meets responsibilities towards children.
- Develop a pro-social identity for positive child outcomes: Promote children's individual strengths and capacities to develop their pro-social identity for sustainable desistance[5], leading to safer communities and fewer victims. All work is constructive and future-focused, built on supportive relationships that empower children to fulfil their potential and make positive contributions to society.
- Collaborate with children: Encourage children's active participation, engagement and wider social inclusion. All work is a meaningful collaboration with children and their carers.
- Promote diversion: Promote a childhood removed from the justice system, using pre-emptive prevention, diversion and minimal intervention. All work minimises criminogenic stigma from contact with the system.

(YJB 2021: 10–11)

Child first as an expansionist principle, not a reductionist model

The Child First principle explicitly questions and challenges established adult-centric, adulterising and interventionist, labelling and criminalising constructions of children and young people (when they offend) as risky and threatening 'offenders' (Case 2021), encompassing a range of theoretical, ideological and principled assumptions about the nature of childhood and children's evolving capacity (Smith 2011). Crucially, Child First promotes contextualised youth justice by considering criminogenic influence and intervention effectiveness within and between the range of contexts inhabited and experienced by young people, not simply the micro-level contexts of rational decision-making and risk factor influence prioritised by ARFTs, DCP and the 'What Works' framework (see Chapter 2). Child First advocates for constructions of children, offending and youth justice that fully incorporate contextual influences at the micro-level (e.g. positive identity development, desistance), the meso-level (e.g. collaboration and positive relationships with children) and the macro-level (e.g. addressing structural disadvantage, the cultural construction of children as children, diversion from criminogenic systemic contexts). Child First is now the guiding principle for all policy, strategy and practice across the YJS of England and Wales. In addition, it has been formalised as a key reform principle for youth justice in Northern Ireland (DoJ 2021) and is increasingly influential as a shaper of policy and practice in a host of youth justice systems across the globalised Western world, including China (see 'In focus box' below), Scotland, Ireland, New Zealand, Canada, the USA and Australia (Case and Hazel 2023; see also Gray and Smith 2024).

In focus: Child first principles in China

A series of key normative principles can be identified as underpinning contemporary juvenile justice in China (Jou, Chang and Hebenton (2014), several of which are closely related to the Child First principle and its component tenets:

'Education First and Punishment Second' Principle: The judicial authority is required to fully consider the unique characteristics of the juvenile in terms of their age and physical and mental development (i.e. see children as children) and pinpoint where education can best achieve the aims of reform. 'Punishment second' (i.e. equivalent to the 'offender second' element of the CFOS principle) emphasises the appropriate use of punishment to best support juvenile rehabilitation, not simply punishment as 'deterrence' (Cheng and Yu 2013).

'Simplification' Principle: Juvenile justice in China seeks to protect the mental and physical health of juveniles, and judges are required to clearly explain the legal rights of juveniles to them in order to eliminate any associated fear of the system among juveniles. This principled approach is pursued in the more general context of educating and reforming, rather than punishing (Ye 2013), similar to the Child First ethos of promoting child-friendly/appropriate treatment and avoiding criminalisation and stigmatisation.

'Best Interests' Principle: A core principle of juvenile justice in China since amendments to the juvenile protection law in 2006, the 'Best Interests' principle holds that the physical, spiritual, mental, moral and social development of the juvenile is assumed as the first priority in juvenile justice contexts (i.e. Child First). Furthermore, the individual needs of the young person must be recognised, regardless of the nature of the crime committed, and their basic welfare and rights must be well protected throughout the investigation, court processes and into aftercare (Yan 2012).

'Teach and Instruct' Principle: When the juvenile is arrested, the psychological change of identity from a 'good citizen' to a 'criminal offender' (i.e. 'offender first') may create complex mental pressures for the juvenile/child. For example, the potential loss of freedom and associated fears of punishment, together with damage to harmonious community relations, can make it difficult for juveniles to reflect on their behaviour (Jou, Chang and Hebenton 2014). Consequently, combining moral instruction with allowing juveniles to consider the consequences of their actions can enable and empower them to have the courage and confidence to reform (Jou, Chan and Hebenton 2014; Ye 2013), for example, through the development of positive identity (i.e. tenet two of Child First).

Child First supersedes traditional 'models' of youth justice (e.g. welfare, justice), whilst actively challenging and rejecting hegemonic, reductionist, adult-centric and neo-correctionalist risk management paradigms that are anchored in pathologising notions of the 'problem child' (see the detailed critique by Case 2022). Accordingly, Child First offers a guiding principle for reconstructing understandings of 'youth offending' and a relational, dynamic and contextual force for change in how children experience youth justice (Case and Hazel 2023). The principle promotes a radical, expansionist cultural and practical shift for youth justice, presenting a progressive philosophy and a methodical and reasoned way of thinking about youth offending and about applying the evidence-base for effective youth justice that moves beyond conceptual, systemic and practical reductionism. As such, Child First has been conceptualised as at once a 'philosophy of positive youth justice' (Haines and Case 2015: 1) and a 'philosophical stance' (Bateman 2020) – a guiding set of principles, objectives, understandings and experiences that frame and animate professional knowledge, skills and practice (Case and Haines 2020). Ultimately, Child First is intended to produce a 'common language' with which stakeholders across youth justice systems can make decisions in an evidence-informed way that will lead to positive outcomes and behaviour for young people (constructed as 'children') and so will prevent offending, protect the public, make communities feel safer and improve the lives of young people (Case and Hazel 2023). However, contextual challenges remain for realising Child First Across the youth justice policy commerce strategy and practise contexts of nation states in the globalised Western world:

- **Reconciling Child First with rights-based Child-Friendly Justice:** Both Child First and children's rights-based Child-Friendly Justice approaches highlight the importance of ensuring that 'children' (not young people) are treated with regard to their age and understanding, in a manner that takes account of their circumstances and needs. Both espouse the importance of diversion as a formal and explicit principle for keeping children out of formal youth justice systems, avoiding stigmatising and labelling children and preventing children from further offending. Both approaches promote the importance of children participating in processes and decision-making about their lives (Kilkelly, in Case and Hazel 2023). However, whilst sharing broadly similar principles, values and evidence-bases with Child-Friendly Justice (Case and Browning 2021), Child First makes relatively few explicit references to children's rights beyond tenet one's 'prioritisation of the best interests of children' (YJB 2024: 10) and 'recognising children's 'particular needs, capacities, rights and potential' through practice that is 'child-focused, developmentally informed, acknowledges structural barriers and meets responsibilities towards children' (YJB 2023: 10). These limited references to 'rights' allegedly make clear that children's rights considerations are only one (marginalised) element of the broader Child First approach (Kilkelly, in Case and Hazel 2023).

- **Addressing neglected youth justice contexts:** Critics argue that there are particular areas of substance where Child First could be considered underdeveloped and could have its credibility and potential impact tested going forwards (Gray and Smith 2024; Kilkelly, in Case and Haines 2023; Bateman 2020). For example, the Child First movement appears relatively silent on tackling *disproportionate ethnic minority contact with youth justice systems*, despite acknowledging 'structural barriers' as part of the commitment to prioritising the child's best interests. In addition, it has been asserted that the YJB's 'Child First' agenda continues to dematerialise the *personal and social problems* of children who offend, acknowledging the existence of 'structural inequalities,' but with limited discussion of how these barriers will be challenged (Gray and Smith 2024). Instead, the emphasis remains on changing the child and improving the delivery of youth justice (Bateman 2020). Furthermore, Child First advocates (e.g. the YJB) remain relatively silent on the *use of detention with children*, with limited, if any, acknowledgement that in some instances custody may be inevitable and necessary, either because of the harm caused by the child's offending or the risk they pose to public safety, as there will not be any safe alternative (Bateman 2020). The YJB is also relatively silent, thus far at least, on the *court process* and does not address how children are to enjoy that most fundamental of rights, a fair trial, with proportionate sentencing and Child-Friendly procedures, especially when subjected to adult proceedings (although, see Hollingsworth, in Case and Hazel 2023). Finally, according to Kilkelly (in Case and Hazel 2023), more research is required to articulate what Child First means in the context of *serious youth offending*, where the political priorities of public safety and punishment may, at times, require an approach driven by risk assessment, rather than diversion. In this respect, it is important that the Child First model can be articulated not just as the model that is best for children, but one that is best for everyone, including the communities and individuals who are the victims of (serious) youth crime.
- **Realisation in a range of broader (non-community) youth justice contexts:** Arguably, it is not yet clear how Child First will become embedded into practice throughout youth justice systems in different contexts, organisations and systems (see Day 2022; Case and Browning 2021a). Whilst the evidently growing adoption of Child First across youth justice systems, most notably in community contexts, is important, more widespread policy adoption and legislative change (e.g. within partner agencies and support systems working with children) may be required so that the principle is embedded in practice throughout youth justice systems, realised in non-community youth justice systemic contexts (e.g. policing, courts, custody)

and translated into related support systems (e.g. social care, education, health). Relatedly, if not all stakeholders in these different youth justice and related contexts expressly adopt or attempt to integrate Child First, this could result in policy confusion, translating into mixed messages for practitioners (Day 2022). Finally, Child First's progressive approach to youth justice may be tested if public priorities such as community safety and victims' rights are seen in competition with Child First; political support is essential to prevent a return to punitive responses.

- **Evolving the Child First evidence-base:** Conceptually, empirically and academically, there is a need to continue to build an evidence-base of outcomes from applying Child First concepts with different children in different ways in different contexts. There must also be recognition that there are still conceptual debates about concepts within Child First that need to be played out, which, of course, is how any field of knowledge progresses. For instance, there is ongoing debate about how much Child First youth justice can be aligned with the concept of 'desistance theory' which first emerged from the adult literature (Wigzell, Paterson-Young and Batemen 2024). It has been noted that as policy and practice further operationalise Child First, there are and will continue to be differences of opinion over key issues, such as the appropriateness of child custody, how to respond to disproportionality and serious youth violence and how to integrate children's rights considerations more thoroughly, that will need to be navigated by academics and other stakeholders (Haines and Thomas, in Case and Hazel 2023). Additionally, as the evidence-base and contemporary understandings in youth justice research grow, the academic community will need to continue to be fully engaged with how this should be interpreted for policy and practice and incorporated into the Child First principle. At the same time, it is important to acknowledge that the Child First approach remains in its infancy, and like any new policy direction, it will take time to become successfully embedded in practice.

In summary, Child First presents as a potentially effective vehicle for evidence-based, progressive reform in youth justice contexts. Moreover, the progress so far has been made within existing legislation (which is still offender-focused) and within contexts of uncertainty from socio-political and socio-economic upheaval (Brexit) and a global pandemic (COVID-19). Whilst undeniably still on a journey of conceptual, evidential and practical development and whilst needing to fully address relatively overlooked issues in its development thus far (e.g. disproportionality), it has already been demonstrated that there is clear potential for the Child First principle to serve as a valid and sustainable blueprint internationally for a cutting-edge, principled and 'positive' approach to working with children and young people who come into contact with youth justice systems.

Child first in five contextualised pieces

1. **Expansionism to challenge reductionism:** Child First offers a progressive philosophy of youth justice mobilised by a series of evidence-based principles/tenets that promote expansionist, contextualised understandings of and responses to youth offending that have challenged the reductionism of dominant Positivist and Neo-correctionalist approaches.
2. **Broader contextual influences:** A range of meso- and macro-level contextual influences have shaped the development and evolution of Child First, including socio-economic changes, socio-political dynamism due to major national and global events, expanding evidence-bases and principled debates.
3. **Contextualised principles:** Child First is at once a philosophy, strategy and model, sensitive to the youth justice and related contexts experienced by children and populated by interconnected principles/tenets: Seeing children as children, promoting prosocial identity development/positive outcomes, collaboration with children and diversion from criminogenic stigma in systemic contexts.
4. **Systemic context:** The Child First principle and its associated tenets promote understandings of youth offending, youth justice responses and associated evidence-bases across a range of systemic contexts, including out-of-court, in the community, in custody and during resettlement following custody, underpinning these responses with universal and contextualised principles such as relationship-building and the realisation of children's rights.
5. **Contextual challenges:** The successful evolution and realisation of Child First across youth justice systems remain dependent (to some degree at least) on the approach attending to a series of contextual challenges, including potential reconciliation with rights-based Child-Friendly Justice, addressing relatively neglected issues (e.g. ethnic disproportionality, serious youth offending, social justice), effective translation in a range of (non-community) youth justice contexts and continuing to evolve its evidence-base to address these challenges.

Addressing the problem of decontextualised youth justice

This chapter has introduced the emerging complexity and hybridity of youth justice models, rationales and principles and subsequently unpacked a group of contextualised youth justice responses designed to challenge the reductionist, decontextualising weaknesses of dominant justice-based and contemporary punitive, neo-liberal and neo-correctionalist approaches (see Chapter two). The initial discussion of 'Community Crime Prevention' (CCP) noted how this approach challenges the reductionist and individualising nature of Developmental Crime Prevention (its corresponding model within the broader Social Crime Prevention framework) by offering explicitly

Table 4.1 Summarising the extent and nature of contextualisation in contextualised youth justice responses to youth offending

Response category	*Criminogenic influences targeted*	*Approach*	*Psychosocial bias?*	*Contextual influence?*
Community Crime Prevention	Conditions in the physical and social environment Social conditions in residential communities	Comprehensive Community Initiatives (CCIs) Community organisation, defence, development, mentoring, policing, order maintenance, structural change	Some (tendency to target individual risk factors)	Yes – socio-structural, community
EMMIE	Contextual factors shaping 'mechanisms of change' in interventions	Effects, Moderators, Mechanisms, Implementation and Economic costs relating to interventions	No, but capable of identifying this in interventions and their evaluation	Yes – focused on identifying and explaining contextual influence
Realist Synthesis	'What works for whom, in what circumstances'	Targeting relationships between Contexts, Mechanisms and Outcomes in interventions		
Child-Friendly Justice	Adult-centric, punitive, discriminatory youth justice policies and practices Neglect of the requirements of international children's rights instruments	Compliance with children's rights instruments; children's rights as universal and unconditional Rights-based, child-centric youth and juvenile justice systems	No	Yes – focused on socio-structural, socio-political, systemic and relational contexts
Child First	Adult-centric, adulterising, punitive, neo-correctionalist, criminalising discriminatory youth justice policies and practices	Positive Youth Justice, Constructive Resettlement See children as children Prosocial identity development for positive child outcomes Collaboration Promoting diversion, minimising stigmatising system contact	No, explicitly critical of and oppositional to such bias	Yes – micro-level positive identity development, meso-level positive, collaborative relationships, macro-level structural disadvantage, diversion from stigmatising systems, cultural constructions of children

social, contextualised understandings of and responses to youth offending by modifying criminogenic conditions in young people's physical and social environments. This was followed by an exploration of the contextualised evaluation framework of 'Realist Synthesis' (including the associated 'EMMIE' framework), which challenged the decontextualised 'What Works' approach by considering 'what works, for whom, in what circumstances?' through an examination of the 'Contexts' (in which youth offending and youth justice take place), 'Mechanisms' (of change promoted by intervention) and 'Outcomes' that underpin intervention 'effectiveness.' There was then a critical review of 'Child-Friendly Justice' as a progressive and expansionist approach to youth justice in the Western world that is explicitly situated within an international children's rights context that advocates for bespoke structural and systemic principles and processes to be applied with young people who offend, including welfare-based approaches and the use of minimum necessary intervention and diversion, all delivered in youth justice systems that are distinct from adult criminal justice systems. Finally, the principle, strategy and model of 'Child First' justice were presented as an expansionist challenge to reductionist youth justice, mobilised by a series of principles/tenets promoting broader evidence-based understandings of and responses to youth offending. It was argued that Child First justice is able to accommodate a range of meso-level (e.g. relational, interpersonal, procedural) and macro-level (e.g. cultural, structural, systemic) contextual influences in its constructions of youth offending and evidence-based, effective youth justice interventions.

By way of summary, Table 4.1 below illustrates the extent and nature of the (de)contextualisation discernible within the youth justice models, strategies and interventions reviewed thus far.

Notes

1 However, whilst the 'What Works' approach to evaluation has been criticised for similar reasons in other research fields (Thornton et al. 2019), the dominance of this approach in youth justice is largely unchallenged (Sherman 2009; Hope 2005, 2009; but see Realist Synthesis section).
2 Neither disposal is an 'intervention,' but rather a broad disposal within which a range of interventions can be delivered.
3 Relatedly, Johns, Williams and Haines (2016: 18) found that a trusting supervisory relationship was perceived by young people as the central factor in their movement away from crime. This highlighted the critical role of such relationships in facilitating a sense of agency and optimism, through consistent and persistent emotional and practical support, and a belief in the person's capacity to change, which in turn increases the likelihood of desistance.
4 Defined as 'children' by Child First advocates, in line with the UNCRC definition of a 'child' as an individual below the age of 18 (Haines and Case 2015).
5 For a detailed discussion of the concept and operation of 'desistence' in the Child First context, see the edited text 'Desistence and Children' (Wigzell, Paterson-Young and Bateman 2024).

5 Reimagining youth offending and youth justice 'in context'

This book has addressed the under-explored and much-neglected challenge of understanding youth offending 'in context.' In doing so, it explored the contexts within which criminogenic influences operate and within which youth justice interventions are adjudged to be 'effective.' These contexts have been evidenced and understood as relational and dynamic, operating in similarly dynamic and emergent ways over time at multiple levels of the social system (see Greenhalgh and Manzano 2021). Contextualised examination has enabled a detailed critique of traditionally dominant explanations of youth offending, youth justice intervention responses and approaches to knowledge and evidence generation within the youth justice sector as overwhelmingly 'reductionist' – over-simplified, individualised, partial and decontextualised. It has been established that such explanatory, responsive, methodological and evidential reductionism has been founded in the operationalisation of 'context' in static, immediate ways as observable features (e.g. space, place, people, things) operating at fixed points in time in linear, deterministic ways (ibid). Consequently, it has been asserted throughout that 'youth offending' and 'youth justice' interventions are dynamic, contingent and contested social constructions created by powerful individuals, groups and institutions (i.e. influencers) and influencers operating in relational and dynamic contexts within and between different levels of social systems (macro, meso, micro). As a result of applying this critical, contextualised lens throughout, it is now possible for youth offending and youth justice to be better understood 'in context.'

Understanding youth offending and youth justice in context

The problems and limitations of decontextualised explanations of youth offending were introduced in the opening chapter by critically exploring the explanatory theories that have dominated Criminology in the globalised Western world. Most notable and influential among these explanations have been Classicism, Individual Positivism and Artefactual Risk Factor Theories (ARFTs), which situate the causes and predictors of youth offending within/internal to the individual young person. These 'individualising' theories were characterised as 'reductionist' because they restrict, minimise and narrow

DOI: 10.4324/9781003498100-6

explanations by neglecting potentially complex, comprehensive and contextualised criminogenic influences on youth offending (see Chapter 1). Consequently, explanations have often been reduced to a focus on over-simplified, partial and decontextualised factors operating in linear, deterministic ways within static, temporally fixed contexts. The opening chapter demonstrated how this 'explanatory reductionism' and partiality towards micro-level criminogenic influences have been privileged at the expense of examining a broader range of meso-level situational, relational, interactional, systemic and experiential influences and macro-level economic, political, socio-structural, demographic influences and cultural biases (e.g. ethnocentric, androcentric, class-centric, adult-centric) on how youth offending is understood.

The corollary of decontextualised explanations, decontextualised youth justice intervention responses, was then addressed. The second chapter outlined the overarching 'ideal type' models, rationales and principles that have shaped socio-historical constructions of youth justice across Western youth justice systems, charting their trajectory from the long-standing 'welfare versus justice debate' into more punitive, neo-liberal and neo-correctionalist models underpinned by developmental, individualising and risk-based approaches. There was detailed discussion of 'evidence-based' youth justice and its realisation through actuarial risk management, underpinned by evidence from ARFTs and animated by the 'Risk Factor Prevention Paradigm' and the closely associated 'What Works' framework for evaluating intervention 'effectiveness' (see Chapter 2). It was concluded that the reductionist, developmental, individualising, risk-based lens that has dominated explanations of youth offending and has shaped 'evidence-based' and 'effective' youth justice responses has perpetuated a decontextualised focus on 'treating' and 'correcting' problems and deficits located in individualised, psychosocial domains of young people's lives. This reductionist, responsive partiality has come at the expense of identifying and targeting broader, contextualised influences on youth offending that may be criminogenic, both in their own right and through interactions with potential psychosocial criminogenic influences.

The necessary task of explaining youth offending in context was subsequently tackled by outlining and evaluating explanatory theories that have examined the criminogenic role of contextual influences to varying degrees (see Chapter 3). This critical process began with the theories of 'Sociological Positivism' that have focused on sociological, immediate and broader social, socio-structural and socio-systemic criminogenic influences situated externally to/outside of the individual young person. Subsequent discussion of the category of 'Quasi-Contextualised Risk Factor Theory' noted how it has incorporated contextual considerations of the criminogenic interactions between psychosocial risk factors, structural context, informal/formal social controls and critical life events, whilst also considering that criminogenic influence may not necessarily be deterministic because young people can construct, make meaning of, negotiate and resist their exposure to risk, which can shape their pathways into/out of crime. Theories of 'Critical Criminology' were interrogated in terms of their central argument that 'crime' is a product of unequal power relations in society and that it operates as the social construction of powerful groups, which typically disadvantages less powerful groups. As such, these critical theories were presented as challenging the traditional, orthodox Classical-Positivist construction of 'crime' and the 'problem' of youth offending as uncontested facts. The chapter ended with the critique offered by 'Left Realism,' which has asserted that theories of Critical Criminology have idealised and under-estimated the realities/real-world contexts of youth offending and its impact on victims and communities. Taken together, therefore, the third chapter explored contextualised criminogenic, criminalising and cultural influences situated at different levels of the social system that shape how youth offending is constructed and reconstructed in different places at different times.

The final thematic chapter considered how youth offending has been responded to in context through contextualised interventions that have addressed the decontextualising limitations of their predecessors. This contemporary group of principles, methodologies and related interventions has introduced a necessary theoretical, conceptual and methodological 'expansionism' to youth justice methodologies, evidence-bases and understandings of 'effective' intervention (see Chapter four). Initial discussion of the emerging complexity and hybridity of contextualised approaches to constructing youth justice in contemporary Western world youth justice systems was consolidated by detailed analysis and evaluation of four contemporary categories of contextualised youth justice intervention responses. The opening critical review focused on the application and effectiveness of 'Community Crime Prevention' interventions that examine the social contexts within which young people offend, enabling the identification and targeting of the social causes of youth offending, rather than trying to treat or correct criminogenic symptoms located within the individual. This was followed by a critique of the contextualised 'EMMIE' and 'Realist Synthesis' frameworks for designing, administering and evaluating (youth) crime prevention programmes that identify 'what works for whom, in what circumstances, in what respects, and how?' Subsequent contextualised evaluation focused on the progressive and expansionist Child-Friendly Justice approach to conceptualising and delivering youth justice, which is explicitly situated within a children's rights context. It was explained that 'Child-Friendly Justice' advocates for the construction of bespoke structural and systemic contexts and processes for young people ('children') who offend, notably welfare-based and prevention-focused minimum necessary intervention delivered in youth justice systems that are distinct from adult criminal justice systems. Finally, the principle, strategy and model of 'Child First' justice was evaluated as an expansionist challenge to reductionist youth justice that has been mobilised by a series of principles/tenets promoting broader, more contextualised evidence-based understandings of and responses to youth offending. There was discussion of the incorporation within Child First of a range of meso-level (e.g. relational, interpersonal, procedural) and macro-level (e.g. cultural, structural, systemic) contextual influences that have shaped its development, including consideration of socio-economic changes, socio-political dynamism, evolving evidence-bases and principled debates. The chapter concluded that contextualised research and practice methodologies and perspectives have enabled key stakeholders (e.g. politicians, policymakers, strategists, practitioners, academics, children themselves) to better articulate and conceptualise the criminogenic influences in children's lives and the ways in which youth justice interventions can be expected to work.

Following this summary of the key thematic chapters across the book, it is important to provide a contextualised and critical overview of the challenges and opportunities that must be addressed in order to formulate more expansionist, constructed, comprehensive, complex, dynamic and relational 'in context' solutions to youth offending.

The challenges of resilient evidential, explanatory and responsive reductionism

It has been explained that rapid globalisation accelerated the construction of 21st-century socio-political contexts of youth justice wherein intervention responses were required to be defensible, accountable, transparent and informed by 'evidence' (e.g. from research, official statistics). These globalised and modernising pressures created/constructed an explanatory 'Zeitgeist' (i.e. defining spirit/mood of the time) within youth justice for 'evidence-based' policy and practice. This Zeitgeist was animated in political, practice, empirical and academic contexts by the rapid rise to dominance of individualising explanatory theories, with an accompanying insensitivity to the socio-structural and political contexts within which young people (who offend) live and interact. In particular, the persistent risk-led reductionism of evidence-based policy and practice has reflected and encouraged a contemporary strategic climate/context of conflict and ambivalence in 21st-century Western youth justice systems, illustrated by uncertainty regarding how best to 'do' youth justice. This conflict and ambivalence have seemingly precipitated 'cognitive dissonance' (i.e. holding two conflicting thoughts or ideas simultaneously) in youth justice contexts, exemplified by stubborn reliance on risk-led understandings of youth offending that are incongruent with emerging evidence-based and principled contexts recommending more sensitive (e.g. child-centric, non-criminalising, rights-based), therapeutic (Gray and Smith 2024) and trauma-informed (Cox 2021) constructions of youth offending to inform similarly-contextualised youth justice interventions. Youth justice stakeholders in national contexts (e.g. England and Wales, the USA, Australia) have been compelled to perpetuate reductionist risk reliance in the development of policies, strategies and practices, guided by an evidence-base shaped predominantly by individualising, psychosocial explanations, RFPP-led interventions and the experimental 'What Works' evaluation framework. Simultaneously, these same stakeholders have been encouraged to generate new, improved, progressive evidence-bases (e.g. relating to Child-Friendly Justice, Child First, Realist Synthesis) that are fit-for-purpose in addressing the contextual and constructed complexity of young people's lives[1] (Case, Browning and Hampson 2024), the structurally generated harms that young people experience and the failure of state agencies to meet young people's wider social needs (Gray and Smith 2024).

The context of cognitive dissonance outlined above begs the question of why self-fulfilling, self-validating, reductionist and decontextualising risk-based youth justice persists and remains so resilient in the context of sustained critiques and rapidly developing evidence-bases that are incongruent with and even openly oppositional to the RFPP. One potential answer lies in the continued impotence of criminological critique and its failure to exert significant impact on evidence-based policy development in youth justice, akin to the alleged limited impact of 'Public Criminology' and academic criminologists (Loader and Sparks 2013; see also Young 2016). Another compelling explanation lies in the sustained and significant investment of money, time and political capital in the reductionist and decontextualising risk management agenda within and between different contexts/levels of the social system (often macro- and meso-level) that have influenced the social construction of youth offending and youth justice, for example, contexts that are:

- Political: Relational and dynamic contextual features supporting specific political imperatives, agendas and ambitions, which can be located within governments, political parties, individual politicians and external stakeholder organisations (Case 2024).
- Economic: Justification of longstanding financial commitments to developing and implementing risk assessment instruments or funding research based on the methods and paradigms of ARFTs (Bateman 2020).
- Systemic: Prioritisation of the risk-led processes of assessment, intervention and inspection that have perpetuated conceptual partiality (e.g. constructing, validating and applying evidence from ARFTs).
- Strategic: Fulfilling national and local government requirements to produce risk-informed policy and practice guidance, including practice guidance for organisations that will be inspected against risk-based criteria (Case et al. 2023).
- Practical: Meeting political, economic and strategic commitments to actuarial risk management by training, educating and 'hard schooling' youth justice staff in risk management approaches and their associated evidence-bases (Youth Justice Institute 2020; Stephenson and Allen 2018).
- Evidential: Self-perpetuating and uncritically validating partiality for particular forms and uses of 'evidence' (e.g. from ARFTs) at the expense of generating alternative evidence-bases that could serve as a 'complicating

inconvenience' (Goldson 2010: 70) in different contexts, politically, economically, strategically and practically (Case 2024).

Bifurcation as reductionist partiality, not expansionist evolution

Evidential reductionism and growing cognitive dissonance across Western youth justice systems have reinforced and been reinforced by explanatory and responsive 'bifurcation' (i.e. a split along two separate pathways or branches). Nearly a decade ago, when reflecting on the possible future of criminological theory, Ferrell and Hayward (2015) offered the following prediction:

> We suspect that Criminology will continue to bifurcate. On the one hand the logic of positivism and Positivist methodologies operates as an intellectual self-fulfilling prophecy, creating methodological residues that masquerade as objective research findings .... On the other hand, and largely in opposition, alternative criminological paradigms continue to percolate and build momentum.

This predicted bifurcation of explanatory theory in Criminology has manifested in the persistent and resilient popularity of individualising explanations of youth offending (see Chapter 1). Hegemonic theories continue to promote understandings of young people who offend as hopeless, helpless and damaged individuals unable to resist the criminogenic effects of exposure to predetermined causes of offending (typically constructed as individual deficits and risks) without adult-led intervention, treatment and management. Crucially, however, explanations from Sociological Positivism, Quasi-Contextualised Risk Factor Theories, Critical Criminology and Left Realism (see Chapter 3), consolidated by responses from CCP, Realist Synthesis, Child-Friendly Justice and Child First (see Chapter 4), have expanded and evolved the explanatory and responsive focus in policy, practise and academic contexts on examining the socio-structural and economic contexts and interactions that can encourage offending among (typically working-class) young people.

The clear and present danger with this evolving explanatory and responsive bifurcation, however, is that stakeholders could 'throw the baby out with the bathwater' by dismissing the explanatory and responsive value and utility of what they view as competing theories and paradigms in order to promote the validity and status of their own preferred theories and paradigms. Relatedly, schools of thought may fall into explanatory siloes (e.g. Positivism vs Critical Criminology explanations, RFPP-based vs Child First-based responses), refusing to communicate or share ideas with their explanatory 'rivals,' defending their own favoured theories and tending to reject or ignore criticisms, especially from theoretical or practice 'opponents.' This form of partiality is known as 'theoreticism' (Burkhead 2006). It can be compounded and perpetuated by 'territorialism,' wherein like-minded researchers hold their own meetings, have their own specialised journals and publishers and ignore other journals and books. Moreover, open communication and constructive dialogue between proponents of ostensibly competing explanatory theories or responsive paradigms may diminish over time, and the little mutual communication that remains can become harder and more conflictual, whilst stereotypes and prejudices about other forms of explanation or response begin to dominate (Bruinsma 2016). Such deliberate partiality (bias) perpetuates explanatory and responsive reductionism, at least in academia, by encouraging academics 'to oversimplify each other's positions ... failing to make careful conceptual distinctions and [making] partisan attacks' (Blalock 1979: 881, in Bruinsma 2016). Therefore, as a consequence of the partiality and partisanship evidenced and threatened through explanatory and responsive bifurcation, even those stakeholders seeking to explain and respond to youth offending in context could risk straying into reductionism, partiality and (ironically) decontextualisation by dismissing the merits of micro-level, individualising, psychosocial understandings and their potential to complement and augment expansionist, contextualised understandings of youth offending.

These potential barriers and challenges to explanatory and responsive validity, comprehensiveness and effectiveness in youth justice systems would seem to recommend the pursuit of explanatory and responsive integration over bifurcation. Looking across the respective criminological schools of thought and paradigms to identify and accommodate their most developed and compelling explanations, responses, methodologies and evidence-bases could provide integrated, complementary and multi-faceted, 'in context,' expansionist understandings of youth offending. These more suitably complex understandings could then inform equivalent 'in context' responses containing programme theories and targeting mechanisms of change – offering enhanced explanatory power, utility, applicability and contextual-sensitivity to understandings of youth offending and youth justice.

The opportunities of emerging evidential, explanatory and responsive expansionism

Expanding the breadth and depth of the evidence-bases surrounding criminogenic influences and effective interventions is both a challenge to explanatory and responsive reductionism and an opportunity for informing understandings of youth offending and responsive youth justice interventions that are suitably contextualised, complex and integrated. Explanatory and responsive expansionism challenges and undermines the explanatory reductionism illustrated by the intransigent 'risk reliance' (e.g. uncritical adherence to evidence from ARFTs) across youth justice systems internationally (Case 2022) documented across this book. Moreover, 21st century economic pressures and sustained challenges to reductionist risk approaches from stakeholders have motivated the youth justice sector to broaden its evidential ambitions towards more expansionist (e.g. contextualised, constructed, comprehensive) empirical, academic and practice evidence-bases to explain youth offending and to inform youth justice responses/interventions. This contemporary explanatory open-mindedness has not necessarily been reflexive or principled in origin or motive at all times, however, nor could it hope to be in the politically charged and economically driven contexts of youth justice systems (see Case and Hampson 2019; see also Wigzell, Paterson-Young and Bateman 2024). Indeed, a central driver of expansionist evidence generation in the youth justice sector has been socio-economic austerity and the consequent dramatic reduction of resources and the systemic and organisational pragmatism that this has catalysed (Case 2024). That said, austerity-driven service retrenchment has gone some way to addressing conflict and ambivalence, cognitive dissonance and bifurcation within youth justice systems by simultaneously discouraging centralised prescriptions from youth justice policymakers regarding the nature of evidence generation and its application in practice and encouraging decentralised, localised practice innovations, mediations and discretion, precipitating a degree of tentative expansionist innovation at the local level (Bateman 2020).

The changing context of evidence production in Western youth justice systems has precipitated interest in empirical youth justice evidence-bases, both old and new. For example, there has been a resurgence of interest in historically popular aetiological/theoretical movements ('the old') such as Restorative Justice (Restorative Justice Council 2017), diversion and systems management (Smith 2020; Kelly and Armitage 2015) and Social Control Theory (Case and Browning 2021); the latter two featuring prominently in the construction of Child First, for example (Haines and Case 2015). There has been a concurrent push to develop new evidence-bases around the modern, progressive and anti-Positivist and anti-risk approaches ('the new'), such as those focused on relationship-based practice and engagement methods (Case and Hazel 2023), trauma-informed working (YJB 2024), Constructive Resettlement (Hazel and Bateman 2020; see also Chapter 4), and the development of 'Child First' Positive Youth Justice (Haines and Case 2015; see also Case and Browning 2021). These old and new evidence-bases are being further developed (e.g., re-constructed) through a combination of re-application (e.g. repurposing established evidence-bases in contemporary youth justice contexts), modernisation (e.g. updating or reframing existing evidence-bases) and innovation (e.g. creating new evidence-bases reflecting new ways of thinking). This multi-faceted approach to evidential, explanatory and responsive expansionism strongly recommends expanding the evidence-based and contextualised design, implementation and evaluation of youth justice interventions through the Realist Synthesis approach (see Appendix 3). However, innovative, in-context approaches to understanding youth offending have been illustrated most clearly by the evolution of the evidence-based and contextualised 'Child First' principle of youth justice.

The contextualising promise of 'Child First'

The emergence of Child First as a central strategic objective across youth justice systems in the globalised Western world (Case and Hazel 2023) offers a prime example of the expanding evidential, explanatory and responsive purview of understandings of youth offending. The tenets of Child First were designed to guide the collection and interpretation of contextualised, economic and socio-structural explanatory evidence as a means of informing contextualised understandings of youth offending and similarly contextualised understandings of effective youth justice interventions. Child First explicitly encourages evidence generation across a range of life domains and systemic contexts (e.g. welfare, education, social care) that can help stakeholders to contextualise the 'multiple complex needs' of children who offend (Bateman and Wigzell 2019) and to inform responses that address children's best interests, needs, rights, strengths and capacities in constructive, collaborative and non-criminalising ways (Haines and Case 2015; see also Case and Browning 2021).

The journey of Child First has been one of maturation in content, status and application. As the 'CFOS' principle (Haines and Case 2015), it started as an academic concept that built into a powerful and detailed critical commentary exposing the dangerous, criminogenic state of adult-centric and risk-based youth justice internationally. The principle then developed a research evidence-base of its own and soon found itself articulating contemporary academic understanding of what was important in youth justice (Case and Hazel 2023). Subsequently, Child First has been translated into policy and practice contexts with a 'theory of change' (i.e. promoting prosocial identity development) to achieve overall system aims, to inform policy decisions and to underpin the standards to which youth justice professionals adhere. It will now, of course, need to be embedded into policy, practice, discourses and system cultures (see also Chapter four). However, a series of contextualised, macro- and micro-level policy, practice and systemic (macro- and meso-level) challenges and opportunities remain for the realisation of Child First justice, notably:

- **Macro-level rationalisation of a distinct 'Child First' systemic context:** Child First is a principle intended to guide decision-making at both policy and practice levels within youth justice systems that addresses the objective of achieving positive outcomes for young people (Hazel and Williams, in Case and Hazel 2023). Providing contemporary, evidence-based understandings from research could potentially lead policymakers to ask themselves those bigger questions for system reform, such as whether the system context may limit the extent to which a truly Child First approach can operate. For example, Bateman (in Case and Haines 2023) questions whether youth justice systems are bound by a close relationship with adult criminal justice systems and the punitive overtones that such a relationship carries. This raises the question of whether Child

First-based youth justice systems should operate within 'justice' environments/contexts at all, or instead be integrated with children's services contexts. As Child First is becoming increasingly embedded in youth justice policy and practice contexts and draws in wider stakeholders and support systems, there is a continued need to navigate the diverse concerns and priorities of partners working with children experiencing problems within and outside of youth justice systems (Haines and Thomas, in Case and Hazel 2023; Case 2024). Relatedly, Byrne (in Case and Haines 2023) questions whether youth justice should mirror children's social care and education by falling within the purview of education rather than justice departments in order to provide a fully contextualised approach to addressing children's multiple complex needs and problematic experiences.

- **Macro- and meso-level reductionist partiality of 'effective practice':** Reductionist, risk-led discourses persist as a significant barrier at both policy and practice levels in youth justice contexts of 'effective practice.' This discourse privileges particular methodologies, notably the quasi-experimental RFPP and SMS-based 'What Works' evaluation framework. A danger of this partiality lies in how it downplays the importance of a broader range of contextualised criminogenic factors to intervention 'effectiveness,' including structural and systemic (macro) and relational and interactional (meso) influences (Case 2024). Furthermore, biases in evidencing intervention 'effectiveness' can slant youth justice towards prioritising whether interventions make a difference to youth offending outcomes, rather than also focussing on why and how this difference may occur, for whom and in what circumstances (see Realist Synthesis). A Child First evidence-base for effective practice needs to measure 'effectiveness' differently, not based on quasi-experimental, quasi-Positivist methods, but based on whether interventions make a difference to positive child outcomes and whether they can usefully explain why and how a difference occurs, including the recognition of contextual influences. There is an associated need to develop appropriate success measures and indicators to capture positive child outcomes, including the development of pro-social identity – the 'theory of change' for Child First.
- **Meso-level realisation of Child First through engagement mechanisms:** Operationalising and realising Child First in real-world practice contexts is an ongoing challenge for youth justice professionals. Understandings of what Child First means and looks like in youth justice practice contexts remain under-developed (Day 2022; Case and Browning 2021a), especially relative to the level of existing commitment to the principle in policy and strategy rhetoric (Case 2024). There is an urgent work needed, therefore, to help stakeholders working within (and even beyond) different youth justice contexts (e.g. policing, courts, community youth justice teams, custody, resettlement) to understand what to do, and then to ensure that Child First approaches are embedded through guidance,

tools or adapting processes as appropriate (Case and Browning 2021a). Although some tools are available to help practitioners work in constructive ways (e.g. Hazel and Bateman 2020), there is little clear guidance regarding how the 'common language' of Child First should be voiced in their specific contexts. Perhaps the most basic challenge to practitioners is how to better achieve children's engagement and meaningful collaboration throughout (and even beyond) youth justice systems, not least in ensuring that children even understand what is happening to them in youth justice contexts (e.g. in court – Hollingsworth, in Case and Haines 2023).

Integrating contextualised youth justice perspectives: Aligning child first with rights-based child-friendly justice

An even broader contextual challenge and opportunity presents itself in linking Child First to the children's rights approach that underpins Child-Friendly Justice (see Chapter 4); a challenge and opportunity that could have significant benefits for understanding and responding to youth offending in context. A closer alignment of these complementary perspectives could strengthen the perspective that children who enter youth justice systems are rights holders and are worthy of respect, dignity, having their needs met and having a say in their lives (Kilkelly, in Case and Hazel 2023). Although Child First is not exclusively rights-based (see also Chapter 4), critical commentators have asserted that Child First could consider closer and more explicit alignment and overlap with rights-based forms of Child-Friendly Justice (Lynch and Liefaard 2020). Employing rights-based language and rights principles more explicitly and consistently in Child First youth justice contexts would reinforce that Child First embodies evidence-based good practice and would consolidate the approach with the legal weight of an almost universally adopted and evidence-based set of international standards (e.g. the UNCRC). However, it is also acknowledged that a significant challenge remains in that rights-based language and foci have not been politically acceptable in certain international jurisdictions and national policies to this point. For example, Australia has shown clear reluctance to engage with the rights-based approach to children in law and policy (Ogilvie et al. 2024), whilst New Zealand has preferred to base its national children's strategy on the concept of 'well-being,' reflecting a concern that rights ar 'too individualistic' (Lynch 2021). At the same time, if this opposition or reluctance can be overcome, the integration of a children's rights-based approach within Child First offers a huge opportunity to improve the experiences of and outcomes for children in youth justice contexts. With specific regard to the tenets of Child First, for example:

- **See children as children:** Giving Child First a more explicit rights basis would predicate the principle on children having the status of rights holders, worthy of dignity and respect. This alignment with children's rights perspectives would place more emphasis on the child's development (UNCRC Article 6) and recognition of the specific vulnerabilities, needs and circumstances of 'children in conflict with the law' (Article 40). Whilst Child First already commits to prioritising the child's best interests, a greater emphasis on 'all children,' through the UNCRC non-discrimination principle (Article 2), would highlight children's fundamental right to equal treatment. This is especially important given the disproportionate involvement in youth justice systems of children from minority backgrounds and the importance of children's unconditional access to their rights, regardless of their background, status or any structural barriers (Kilkelly 2023).

- **Develop pro-social identity for positive child outcomes:** Alignment of the second tenet of Child First with children's rights perspectives such as Child-Friendly Justice would be facilitated by the UNCRC's focus on the child's right to education and development (Articles 6, 28, 29) and the child's right to health (Article 24). Whilst Child First already highlights the importance of supportive relationships in helping children who offend to develop prosocial identities that encourage positive outcomes, explicit recognition of the UNCRC recommendations to support children through their family and community (Articles 5, 18, 37), along with the state's duty to provide support to the family in return (Article 18), could enhance the effectiveness of both Child First and Child-Friendly Justice (Kilkelly, in Case and Hazel 2023) as contextualised means of understanding and responding to children's offending.
- **Collaborate with children:** Explicit reference to the child's right to be heard (Article 12) could reinforce the child's voice in youth justice decision-making contexts (e.g. sentencing, assessment, intervention planning), whilst respecting their status as agents and actors in their own lives. Whilst children's engagement in interventions, programmes and services can have different meanings to proponents of Child-Friendly Justice and Child First, UNCRC participation rights can co-exist with concepts of engagement and collaboration in a mutually enforcing manner (Kilkelly et al. in Case and Hazel 2023). For example, referencing the 'Guidelines of the Committee of Ministers of the Council of Europe on Child-Friendly Justice' (Council of Europe 2010) in this context would be an important way to highlight the duty to make decision-making systems and processes accessible to children across youth justice systems and to ensure children are supported, informed and guided before, during and after decision-making processes in different youth justice contexts.
- **Promote diversion:** According to Kilkelly (in Case and Haines 2023), there is straightforward reference to be made to the children's rights approach and the UNCRC in this final tenet of Child First, for example, in relation to the child's right to diversion from formal adjudication (Article 40) and diversion from detention (Article 37). The importance of this latter point cannot be overstated. Although Child First clearly

espouses diversion and minimising children's criminogenic and stigmatising contact with youth justice systems, the integration within Child First of the rights-based principle of detention (custody) as a last resort could further support the active prioritisation of alternatives to detention (see also Lynch and Liefaard 2020). This would be especially important as a means of ensuring the application of Child First principles to *all* children, including those at the 'deep end' of youth justice systems, for whom long periods of detention are more likely.

In summary, pursuing common ground between Child First and children's rights-based 'Child-Friendly Justice' would encourage expansionist, contextualised understandings of children who offend and similarly expansionist, contextualised youth justice responses that could incorporate the respective merits of each progressive, expansionist and child-centric approach. Such alignment could support the implementation of the Child First principle, as international children's rights instruments provide important guidance as to how to improve children's rights compliance in domestic legal systems. Consequently, Child First would be strengthened by recourse to children's rights, whilst adopting a rights lens could also give the principle and its manifestation in youth justice approaches increased international relevance and applicability in a way that would extend its reach far beyond current jurisdictional boundaries (Kilkelly, in Case and Hazel 2023).

Conclusion: Reimagining youth offending and youth justice in context

The arguments across this book have realised the proposed 'CASE studies' approach to developing 'in context' understandings of youth offending and youth justice by Contextualising and Analysing established explanations and responses in order to inform Solutions for constructing complex and contextualised explanations and responses that Evolve evidence-generation, knowledge and understanding. A critical lens has been adopted throughout to facilitate understanding of youth offending and youth justice as complex, constructed and contextualised, further enabling challenge of dominant explanations and responses as reductionist: oversimplified (factorised, linear, deterministic), individualised (focused on the individual and micro-level contexts), partial (incomplete, biased) and decontextualised (ignoring or marginalising the influence of broader, dynamic, meso- and macro-level contexts). It has been established that this reductionism perpetuates and is perpetuated by the privileging of narrow, restricted quantitative, experimental methodologies that encourage linear, deterministic and decontextualised (although often evidence-based) understandings of youth offending that individualise criminogenic influences and how these influences operate to render youth justice interventions 'effective.' This methodological, explanatory and responsive partiality has reinforced and been reinforced by cultural, disciplinary, socio-structural and power-based biases in the creation of the knowledge and evidence that underpin understandings of youth offending, notably the biases of androcentrism, ethnocentrism, class-centrism and adult-centrism. Therefore, the dominant, reductionist understandings of youth offending and youth justice in the globalised Western world should *not* be understood as unequivocal facts, but as the dynamic, contingent and contested 'social constructions' of powerful individuals, groups and institutions at particular times, in particular places and operating within and between different levels or 'contexts' of the social system. These social constructions are inherently dynamic (i.e. varying wildly and rapidly over time and place), contingent (i.e. dependent on dynamic socio-historical, cultural, economic and political context) and contested (i.e. subject to dynamic, contingent debate, disagreement and difference). As such, the multi-levelled contexts within which criminogenic influences operate are essentially dynamic, rather than static, immediate and temporally-fixed. They consist of relational features that shape the mechanisms through which youth offending (and desistance from it) occurs and through which youth justice interventions work and fail, thus indicating that context operates in a dynamic, emergent way over time and at multiple levels of the social system (after Greenhalgh and Manzano 2021). With all of this in mind, a set of '5Cs' emerge as potential 'solutions' for understanding youth offending in context:

Five 'solutions' for understanding youth offending in context

1. **Challenging** the dominant explanations of and responses to youth offending in Western youth justice systems is essential and long-overdue, as these have been founded on overwhelmingly reductionist, over-simplified and partial (biased and incomplete) theories, understandings, methodologies, evidence-bases and the partial constructions and representations of political rhetoric, policy preferences, media distortions and public opinion.
2. **Complexity** of theory, methodology, analysis, discussion and recommendations is a tool for challenging reductionism and for collecting evidence, synthesising argument and evaluating understandings that underpin expansionist (e.g. integrated, multi-levelled, contextualised) understandings of criminogenic influence on youth offending and how 'effective' youth justice interventions can function to change young people's behaviour.
3. **Construction** is an essential critical lens and vehicle for challenging reductionism and for integrating complexity within understandings of 'youth offending' and 'youth justice' – fundamental concepts that must be analysed as dynamic, contested and contingent social constructions.
4. **Child-centrism** should be the touchstone for producing suitably challenging, complex and constructed understandings of youth offending and youth justice; challenging the adult-centric and stigmatising nature of traditional approaches and promoting principled, progressive and

effective practice with children (e.g. Child-Friendly Justice, Child First) in youth justice systems.

5. **Contextualisation** should be the basis for challenging reductionism and for developing complex, constructed and child-centric understandings of youth offending and youth justice. Without adherence to this recommendation, traditional limitations and problems will persist, and youth offending and youth justice cannot be appropriately understood, explained or responded to 'in context.'

Note

1 At the time of writing, an excellent example of this strategic and practical incongruence can be found in the YJS of England and Wales, where youth justice professionals continue to have their practice inspected through a staunchly risk-led framework favoured by one governance organisation (HMIP 2022), whilst having this same practice guided and shaped by anti-risk, Child First principles promoted by a different governance organisation (YJB 2024; see also Case and Browning 2021a).

Appendix 1
Explaining youth offending by girls (adapted from Case 2021)

Steve – In your view, to what extent has an understanding of girls who offend been a meaningful component of our explanations of youth crime over time?

Gilly – Historically, there has been an emphasis on female offending as biological, as well as a preoccupation with its assumed sexual and/or psychological causes. Psychological theories have frequently situated the origins of girls' offending within deficient families. For example, Thomas (1907) described women/girls as 'anabolic' (passive), compared with men/boys who are 'katabolic' (active), thus assuming essential physiological sex differences. He further argued that females have more varieties of love in their nervous systems than males and are thus naturally led into sexual 'offences' such as prostitution. In his later work, Thomas (1923) defined girls according to their domestic and sexual roles – dominated by biological imperatives and emotional and irrational impulses. He viewed offending primarily as a social pathology rather than a biological abnormality and believed that wayward girls could be 'saved' through early intervention in the form of individual treatment, which would help delinquent, 'undersocialised' girls to readjust.

Several later studies of girls in British institutions in the 1960s and 1970s continued to address an assumed relationship between psychology and delinquency, pointing to high levels of emotional instability, poor self-image and psychological disturbance in incarcerated girls. Others attributed girls' delinquency to a form of psychological 'acting out' due to family dysfunction, sexual dysfunction (ironically, being *either* under-sexualised *or* over-sexualised) or loneliness. It is highly likely that the foregrounding of girls' sexuality as both cause and expression of their offending in much theorising historically has both reinforced and been reinforced by, legal definitions in which girls' delinquent behaviour was understood as sexual, such as the category of 'moral danger' (Sharpe 2011).

The relevance of peers has been historically sidelined and even ignored by theories of girls' offending, which instead have focused on gangs and peer associations as criminogenic. Whilst group solidarity, excitement and status-seeking were believed to be the principal causes of boys' offending, delinquent girls continued to be portrayed as loners and misfits. Since the late 1970s, however, these assumptions have been challenged by studies demonstrating the importance of peers in girls' offending. Moffitt has gone so far as to suggest that, due to the relative absence of biological factors predisposing girls to offending, 'the bulk of antisocial behaviour, *especially by females*, is best understood as a social phenomenon originating in the context of social relationships' (2006: xvi).

A major advance made by feminist criminologists since the 1980s has been to focus attention on the connections, or 'blurred boundaries,' between young women's offending and their victimisation experiences. Although the causal mechanisms between victimisation and offending are not well understood, unresolved traumatic events may result in alcohol and drug (ab)use and behavioural problems, including law-breaking. There is substantial evidence that young people of both sexes caught up in youth justice systems have been victims of crime and harm inflicted at the hands of adults, usually males (see Smith and Thornberry 1995). Studies of criminalised young women have consistently revealed remarkably high rates of childhood victimisation: One North American review reported rates of sexual abuse among justice system-involved girls of between 40–73% (Chesney-Lind and Shelden 2004). Such 'feminist pathways' research underpins the development of 'gender-responsive programming' within youth justice systems.

Steve – Should we consider having gender-neutral theories of youth offending?

Gilly – There is considerable disagreement among theorists today regarding the extent to which gender-neutral theories of crime, derived as they generally are from studies of (exclusively) boys and men, are able to explain offending by girls and women. Added to this is the near-invisibility, in UK-based research at least, of Black and Minority Ethnic (BAME) young women, whose needs and experiences are implicitly subsumed within those of either their white female or their BAME male, counterparts. An important criticism here is that *both* traditional theories *and* feminist theories are overly deterministic about girls' offending and ignore the historical, social, geographical, patriarchal and racialised contexts in which they live and act. Karen Heimer and Stacey de Coster (1999), examined girls' violent offending in the US and have called for a contextualised explanatory approach, which analyses the interaction of structural and cultural factors that may either inhibit or promote crime and violence among girls and boys. They concluded that, although poverty and economic marginalisation increase the likelihood of violent behaviour for both sexes, patriarchal structures and cultural norms sanctioning female violence serve to limit working-class girls' use of violence, resulting in them committing fewer violent crimes. Simultaneously, Heimer and de Coster's finding that girls' emotional bonds to their families inhibit female violence may go some way to explain why some girls *do* become violent if bonds to their families have been damaged, for example, as a result of abuse, conflict or neglect.

Appendix 2 Explaining youth offending by boys (adapted from Case 2021)

Steve – What is the theoretical basis of the masculinities perspective?

Eric – The basis is social constructionism, focussing on distinctions between sex and gender. This approach argues that gender is not innate, but a social construct. Masculinity is 'performed' as a result of both culturally and socially conditioned 'male socialization' and normative gender roles perceived as gender-appropriate in specific socio-economic contexts (Baumgartner 2014). Indeed, Winlow (2002: 41) demonstrates that 'delinquent lower-class male activities [...] are not entirely divorced from wider male culture.' Collier (1998) argues that dominant debates on masculinity and offending revolve around young men's masculinity and their perceived dangerousness, whereby the bodies of young men are criminalised through signifiers (constructions) of a particular kind of masculinity; white and working-class masculinity. Hatty (2000) explains that aggression and violence come to be socially conditioned ideas, whereby males hold an entitlement to aggression, with a clear idea of legitimate forms of aggressive behaviour. The conclusion is that violence and aggression shape a particular form of male identity and masculinity, which in turn is deeply embedded in many forms of violence (Hatty 2000). This link between masculinity and crime has been established by a number of authors (Messerschmidt 2012; Mullins 2006), who all argue that 'doing crime' is 'doing masculinity.' These authors make a clear connection between the ways in which young men define themselves as men and the reasons for their offending behaviour.

Steve – What are the implications of these explanations for youth justice practice with boys and young men?

Eric – Taking into account that the dominant group of young people in contact with youth justice systems are male and that scholars have made clear connections between constructions of masculinity and youth offending, the logical consequence would be to address or at least problematise issues around masculinity in the prevention, intervention, assessment and sanction of young men who have been identified as having committed crime (Baumgartner 2014). Indeed, the call for male-focused practice in the wider provision of social and welfare services has been longstanding (Taylor 2003), but these examples of the importance of male-focused service provision (Cowburn 2010) have not been translated into the context of youth justice practice (Baumgartner 2014). My research into masculinity and youth justice has demonstrated that workers in Youth Offending Teams (YOTs) drew close connections between the masculinity of young men and their offending behaviour. Those working with young men in YOTs in England and Wales construct young men along the lines of 'hegemonic localized masculinity' (Baumgartner 2014). In other words, the ways in which those YOT workers understand masculinity are surprisingly homogenous in terms of:

1. The display of a clear form of aggression, low impulse control, and the avoidance of any display of weakness;
2. That they link this behaviour to some of the main reasons with which they explain young men's offending – the ways in which the young men perform masculinity are through drinking and fighting, the inability to respond to conflict situations other than through drinking and violent behaviour, and the young men's effort to prove their masculinity by showing bravado and attempting to gain kudos, respect and a reputation as 'hard' (Baumgartner 2014).

Less attention here is paid to the young men's vulnerability and how some of the issues around their offending behaviour can be addressed by problematising their masculinity in prevention, assessment, and intervention by adapting male-friendly approaches. Paradoxically though, the YOT workers in my study did not think that 'masculinity' is something they are to problematise with the young men with whom they work. Some reasons for this are that (1) practice guidance does not consider gender as a relevant category in assessment and practice, and (2) practitioners do not feel sufficiently equipped through training to address issues around masculinity. Whilst some gender practices reinforcing negative types of masculinity are clearly present, the opportunity is being missed to address some of the young men's offending behaviour through addressing issues around masculinity (Baumgartner 2014).

Appendix 3
Contextualised youth justice intervention through Realist Synthesis

The emerging evidence-base of Realist Synthesis evaluation in youth justice (see also Chapter four) provides salient lessons for constructing contextualised interventions that are suitably expansionist (non-reductionist) through their prioritisation of understanding youth offending as the dynamic product of relationships between contexts, mechanisms and outcomes. In particular, evidence implicates the need to expand the contexts within which intervention 'effectiveness' is evaluated, to identify 'programme theories' as standard when planning interventions, to prioritise child-centric programme theories and mechanisms of change within interventions, to deliver these interventions within child-centric contexts and to identify a broader range of child-centric outcomes to signify intervention effectiveness. Five recommendations emerged to support these aims (after Sutton et al. 2022):

1. **Context: Expand the evidence-base for intervention 'effectiveness'**

It has been established that there is a pressing need to collect a more comprehensive breadth and depth of evidence to inform youth justice intervention planning because dominant approaches have presented a reductionist, partial, individualised and decontextualised picture of the causes of youth offending and effective youth justice responses. A conceptual and practical evolution from reductionism to expansionism in constructing and understanding youth offending in interventions would be facilitated by routine, detailed consideration of a broader range of potential implementation issues (moderators), programme theories and mechanisms of change, context-mechanism interactions/relationships and possible outcomes for children (hard, intermediate, soft). Accordingly, increasing the use of qualitative and contextualised evaluation frameworks, most notably Realist Synthesis (but including EMMIE), could also help to prioritise this essential source of evidence of intervention effectiveness (Case et al. 2022; Tompson et al. 2020). As such, qualitative evidence (e.g. regarding where, for whom, how and why an intervention works) can complement and extend (rather than replace) potentially informative quantitative evidence of effectiveness (e.g. in relation to what and how much intervention works).

2. Mechanisms: Prioritise 'programme theories' in interventions

Utilising explicit, evidenced 'programme theories' (i.e. how interventions are intended to work) informed by identified 'mechanisms of change' (see Realist Synthesis discussion in Chapter 4) would enhance contextualised understandings of youth offending that can be targeted by similarly contextualised youth justice interventions (Case et al. 2022; Fullerton, Bamber and Redmond 2021; Noble and Hodgson 2016; Bamber et al. 2016). Viewing context as static and conceptualising programme theories in terms of these static contexts rather than viewing contexts as dynamic and containing mechanisms of change privileges superficial, reductionist 'explanations' of intervention effectiveness. Accordingly, the evaluation of interventions as 'effective' and 'What Works' can provide no useful information regarding the mechanisms and processes of change that populate the explanatory 'Black Box' between input/intervention and output/effect (Case et al. 2022). However, emerging research evidence offers strong support for the centrality and importance of identifying, designing, integrating and evaluating clear, well-informed, robust and useful programme theories within 'effective,' contextualised preventative interventions in youth justice systems (Sutton et al. 2022; Fullerton, Bamber and Redmond 2021; Center for Youth Impact 2017). Ideally, contextualised, these programme theories and their related outcome measures should be child-centric (e.g. grounded in Child-Friendly Justice and/or Child First), should prioritise the engagement of children through positive relationships and should be agreed as part of constructive, positive relationships between all key stakeholders (including children) who experience and are responsible for the design, implementation and ultimate success/failure of youth justice intervention (Creaney and Burns, in Case and Hazel 2023).

3. Mechanisms: Prioritise child-centric programme theories for interventions

In order to be effective and sustainable (e.g. to engage children within interventions), evidence suggests that programme theories should move away from partial, individualising, responsibilising, stigmatising, punitive, controlling and compliance-led conceptualisations of youth offending and move towards more child-centric (e.g. Child-Friendly, Child First) constructions and explanations grounded in prosocial identity development, engagement and promoting intrinsic motivation in contexts of positive relationships (Sutton et al. 2022). Indeed, the Realist Synthesis evaluation has identified four fundamental elements of and contextualised programme theories that can promote effective child-centric support and intervention for children who offend (Case et al. 2022; Fullerton, Bamber and Redmond 2021; Bamber et al. 2016): activities (interventions and the contexts in which they are implemented), mechanisms of change (feelings and experiences leading to positive outcomes), intermediate outcomes (values, attitudes, knowledge, skills and behaviours developed when participating in activities) and impacts (longer-term effects/outcomes). Such expansionist conceptions of context (e.g. focussing on children's youth justice journeys and intervention experiences) as relational, dynamic, complex and non-linear, perceive change as a process rather than an organised, linear sequence, which makes plotting programme theories/mechanisms using traditional outcome patterns difficult (see Noble and Hodgson 2016), this challenging and undermining traditional risk-based and 'What Works' intervention approaches.

4. **Contexts-Mechanisms: Child-centric contexts and programme theories**

Child-centric 'mechanisms of change' are triggered by child-centric programme theories most effectively within three broad contexts. Firstly, 'environment and relationships' are crucial contexts in enabling learning and development experiences, and critical to engaging children and promoting prosocial identity development for positive outcomes that are driven by intrinsic (rather than extrinsic) motivation to engage and change (Fullerton, Bamber and Redmond 2021). Relationship-based practice and intervention promote prosocial identity development/positive outcomes by encouraging children to feel trust/trusted, respected (not judged/punished), safe and secure and by addressing children's needs, strengths, capacities and rights as mechanisms of change (Center for Youth Impact 2017). Secondly, the 'nature and delivery of intervention activities' can be crucial influences, so it is important to design and deliver interventions in contexts where children feel a sense of positive challenge, enjoyment, satisfaction, purpose, achievement and contribution (Sutton et al. 2022). These mechanisms of change can have a reciprocal relationship with intrinsic motivation and provide children with a purpose to achieve something concrete, boost their self-confidence and enable them to become more aware of their own skills, attitudes and behaviour. Finally, Realist Synthesis evaluation evidence indicates that 'community' is a crucial intervention context. It is vital to design and deliver activities in contexts where children feel included and connected to the community and empowered to change their own lives and the services they receive, for example, through co-design and co-collaboration.

5. **Outcomes: Identify child-centric outcomes to assess intervention effectiveness**

It is crucial that the evaluation of contextualised, child-centric interventions in youth justice contexts integrates alternative outcome measures to complement and augment reductionist, partial and decontextualised, hard, 'binary' (yes-no) outcome measures focused on simply preventing offending. Whilst hard outcome measures remain important distal (longer-term) indicators of youth justice intervention effectiveness (Center for Youth Impact 2017), there are benefits to focussing on complementary, additional intermediate and proximal (shorter-term) outcome measures that are more holistic (i.e. less reductionist), contextualised and child-centric (e.g. positive, promotional, prosocial and sustainable – see also Fullerton, Bamber and Redmond 2021). 'Intermediate' outcomes are more often located at the relational (inter-personal) level, such as strong family relationships, community connections, trust, empathy, confidence in adult professionals and processes (legitimacy), engagement and relationship-building with professionals (YJB 2016), shared understandings and decision-making, bonding/attachment and increased social capital (see also Fullerton, Bamber and Redmond 2021). 'Soft' outcome measures can be 'intrinsic' (i.e. internal to/within the individual child) or 'extrinsic' (i.e. external to/outside of the child). Those most commonly identified in empirical research include values (e.g. respect for others, empathy), feelings (e.g. security, resilience, feeling valued and listened to), attitudes and non-cognitive skills (e.g. aspirations, responsibility, self-esteem/confidence), knowledge and skills (e.g. socio-emotional, communicative, problem-solving) and behaviours (e.g. agency, decision-making, positive relationships).

Bibliography

Agnew, R. (2005) *Why Do Criminals Offend? A General Theory of Crime and Delinquency*. Oxford: Oxford University Press.

Agnew, R. and Kaufman, J. (2017) *Anomie, Strain and Subcultural Theories of Crime*. London: Routledge.

Ahonen, L., Farrington, D., Pardini, D. and Stouthamer-Loeber, M. (2021) Cohort profile: The Pittsburgh youth study. *Journal of Developmental and Life-Course Criminology,* 7: 481–523.

Aichhorn, A. (1925) *Wayward Youth*. New York: Meridian Books.

Akers, R. (1985) *Deviant behavior: A social learning approach*. Belmont, CA: Wadsworth.

Akers, R.L. (1991) Self-control as a general theory of crime. *Journal of Quantitative Criminology*, 7: 201–211.

Akers, R.L. (2017) Rational choice, deterrence, and social learning theory in criminology: The path not taken. In: M. Natarajan (ed.), *Crime Opportunity Theories Routine Activity, Rational Choice and their Variants*. London: Routledge.

Alder, C. and Wundersitz, J. (1994) New directions in juvenile justice reform in Australia. In C. Alder and J. Wundersitz (eds.), *Family Conferencing and Juvenile Justice: The Way Forward or Misplaced Optimism?* Canberra: Australian Institute of Criminology.

Andrews, D.A. and Bonta, J. (2010) *The Psychology of Criminal Conduct*. London: Routledge.

Archer, D., Longstaff, E. and Skinns, L. (2002) *Promising Prevention: A Review of Promising and Effective Approaches to Preventing Offending by Young People*. London: ARCS.

ARCS Ltd (2008) *Reviewing the Effectiveness of Community Safety Policy and Practice – An Overview of Current Debates and their Background*. Montreal: International Centre for the Prevention of Crime.

Armstrong, D. (2004) A risky business? Research, policy, governmentality and youth offending. *Youth Justice*, 4(2): 100–116.

Arnull, E. and Fox, D. (2016) *Cultural Perspectives on Youth Justice. Connecting Theory, Policy and International Practice*. London: Palgrave.

Ashcroft, J., Daniels, D. and Hart, S. (2004) *Evaluating GREAT: A School-Based Gang Prevention Program*. Washington, DC: National Institute of Justice, US Department of Justice.

Astbury, B. (2018). Making claims using realist methods. In: N. Emmel, J. Greenhalgh, A. Manzano, M. Monaghan, and S. Dalkin (eds.), *Doing Realist Research* (pp. 59–78). London: Sage Publications Ltd.

Axford, N., Morpeth, L., Bjornstad, G., Hobbs, T. and Berry, V. (2022) "What works" registries of interventions to improve child and youth psychosocial outcomes: A critical appraisal. *JournalChildren and Youth Services Review*, 137: 106469

Azeredo, A., Moreira, D., Figueiredo, P. and Barbosa, F. (2019) Delinquent behavior: Systematic review of genetic and environmental risk factors. *Clinical Child and Family Psychology Review*, 22: 502–526.

Bailleau, F. and Cartuyvels, Y. (eds.) (2002) La justice pénale des mineurs en Europe. *Déviance et Société*, 26(3), special issue, 255–269.

Baker, K. (2005) Assessment in youth justice: Professional discretion and the use of Asset. *Youth Justice*, 5: 106–122.

Bamber, J., Brolly, C., Mills, E. and Farrar, C. (2016) *Lessons from the Literature: Building Relationships with Detained Young People to Improve Pro-social Outcomes*. Dublin: Oberstown Children Detention Campus (Oberstown. Retrieved December 5).

Bandura, A. (1973) *Aggression: A Social Learning Analysis*. Englewood Cliffs, NJ: Prentice Hall.

Bandura, A. (1986) The explanatory and predictive scope of self-efficacy theory. *Journal of Social and Clinical Psychology*, 4(3): 359–373.

Barry, M. (2006) *Youth Offending in Transition*. London: Routledge.

Basto-Pereira, M. and Farrington, D. (2020) Lifelong conviction pathways and self-reported offending: Towards a deeper comprehension of criminal career development. *The British Journal of Criminology*, 60(2): 285–302.

Bateman, T. (2020) *The State of Youth Justice 2020: An Overview of Trends and Developments*. London: NAYJ.

Bateman, T. and Pitts, J. (eds.) (2005) *The RHP Companion to Youth Justice*. Lyme Regis: Russell House.

Bateman, T. and Wigzell, A. (2019) Exploring recent trends in youth justice reconvictions: A challenge to the complexity thesis. *Youth Justice,* 252–271.

Bates, K.A., Bader, C.D. and Mencken, F.C. (2003) Family structure, power-control theory and deviance: Extending power-control theory to include alternate family forms. *Western Criminology Review*, 4(3): 170–190.

Baumgartner, E. (2012) And then there were the men–masculinity and the youth justice system in England and Wales. *Graduate Journal of Social Sciences, Special Edition: 'Gendered Subjects'*, 9(3): 79–86.

Baumgartner, E. (2014) Boys will be boys, or will they? A study of youth offending team practitioners' constrictions of masculinity of the young men with whom they work. Durham University: Unpublished Thesis. Available at: http://etheses.dur.ac.uk/10607/.

Beck, U. (1992) *Risk Society: Towards a New Modernity*. London: Sage.

Becker, H. (1963) *Outsiders: Studies in the Sociology of Deviance*. New York: The Free Press.

Beckman, M. (2004) Neuroscience: Crime, culpability, and the adolescent brain. *Science*, 30: 596–599.

Bedoya, A. and Portnoy, J. (2022) Biosocial criminology: History, theory, research evidence, and policy. *Victims and Offenders*, 18(8): 1599–1629.

Benai, R. (2019) Concentric zone theory. In: A. Orum (ed.), *The Wiley Blackwell Encyclopedia of Urban and Regional Studies*. London: Wiley.

Bentham, J. (1970) *An Introduction to the Principles of Morals and Legislation*, edited by J.H. Burns and H.L.A. Hart. London: Athlone Press.

Bernard, T.J., Snipes, J.B., Gerould, A.L. and Vold, G.B. (2015) *Vold's Theoretical Criminology*. Oxford: Oxford University Press.

Bishop, D.M. and Farber, H.B. (2007) Joining the legal significance of adolescent developmental capacities with the legal rights provided by in re Gault. *Rutgers Law Review*, 60(1): 125–172.

Blyth, M., Solomon, E. and Baker, K. (2007) *Young People and Risk*. Bristol: Policy Press.

Boaz, A. and Ashley, D. (2003) *Fit for Purpose? Assessing Research Quality for Evidence Based Policy and Practice*. Working Paper 11, ESRC UK Centre for Evidence Based Policy and Practice. London: Queen Mary, University of London.

Boccio, C, Schwartz, J.A. and Beaver, K.M. (2022) The influence of low self-control and thoughtfully reflective decision making on criminal justice processing. *American Journal of Criminal Justice*, 47, 506–525.

Boeck, T., Fleming, J. and Kemshall, H. (2006) The context of risk decisions: Does social capital make a difference? *Forum: Qualitative Social Research* [On-line Journal], 7(1), Article. 17. Available at: www.qualitative-research.net/fqs-texte/1–06/06–1-17-e.htm.

Bottoms, A.E. and McClintock, F.H. (1973) *Criminals Coming of Age. A Study of Institutional Adaptation in the Treatment of Adolescent Offenders*. London: Heinemann.

Box, S. (1983) *Power, Crime, and Mystification*, London: Routledge.

Brantingham, P.J. and Faust, F.L. (1976) A conceptual model of crime prevention. *Crime & Delinquency*, 22(3): 284–296.

Bradshaw, P.J. and Smith, D.J. (2005) *Gang Membership and Teenage Offending*. Edinburgh Study of Youth Transitions and Crime Research Digest No. 8. Edinburgh: Edinburgh University.

Brayne, S. (2020) I'm a sociologist who studies how police use data: Relying on algorithms can further bias and inequality — but it doesn't have to be that way. Available at: https://www.businessinsider.com/sociologist-who-studies-police-and-data-algorithm-can-further-bias-2020-6?r=US&IR=T.

Bredewold, F. and Tonkens, E. (2021) Understanding successes and failures of family group conferencing: An in-depth multiple case study. *British Journal of Social Work*, 51(6): 2173–2190.

Bronfenbrenner, U. (1995) Developmental ecology through space and time: A future perspective. In: P. Moen, G. H. Elder, Jr., and K. Lüscher (eds.), *Examining Lives in Context: Perspectives on the Ecology of Human Development* (pp. 619–647). New York: American Psychological Association.

Bronfenbrenner, U. and Morris, P.A. (2007) The ecology of developmental processes. In: W. Damon and R.M. Lerner (eds.), *Handbook of Child Psychology: Vol 1: Theoretical Models of Human Development*. New York: Wiley.

Brownfield, D. (2018) Subcultural theories of crime and delinquency. In: J. Hagen (ed.), *Criminological Controversies*. London: Routledge.

Browning, K., Huizinga, D., Loeber, R. and Thornberry, T.P. (1999) Causes and Correlates of Delinquency Program. Fact Sheet.Washington, DC: U.S. Department of Justice, Office of Justice Programs, Office of Juvenile Justice and Delinquency Prevention.

Bruinsma, G. (2016) Proliferation of crime causation theories in an era of fragmentation: Reflections on the current state of criminological theory. *European Journal of Criminology*, 13(6): 659–676.

Bunge, M. (2006) *Chasing Reality: Strife over Realism*. Toronto: University of Toronto Press.

Burkhead, M.D. (2006) *The Search for the Causes of Crime. A History of the Theory in Criminology*. Jefferson & London: McFarland.

Butts J., Pelettier, E. and Kazemian, L. (2018) *Positive Outcomes: Strategies for Assessing the Progress of Youth Involved in the Justice System*. New York: John Jay Research and Evaluation Centre.

Cabot, R. (1940) A long-term study of children: The Cambridge-somerville youth study. *Child Development*, 11(2): 143–151.

Case, S. (2021) *Youth Justice: A Critical Introduction*. Abingdon: Routledge.
Case, S., Johnson, P., Manlow, D., Smith, R. and Williams, K. (2017) *Criminology*. Oxford: Oxford University Press.
Case, S.P. (2006) Young people 'at risk' of what? Challenging risk-focused early intervention as crime prevention, *Youth Justice*, 6(3): 171–179.
Case, S.P. (2007) Questioning the 'evidence' of risk that underpins evidence-led youth justice interventions. *Youth Justice*, 7(2): 91–106.
Case, S.P. (2022) Challenging the reductionism of 'evidence-based' youth justice. *Sustainability*, 13(4): 1735.
Case, S.P. (2024) *Youth Justice: Towards a Contextualised Understanding of Policy-Making*. Bristol: BUP.
Case, S.P. and Browning, A. (2021a) The child first strategy implementation project. Available at: https://www.lboro.ac.uk/subjects/social-policy-studies/research/child-first-justice/#:~:text='Child%20First'%20Justice%20is%20a,rather%20than%20as%20'offenders'.
Case, S.P. and Browning, A. (2021b) Child first: The research evidence-base. Available at: https://www.lboro.ac.uk/subjects/social-policy-studies/research/child-first-justice/#:~:text='Child%20First'%20Justice%20is%20a,rather%20than%20as%20'offenders.
Case, S.P. and Browning, A. (2021c) *Child First: The Evidence-Base*. Loughborough: Loughborough University for the YJB.
Case, S.P., Browning, A. and Hampson, K. (2024) The child first strategy implementation project – translating strategy into practice. *Youth Justice*, 24(2): 204–230.
Case, S.P., Clutton, S. and Haines, K.R. (2005) Extending Entitlement: A Welsh Policy for Children, *Wales Journal of Law and Policy*, 4(2): 187–202.
Case, S.P. and Haines, K.R. (2009) *Understanding Youth Offending: Risk Factor Research Policy and Practice*. Cullompton: Willan.
Case, S.P. and Haines, K.R. (2018) Transatlantic 'positive youth justice': Coherent movement or disparate critique? *Crime Prevention and Community Safety*, 20(3): 208–222.
Case, S.P. and Haines, K.R. (2011) Protection, prevention and promotion: The restricted evolution of the protective factor in criminological research. *Social Work Review*, 2: 109–122.
Case, S.P. and Haines, K.R. (2020) Abolishing youth justice systems: Children first, offenders nowhere. *Youth Justice Journal, Early View*, 3–17.
Case, S. and Hampson, K. (2019) Youth justice pathways to change: Drivers, challenges and opportunities. *Youth Justice*, 19(1): 25–41.
Case, S.P. and Hazel, N. (2023) *Child First: Developing a New Youth Justice System*. London: Palgrave.
Case, S., Sutton, C., Monaghan, M., Greenhalgh, J. and Wright, J. (2022) Understanding preventative intervention in youth justice. https://www.lboro.ac.uk/subjects/social-policy-studies/research/child-first-justice/understanding-preventative-intervention/
Catalano, R.F., Berglund, M.L., Ryan, J.A., Lonczak, H.S. and Hawkins, J.D. (2004) Positive youth development in the united states research findings on evaluations of positive youth development programmes. *Prevention and Treatment, 5*(15): 98–124.
Catalano, R.F. and Hawkins, J.D. (1996) The social development model: A theory of anti-social behaviour. In: J. Hawkins (ed.), *Delinquency and Crime: Current Theories*. Cambridge: Cambridge University Press.
Catalano, R.F. et al. (2017) Mediating the effects of poverty, gender, individual characteristics, and external constraints on antisocial behavior: A test of the

social development model and implications for developmental life-course theory. In: D Farrington (ed.), *Integrated Developmental and Life-Course Theories of Offending*. London: Routledge.

Cavadino, M. and Dignan, J. (2013) *Penal Systems: A Comparative Approach*, 2nd edition. Thousand Oaks, CA and New Delhi: Sage Publications.

Center for Theory of Change (2024) Available at: https://www.theoryofchange.org/.

Center for Youth Impact (2017) Grantee level theory of change. Available at: https://www.youthimpact.uk/yif-learning-project/grantee-level-theory-change.

Chambliss, W.J. (1975) Toward a political economy of crime. *Theory and Society*, 2(1): 149–170.

Chapman, T. and O'Mahony, D. (2007) Youth and criminal justice in Northern Ireland developments in social work with offenders. In: G. McIvor and P. Raynor (eds.), *Developments in Social Work with Offenders* (pp. 99–131).

Cheng, J. and Yu, M.Y. (2013) The thoughts of perfection the juvenile criminal justice system in China. *Law and Society*, 9: 55–56.

Chesney-Lind, M. and Shelden, R.G. (2004) *Girls, Delinquency and Juvenile Justice* (3rd ed.). Belmont, CA: Wadsworth.

Child Rights Network (2024) Minimum ages of criminal responsibility in the Americas. Available at: https://archive.crin.org/en/home/ages/Americas.html (Accessed August 2024)

Christiansen, K.O. (1974) Seriousness of criminality and concordance among danish twins. In: R. Hood (ed.), *Crime, Criminology and Public Policy*. New York: Free Press.

Clarke, R.V.G. (1987) Rational choice theory and prison psychology. In: B.J. McGurk, D. Thornton, and M. Williams (eds.), *Applying Psychology to Imprisonment: Theory and Practice*. London: HMSO.

Cloward, R. and Ohlin, L. (1960) *Delinquency and Opportunity*. New York: Free Press.

Cohen, A. K. (1955) *Delinquent Boys: The Culture of The Gang*. New York: The Free Press.

Cohen, L.E., Kluegel, J. and Land, K. (1981) Social inequality and predatory criminal victimization: An exposition and test of a formal theory. *American Sociological Review*, 46: 505–524.

Cohn, E., Farrington, D. and Iratzoqui, A. (2020) Changes in the most-cited scholars in 20 criminology and criminal justice journals between 1990 and 2015 and comparisons with the Asian journal of criminology. *Asian Journal of Criminology*, 16(3): 279–292.

Collier, R. (1998) *Masculinities, Crime and Criminology: Men, Heterosexuality and the Criminal(ised) Other*. London: Sage Publications.

Colvin, M. (2000) *Crime and Coercion: An Integrated Theory of Chronic Criminality*. New York: St Martin's Press.

Committee on the Rights of the Child (CRC) (2008) *UNCRC Concluding Observations*. Geneva: UNICEF.

Committee on the Rights of the Child (CRC) (2019) UNCRC Concluding Observations. Geneva: UNICEF.

Connell, R.W. (2005) *Masculinities*. London: Polity Press.

Cook, T.D. and Campbell, D.T. (1979) *Quasi-experimentation: Design and Analysis for Field Settings*. Chicago: Rand McNally.

Cornish, D.B. and Clarke, R.V.G. (1987) Understanding crime displacement: An application of rational choice theory. *Criminology*, 25: 933–947.

Council of Europe (2008) European Rules for Juvenile Offenders Subject to Sanctions or Measures: Basic Principles 2008. Strasbourg: Council of Europe.

Council of Europe (2010) *The Guidelines of the Committee of Ministers of the Council of Europe on Child-friendly Justice*. Strasbourg: Council of Europe.
Cowburn, M. (2010) Invisible men: Social reactions to male sexual coercion-bringing men and masculinities into community safety and public policy. *Critical Social Policy*, 30: 225–244.
Cox, A. (2021) The new economy of youth justice. *Youth Justice*, 21(1): 107–126.
Crawford, A. (1998) *Crime Prevention and Community Safety: Politics, Policies and Practices*. Harlow: Longman.
Crawford, A. and Evans, K. (2017) Crime prevention and community safety. In: A. Liebling, S. Maruna, and L. McAra (eds.), *The Oxford Handbook of Criminology* (pp. 797–824). Oxford: Oxford University Press.
Crawford, A. and Newburn, T. (2003) *Youth Offending and Restorative Justice*. Cullompton: Willan.
Cullen, F.T. (2005) The twelve people who saved rehabilitation: How the science of criminology made a difference. *Criminology*, 43(1): 1–42.
Cullen, F.T. (2013) *Rehabilitation: Beyond Nothing Works*. Chicago: Chicago University press.
Cullen, F.T. and Jonson, C. (2017) *Correctional Theory: Context and Consequences* (2nd ed.). Thousand: Sage Publications.
Cunneen, C. (2008) Young people and juvenile justice. In: G. Monahan and L. Young (eds.), *Children and the Law in Australia* (pp. 187–203). Australia: LexisNexis.
Cunneen, C. (2020) Youth justice and racialization: Comparative reflections. *Theoretical Criminology*, 24(3): 521–539.
Cunneen, C. and Goldson, B. (2015) Restorative justice? A critical analysis. In: B. Goldson and J. Muncie (eds.), *Youth, Crime and Justice* (2nd ed.). London: Sage.
Day, A. (2020) Time to stop and smell the roses: On 'rushing headlong' into service delivery without really knowing what it is we are doing. *Criminal and Mental Health Behavior*, 5–8.
Day, A. (2022) 'It's a hard balance to find': The perspectives of youth justice practitioners in England on the place of 'risk' in an emerging 'child first' world'. *Youth Justice*, 58–75.
Deakin, J., Fox, C. and Matos, R. (2020) Labelled as 'risky' in an era of control: How young people experience and respond to the stigma of criminalized identities. *European Journal of Criminology*, 19(4): 653–673.
DeKeseredy, W. (2021) *Contemporary Critical Criminology*. London: Routledge.
DeKeseredy, W. and Schwartz, M. (2018) Left realism: A new look. In: W. Dekeseredy and M. Dragiewicz (eds.), *Routledge Handbook of Critical Criminology*. London: Routledge
Division of Violence Prevention (2019) *Preventing Adverse Childhood Experiences (ACEs): Leveraging the Best Available Evidence*. Atlanta: Division of Violence Prevention.
DoJ (2021) Youth justice strategy. Belfast: DoJ.
Downes, D. and Rock, P. (1998) *Understanding Deviance* (3rd edition). Oxford: Oxford University Press.
Dunkel, F. (2014) Juvenile justice systems in Europe – Reform developments between justice, welfare and 'new punitiveness'. *Criminological Studies*, 1.
Durkheim, E. (1895/1964) *The Division of Labor in Society*. New York: Free Press.
Eckhouse, L., Lum, K., Conti-Cook, C. and Ciccolini, J. (2019) Layers of bias: A unified approach for understanding problems with risk assessment. *Criminal Justice and Behavior*, 46(2): 185–209.
Edwards, A. and Hughes, G. (2009) The preventive turn and the promotion of safer communities in England and Wales. In: A. Crawford (ed.), *Crime Prevention Policies in Comparative Perspective*. Cullompton, UK: Willan.

Elder, G.H., Kirkpatrick Johnson, M. and Crosnoe, R. (2004) The emergence of development and life-course theory. In: J. Mortimer and M. Shanahan (eds.), *Handbook of the Life Course* (pp. 3–22). New York: Plenum.

Elliott, D.S., Ageton, S.S. and Canter, J. (1979) An integrated theoretical perspective on delinquent behaviour. *Journal of Research in Crime and Delinquency*, 16: 3–27.

Emmel, N., Monaghan, M., Manzano, A. and Greenhalgh, J. and Dalkin, S. (2018) *Doing Realist Research*. London: Sage Publications Ltd.

Emmel, N., Monaghan, M., Manzano, A. and Greenhalgh, J. and Dalkin, S. (2021) *Doing Realist Research*. London: Sage Publications Ltd.

Eysenck, H.J. (1970) *Crime and Personality*. London: Granada.

Farrington, D.P. (1996) *Understanding and Preventing Youth Crime*. York, UK: JRF.

Farrington, D.P. (2000) Developmental criminology and risk-focussed prevention. In: M. Maguire, R. Morgan, and R. Reiner (eds.), *The Oxford Handbook of Criminology* (3rd ed.). Oxford: Oxford University Press.

Farrington, D.P. (2007) Childhood risk factors and risk-focused prevention. In: M. Maguire, R. Morgan, and R. Reiner (eds.), *The Oxford Handbook of Criminology*. Oxford: Oxford University Press.

Farrington, D.P. (2020) The integrated cognitive antisocial potential (ICAP) theory: Past, Present, and Future. *Journal of Developmental and Life-Course Criminology*, 6(2): 158–171.

Farrington, D.P. (2005) The integrated cognitive antisocial development (ICAP) theory. In D.P. Farrington (ed.), *Integrated Developmental and Life-Course Theories of Offending*. New Brunswick: Transaction.

Feeley, M.M. and Simon, J. (1992) The new penology: Notes on the emerging strategy of corrections and its implications. *Criminology*, 30: 449–474.

Ferrell, J. and Hayward, K. (2015) *Cultural Criminology: An Invitation*. London: Sage.

Ferri, E. (1895) *Criminal Sociology*. London: Unwin.

Fisher, E. and Mehozay, Y. (2019) How algorithms see their audience: Media epistemes and the changing conception of the individual. *Media, Culture and Society*, 41(8): 1176–1191.

Fitzgibbon, K. and O'Brien, W. (2019) A child's capacity to commit crime: Examining the operation of doli incapax in Victoria (Australia), 8(12): 18–33.

Fond, M., Haydon, A. and Kendall-Taylor, N. (2015). Communicating Connections: Framing the Relationship Between Social Drivers, Early Adversity, and Child Neglect. Available at: https://www.frameworksinstitute.org/resources/communicating-connections-framing-the-relationship-between-social-drivers-early-adversity-and-child-neglect/

France, A. (2008) Risk factor analysis and the youth question. *Journal of Youth Studies*, 11(1): 1–15.

France, A., Bottrell, D. and Armstrong, D. (2012) *A Political Ecology of Youth and Crime*. London: Palgrave Macmillan

France, A. and Crow, I. (2005) Using the 'risk factor paradigm' in prevention: Lessons from the evaluation of Communities that Care. *Children and Society*, 19(2): 172–184.

France, A. and Homel, R. (2007) *Pathways and Crime Prevention: Theory, Policy and Practice*. Cullompton: Willan.

France, A. and Homel, R. (2013) *Pathways and Crime Prevention. Theory, Policy and Practice*, 2nd edition. Cullompton: Willan.

France, A. and Utting, D. (2005) The paradigm of 'risk and protection-focused prevention' and its impact on services for children and families. *Children and Society*, 19: 77–90.

Friday, P.C. and Ren, X. (2006) *Delinquency and Juvenile Justice Systems in the Non-Western World*. New York: Criminal Justice Press.
Froggio, G. (2007) Strain and juvenile delinquency: A critical review of Agnew's general strain theory. *Journal of Loss and Trauma*, 12(4): 383–418.
Fullerton, D., Bamber, J. and Redmond, S. (2021) *Developing Effective Relationships Between Youth Justice Workers and Young People: A Synthesis of the Evidence, REPPP Review*. Limerick: University of Limerick.
Furlong, A. and Cartmel, F. (2006) *Young People and Social Change: New Perspectives*. Buckingham: Open University Press.
Garland, D. (2002) *The Culture of Control*. Oxford: Oxford University Press.
Giedd, J.N., Blumenthal, J., Jeffries, N.O., Castellanos, F.X., Liu, H., Zijdenbos, A., Paus, T., Evans, A.C. and Rapoport, J.L. (1999) Brain development during childhood and adolescence: A longitudinal MRI study. *Nature Neuroscience*, 2(10): 861–863.
Glueck, S. and Glueck, E. (1930) *500 Criminal Careers*. New York: Alfred Knopf.
Glueck, S. and Glueck, E. (1950) *Unraveling Juvenile Delinquency*. New York: Commonwealth Fund.
Goddard, H.H. (1914) *Feeblemindedness: Its Causes and Consequences*. New York: Macmillan.
Goddard, T. (2017) The trouble with using risk assessment instruments to quantify the chance of future youth offending. *Sustainability,* 13(21): 11624.
Goddard, T. and Myers, R.R. (2017) Against evidence-based oppression: Marginalized youth and the politics of risk-based assessment and intervention. *Theoretical Criminology*, 21(2): 151–167.
Goffman, E. (1990) *The Presentation of Self in Everyday Life*. London: Penguin.
Goldblatt, P., and Lewis, C. (1998) Reducing reoffending: An assessment of research evidence on ways of dealing with offending behaviour. Home Office Research Study 187. London: Home Office.
Goldson, B. (2005) Taking liberties: Policy and the punitive turn. In: H. Hendrick (ed.), *Child Welfare and Social Policy*. Bristol: Policy Press.
Goldson, B. (2010) The sleep of (criminological) reason: Knowledge-policy rupture and new labour's youth justice legacy. *Criminology and Criminal Justice*, 10(2): 155–178.
Goldson, B. (2014) Youth justice in a changing Europe: Crisis conditions and alternative visions. *Perspectives on Youth*, 1: 39–52.
Goldson, B. and Briggs, D. (2021) *Making Youth Justice: Local Penal Cultures and Differential Outcomes: Lessons and Prospects for Policy and Practice*. London: Howard League.
Goldson, B. and Hughes, G. (2010) Sociological criminology and youth justice: Comparative policy analysis and academic intervention. *Criminology and Criminal Justice*, 10(2): 211–230.
Goldson, B. and Muncie, J. (2015) *Youth Crime and Justice*. London: Sage.
Goldson, B. and Muncie, J. (2021) *Youth Crime and Justice*, 2nd edition. London: Sage.
Goshe, S. (2015) Moving beyond the punitive legacy: Taking stock of persistent problems in juvenile justice. *Youth Justice*, 15: 42–56. DOI: 10.1177/1473225414537930.
Goshe, S (2019) How contemporary rehabilitation fails youth and sabotages the American juvenile justice system: A critique and call for change. *Critical Criminology*, 27: 559–573.
Gottfredson, M.R. and Hirschi, T. (1990) *A General Theory of Crime*. Stanford, CA: Stanford University Press.
Gray, P., Jump, D. and Smithson, H. (2023) *Adverse Childhood Experiences and Serious Youth Violence*. Bristol: Bristol University Press.

Gray, P. and Smith, R. (2024) Youth justice and social harm: Towards a 'theory of the good'. *Criminology and Criminal Justice*, 1–18.

Greenhalgh, J. and Manzano, A. (2022) Understanding 'context' in realist evaluation synthesis. *International Journal of Social Research Methodology*, 5: 583–595.

Greenough, W.T., Black, J.E. and Wallace, C.S. (1987) Experience and brain development. *Child Development*, 58(3): 539–559.

Grove, W.M. and Meehl, P.E. (1996) Comparative efficiency of informal (subjective, impressionistic) and formal (mechanical, algorithmic) prediction. *Psychology, Public Policy and Law*, 2: 293–323.

Gungea, M., Jaunky, V. and Ramesh, V. (2017) Personality traits and juvenile delinquency a critical analysis. *International Journal of Conceptions on Management and Social Sciences*, 5(1): 2357–2787

Hagan, J. (1989) *Structural Criminology*. New Brunswick, NJ: Rutgers University Press.

Hagell, A. and Hazel, N. (2001) Macro and micro patterns in the development of secure custodial institutions for serious and persistent young offenders in england and wales. *Youth Justice*, 1(1): 3–16.

Haines, K.R. and Case, S.P. (2008) The rhetoric and reality of the Risk Factor Prevention Paradigm approach to preventing and reducing youth offending. *Youth Justice*, 8(1): 5–20.

Haines, K.R. and Case, S.P. (2012) Is the scaled approach a failed approach? *Youth Justice*, 12(3): 212–228.

Haines, K.R. and Case, S.P. (2015) *Positive Youth Justice: Children First, Offenders Second*. Bristol: Policy Press.

Haines, K. and Drakeford, M. (1998) *Young People and Youth Justice*. London: Macmillan.

Haines, K. and Thomas, S. (2023) Challenging historical populism. In: S. Case and N. Hazel. (eds.), *Child First: Developing a new youth justice system*. London: Palgrave.

Hammersley, R., Marsland, L. and Reid, M. (2003) *Substance Use by Young Offenders: The Impact of the Normalisation of Drug Use in the Early Years of the 21st Century*. Home Office Research Study No. 261. London: Home Office.

Hannah-Moffat, K. (2018) Algorithmic risk governance: Big data analytics, race and information activism in criminal justice debates. *Theoretical Criminology*, 23(4): 453–470.

Hannah-Moffat, K. (2019) Algorithmic risk governance: Big data analytics, race and information activism in criminal justice debates. *Theoretical Criminology*, 23(4) 453–470.

Hardyns, W. and Pauwels, L. (2017) The Chicago school and criminology. In: R. Triplett (ed.), *The Handbook of the History and Philosophy of Criminology* (pp. 123–139). Wiley-Blackwell.

Harding, C.J. and Becroft, A.J. (2013) 10 Characteristics of A Good Youth Justice System. A paper for The Pacific Judicial Development Programme Family Violence and Youth Justice Workshop. Port Vila, Vanuatu.

Harris, R. (1985) Towards just welfare. *British Journal of Criminology*, 25(1): 31–45.

Hatty, S.E. (2000) *Engendering Violence. Masculinities, Violence and Culture*. London: Sage Publications.

Haw, K. (2007) Risk factors and pathways into and out of crime: Misleading, misinterpreted or mythic? From generative metaphor to professional myth. In: A. France and R. Homel (eds.), *Pathways and Crime Prevention*. Cullompton, UK: Willan.

Hawkins, J.D. and Catalano, R.F. (1992) *Communities that Care*. San Francisco: Jossey-Bass.

Hawkins, J.D. and Weis, J.G. (1985) The social development model: An integrated approach to delinquency prevention. *Journal of Primary Prevention*, 6: 73–97.

Hawkins, J. D., Smith, B.H., Hill, K.G., Kosterman, R., Catalano, R.F. and Abbott. R.D. (2003) 'Understanding and preventing crime and violence. Findings from the Seattle social development project'. In T.P. Thornberry and M.D. Krohn (eds.), *Taking Stock of Delinquency: An Overview of Findings from Contemporary Longitudinal Studies*. New York: Kluwer.

Hazel, N. (2008) *Cross-National Comparison of Youth Justice*. London: YJB.

Hazel, N. and Bateman, T. (2020). Supporting children's resettlement ('reentry') after custody: Beyond the risk paradigm. *Youth Justice*, 21(1): 71–89.

Heimer, K. and De Coster, S. (1999) The gendering of violent delinquency. *Criminology*, 37(2): 277–318.

Henriksen, A., Bengtsson, T. and Henriksen, T. (2024) Crime prevention, support or punishment? Introducing an ambiguous system of youth justice in denmark. *Youth Justice,* 463–479.

Herrnstein, R.J. and Murray, C. (1994) *The Bell Curve*. New York: Basic Books.

Hine, J (2005). Early intervention: The view from on track. *Children and Society*, 19(2): 117–130.

Hine, J. (2006) *Young People, Pathways and Crime: Context and Complexity*. Leicester, UK: Pathways into and out of Crime: Taking Stock and Moving Forward: International Symposium, April.

Hine, J., France, A., Dunkerton, L. and Armstrong, D. (2007) Risk and resilience in children who are offending, excluded from school or who have behaviour problems. Available at: www.pcrrd.group.shef.ac.uk/reports/project_1.pdf (Accessed July 2007).

Hirschi, T. (1969) *Causes of Delinquency*. Berkeley: University of California.

HMIP. (2022) The Risk-Need-Responsivity Model. Retrieved from HMIP: Available at: https://www.justiceinspectorates.gov.uk/hmiprobation/research/the-evidence-base-probation/models-and-principles/the-rnr-model/

Holloway, K., Bennett. T. and Farrington, D. (2005) *The Effectiveness of Criminal Justice and Treatment Programmes in Reducing Drug-related Crime: A Systematic Review*. Home Office Online Report 26/05. London: Home Office.

Hope. T. (1998) Community crime prevention. In: P. Goldblatt and C. Lewis (eds.), *Reducing Reoffending: An Assessment of Research Evidence on Ways of Dealing with Offending Behaviour*. Home Office Research Study 187. London: Home Office

Hope, T. (2005) Pretend it doesn't work: The 'anti-social' bias in the Maryland scientific methods scale. *European Journal on Criminal Policy and Research*, 11(3): 275–296.

Hope, T. (2009) The illusion of control. A response to professor sherman. *Criminology and Criminal Justice*, 9(2): 125–134.

Hopkins-Burke, R. (2016*) Young People, Crime and Justice*. Abingdon, UK: Routledge.

Hough, M. (2010) Gold standard or fool's gold: The pursuit of certainty in experimental criminology. *Criminology & Criminal Justice*, 10(1), 11–22. Available at: http://frameworksinstitute.org/assets/files/ECD/social_determinants_ecd_messagebrief_finalpdf (Accessed October 2020). https://www.icpsr.umich.edu/web/NACJD/studies/36473 (Accessed July 2024)

Huizinga, D. (2017) *Denver Youth Survey Waves 1–5, (1988–1992)*. Available at: https://www.icpsr.umich.edu/web/NACJD/studies/36473

Huizinga, D. and Espiritu, R. (1999) *Delinquent Behavior of Youth in the Juvenile Justice System*. Pittsburgh, PA: National Center for Juvenile Justice.

Jackson, D., Jones, M., Semenza, D. and Testa, A. (2023) Adverse childhood experiences and adolescent delinquency: A theoretically informed investigation of during middle childhood. *International Journal of Environmental Research and Public Health*, 20(4), February: 3202.

Jeffery, C.R. (1977) *Crime Prevention Through Environmental Design*. Beverly Hills, CA: Sage.

Johns, D., Williams, K. and Haines, K. (2016) Ecological youth justice: Understanding the social ecology of young people's prolific offending. *Youth Justice*, 17(1): 3–21.

Johnson, S., Tilley, N. and Bowers, K. (2015) Introducing EMMIE: An evidence rating scale to encourage mixedmethod crime prevention synthesis reviews. *Journal of Experimental Criminology*, 11: 459–473.

Johnston, J., MacDonald, R., Mason, P., Ridley, L. and Webster, C. (2000) *Snakes and Ladders: Young People, Transitions and Social Exclusion*. Bristol, UK: Policy Press.

Joliffe, D., Farrington, D., Piquero, A. and Macloed, J. (2017) Prevalence of life-course-persistent, adolescence-limited, and late-onset offenders: A systematic review of prospective longitudinal studies. *Aggression and Violent Behaviour*, 33: 4–14.

Jones, A.P., Laurens, K.R., Herba, C.M., Barker, G.J. and Viding, E. (2009) Amygdala hypoactivity to fearful faces in boys with conduct problems and callous-unemotional traits. *American Journal of Psychiatry*, 166: 95–102.

Jou, S., Chang, Y. and Hebenton, W. (2014) *Youth Justice in China*. Oxford: Oxford University Press.

Justice Analytical Services (2018) *What Have ACEs Got to do with Justice?* Edinburgh: Scottish Government.

YJB (2024) Strategic Plan. London: YJB.

Kelly, L. and Armitage, V. (2015) Diverse diversions: Youth justice reform, localized practices, and a 'new interventionist diversion'? *Youth Justice*, 15(2): 117–133.

Kemshall, H. (2007) Risk assessment and risk management: The right approach?. In: M. Blyth, E. Solomon, and K. Baker (eds.), *Young People and Risk*. Bristol, UK: Policy Press.

Kemshall, H. (2008) Risk, rights and justice: Understanding and responding to youth risk. *Youth Justice*, 8(1): 21–38.

Kemshall, H., Marsland, L., Boeck, T. and Dunkerton, L. (2006) Young people, pathways and crime: Beyond risk factors. Australian and New Zealand *Journal of Criminology*, 39(3): 354–370.

Kemshall, H., Marsland, L., Boeck, T. and Dunkerton, L. (2007) Young people, pathways and crime: Beyond risk factors. In: A. France and R. Homel (eds.), *Pathways and Crime Prevention. Theory, Policy and Practice*. Cullompton: Willan.

Kemshall, H., Marsland, L., Boeck, T. and Dunkerton, L. (2013) Young people, pathways and crime: Beyond risk factors. In: A. France and R. Homel (eds.), *Pathways and Crime Prevention. Theory, Policy and Practice*. Cullompton: Willan.

Kilkelly, U. (2023) Child first and children's rights. In. S. Case and N. Hazel (eds.), *Child First: Developing a New Youth Justice System*. London: Palgrave.

Kilkelly, U. and Bergin, P. (2021), *Advancing Children's Rights in Detention. A Model for International Reform*. Bristol: Bristol University Press.

Kraemer, H., Stice, E., Kazdin, A., Offord, D. and Kupfer, D. (2001) How do risk factors work together? Mediators, moderators, and independent, overlapping, and proxy risk factors. *American Journal of Psychiatry*, 158: 848–856.

Lacey, R.E. and Minnis, H. (2020). Practitioner review: Twenty years of research with adverse childhood experience scores – advantages, disadvantages and applications to practice. *Journal of Child Psychology and Psychiatry*, 61(2): 116–130.

Laub, J. and Sampson, R. (2003) *Shared Beginnings, Delinquent Lives. Delinquent Boys to Age 70*. London: Harvard University Press.

Laub, J., Sampson, R. and Sweetan, G. (2017) Assessing sampson and laub's life-course theory of crime. In: F. Cullen, J. Wright, and K. Blevins (eds.), *Taking Stock*. London: Routledge.
Lawy, R. (2002) Risk stories: Youth identities, learning and everyday risk. *Journal of Youth Studies*, 5(4): 407–423.
Lea, J. (2014) New deviancy, Marxism, and the politics of left realism. *Theoretical Criminology*, 18(4): 432–440.
Lea, J. (2016) Left realism: A radical criminology for the current crisis. *International Journal for Crime, Justice and Social Democracy*, 8(1): 18–33.
Lea, J. and Young, J. (1984) *What is to be Done About Law and Order?* Harmondsworth, UK: Penguin.
Lemert, E. (1951) *Social Pathology*. New York: McGraw-Hill.
Lemert, E. (1972) *Human Deviance, Social Problems, and Social Control*. New York: Prentice-Hall.
Liefaard, T (2020) Juvenile justice. In J. Todres and S. King (eds.), *The Oxford Handbook of Children's Rights*. New York: Oxford University Press.
Link, B. G. and Phelan, J. C. (2001) Conceptualizing stigma. *Annual Review of Sociology*, 27: 363–385.
Lipsey, M. and Wilson, D. (1993) The efficacy of psychological, educational, and behavioral treatment: confirmation from meta-analysis. *American Psychologist*, 48(12): 1181–1209.
Loader, I. and Sparks, R. (2013) *Public Crimi*nology? London: Routledge.
Loeber, R. and Hay, D.F. (1997) Key issues in the development of aggression and violence from childhood to early adulthood. *Annual Review of Psychology*, 48: 371–410.
Lombroso, C. (1875) *L'uomo delinquente (The Criminal Man)*. Milan: Hoepli.
Lynch, N. and Liefaard, T. (2020) What is left in the "too hard basket"? Developments and challenges for the rights of children in conflict with the law. *International Journal of Children's Rights*, 28(1): 89–110.
Macdonald, R. (2013) Social exclusion, youth transitions and criminal Careers: Five Critical Reflections on "Risk". In: A. France and R. Homel (eds.), *Pathways and Crime Prevention*. Cullompton: Willan.
Lynch, N. (2021) Incorporation of the UNCRC in New Zealand. Intersentia.
Macdonald, R. and Marsh, J. (2005) *Disconnected Youth? Growing Up in Britain's Poor Neighbourhoods*. Basingstoke: Palgrave.
MacDonald, R. and Shildrick, T. (2018) Biography, history and place: understanding youth transitions in teeside. In: S. Irwin and A. Nilsen (eds.), *Transitions to Adulthood through Recession*. London: Taylor and Francis.
Maguire, M., Morgan, R. and Reiner, R. (2007) *The Oxford Handbook of Criminology*. Oxford: Oxford University Press.
Marsh, I. and Melville. G. (2019) *Crime, Justice and the Media*. London: Routledge.
Martinson, R. (1974) What works? – Questions and answers about prison reform. *Public Interest*, 35: 22–54.
Maruna, S., Francis, V., Liddle, M., McAteer, L., Watts, E. and Wright, S. (2008) *Reducing Offending: A Critical Review of the International Research Evidence*. NIO Research and Statistical Series: Report No. 18. Belfast: NIO.
May, M. (1973) Innocence and experience: The evolution of the concept of juvenile delinquency in the mid-nineteenth century. *Victorian Studies*, xvii: 7–29.
McAra, L. (2010) Models of youth justice. In: D.J. Smith (ed.), *A New Response to Youth Crime*. Cullompton, UK: Willan.
McAra, L. (2023) Youth justice in an age of uncertainty: Principles, performance and prospects. In: A. Liebling, S. Maruna, and L. McAra (eds.), *Oxford Handbook of Criminology*. Oxford: Oxford University Press.

McAra, L. and McVie, S. (2007) Youth justice? The impact of system contact on patterns of desistance from offending. *European Journal of Criminology*, 4(3): 315–345.
McAra, L. and McVie, S. (2010) Youth crime and justice: Key messages from the Edinburgh study of youth transitions and crime. *Criminology and Criminal Justice*, 10: 211–230.
McAra, L. and McVie, S. (2015) The case for diversion and minimum necessary intervention. In: B. Goldson and J. Muncie (eds.), *Youth Crime and Justice*. London: Sage.
McAra, L. and McVie, S. (2022) *Causes and Impact of Offending and Criminal Justice Pathways: Follow-up of the Edinburgh Study Cohort at Age* (p. 35). Available at: https://www.research.ed.ac.uk/en/publications/causes-and-impact-of-offending-and-criminal-justice-pathways-foll (Accessed October 2024).
McCarten, K. (2020) *Trauma-Informed Practice*. London: HM Inspectorate of Probation Academic Insights.
McCarthy, P., Laing, K. and Walker, J. (2004) *Offenders of the Future: Assessing the Risk of Children and Young People Becoming Involved in Criminal or Antisocial Behaviour*. London: Department for Education and Skills.
McCord, J. (1978) A thirty-year follow-up of treatment effects. *American Psychologist*, 33(3): 284–289.
Mednick, S.A., Moffitt, T.E. and Stack, S. (1987) *The Causes of Crime: New Biological Approaches*. Cambridge: Cambridge University Press.
Mednick, S. A. and Volavka, J. (1980). Biology and crime. In N. Morris, and M. H. Tonry (eds.), *Crime and Justice*. London: Sage.
Mehozay, Y. and Fisher, E. (2018) The epistemology of algorithmic risk assessment and the path towards a non-penology penology. *Punishment and Society*, 21(5): 523–541.
Mercurio, E. et al. (2020) Adolescent brain development and progressive legal responsibility in the Latin American Context. *Front Psychology*, 11: 627.
Merton, R.K. (1938) Social structure and anomie. *American Sociological Review*, 3: 672–682.
Messerschmidt, J.W. (2012) *Gender, Heterosexuality, and Youth Violence: The Struggle for Recognition*. Plymouth, UK: Rowman & Littlefield Publishers.
Messerschmidt, J. and Tomsen, S. (2017) Masculinities, crime, and criminal justice. In: M. Tonry (ed.), *Oxford Handbooks Online*. New York: Oxford University Press.
Mika, H. and Zehr, H. (2003) A restorative framework for community justice practice. In: K. McEvoy and T. Newburn (eds.), *Criminology, Conflict Resolution and Restoratice Justice*. Basingstoke, UK and New York: Palgrave Macmillan.
Moffitt, T.E. (2006). Life-course persistent versus adolescence-limited antisocial behavior. In D. Cicchetti and D. Cohen (eds.), *Developmental Psychopathology* (2nd ed., Vol. 3, pp. 570–598). New York: Wiley.
MOJ and Welsh Government. (2019) *Youth Justice Blueprint for Wales*. London: Ministry of Justice.
Mooney, J. (2021) 'Left Realism: Taking Crime Seriously', in the Oxford Research. Encyclopedia of Criminology and Criminal Justice, Oxford University Press.
Mullins, C.W. (2006) *Holding your Square: Masculinities, Streetlife and Violence*. Cullompton, UK: Willan Publishing.
Muncie, J. (2008) The 'punitive' turn in juvenile justice: Cultures of control and rights compliance in Western Europe and the USA. *Youth Justice*, 8(2): 107–121.
Muncie, J. (2010) The United Nations, children's rights and juvenile justice. In: W. Taylor, R. Hester, and R. Earle (eds.), *Youth Justice Handbook* (pp. 200–210). London: Routledge.
Muncie, J. (2021) *Youth and Crime* (5th ed.). London: Sage.
Murray, C. (1990) *The Emerging British Underclass*. London: Institute of Economic Affairs Health and Welfare Unit.

Myers, R., Goddard, T. and Davidtz, J. (2021) Reconnecting youth: Beyond individualized programs and risks. *Youth Justice*, 21(1): 55–70.

Nagin, D.S. and Tremblay, R.E. (2005) Developmental trajectory groups: Fact or a useful statistical fiction? *Criminology,* 43(4): 873–904.

Noble, J. and Hodgson, L. (2016) *Theory of Change Guidance*. London: YJB.

Nwalozie, C. (2015) Rethinking subculture and subcultural theory in the study of youth crime–A theoretical discourse. Available at: https://efaidnbmnnnibpcajpcglclefindmkaj/https://core.ac.uk/download/pdf/228197743.pdf (Accessed October 2024).

Nye, F.I. (1958) *Family Relationships and Delinquent Behaviour*. New York: Wiley.

Ogilvie, J., Thompson, C., Lockwood, K., Little, S., Allard, T., Thomsen, L. and Dennison, S. (2024). Examining the characteristics of children who experience contact with the youth justice system in queensland: Implications for the minimum age of criminal responsibility. *CrimRxiv*. https://doi.org/10.21428/cb6ab371.784a5bac

Forde, L. (2021) Welfare, justice, and diverse models of youth justice: A children's rights analysis. *The International Journal of Children's Rights*, 29(4), 920–945. ISSN: 0927-5568.

Park, R. and Burgess, E. (1925) *The City*. Chicago, IL: University of Chicago Press.

Pasquale, F (2015) The algorithmic self. *The Hedgehog Review,* 17(1): 1–7.

Pauwels, J., Svensson, R. and Hirtenlehner, H. (2018) Testing situational action theory: A narrative review of studies published between 2006 and 2015. *European Journal of Criminology*, 15(1): 32–55.

Pavlov, I. (1927/1960) *Conditioned Reflexes: An Investigation of the Physiological Activity of the Cerebral Cortex*. New York: Dover Publications.

Pawson, R. (2006) *Evidence-based Policy: A Realist Perspective*. London: Sage Publications Ltd.

Pawson, R. (2013) *The Science of Evaluation: A Realist Manifesto*. London: Sage Publications Ltd.

Pawson, R. and Tilley, N. (2004) *Realistic Evaluation*, 2nd edition. London: Sage.

Payne, B., Young, G. and Hobson, J. (2022) Restorative practices in schools in Northern Ireland: Towards an 'all school' model. *Irish Probation Journal*, 19: 74–96.

Pearson, G. (1983) *Hooligan: A History of Respectable Fears*. Basingstoke: Macmillan.

Perry, B.D. (2001) Violence and childhood: How persisting fear can alter the developing child's brain. Available at: www.childtrauma.org/CTAMATERIALS/Vio_child.asp.

Pittman, K.J., Irby, M., Tolman, J., Yohalem, N. and Ferber, T. (2003) *Preventing Problems, Promoting Development, Encouraging Engagement Competing Priorities or Inseparable Goals?* Washington: The Forum for Youth Investment.

Pitts, J. (2003) *The New Politics of Youth Crime: Discipline or Solidarity?* Lyme Regis: Russell House.

Pollard, J.A., Hawkins, J.D. and Arthur, M.W. (1999) Risk and protection: Are both necessary to understand diverse behavioral outcomes in adolescence? *Social Work Research*, 23(3): 145–158.

Porteus, D. (2007) The prevention of youth crime: A risky business? In: B. Thom, R. Sales, and J. Pearce (eds.), *Growing Up With Risk*. Bristol, UK: Policy Press.

Powers, E., Witmer, H. and Allport, G.W. (1951) *An Experiment in the Prevention of Delinquency. The Cambridge-Somerville Youth Study*. New York: Columbia University Press.

Pratt, J. and Eriksson, A. (2012) In defence of scandinavian exceptionalism. In: T. Ugelvik and J. Dullum (eds.), *Penal Exceptionalism? Nordic Prison Policy and Practice*. London: Routledge.

Prelow, H., Loukas, A. and Jordan-Green, L. (2007) Socioenvironmental risk and adjustment in Latino youth: The mediating effects of family processes and social competence. *Journal of Youth and Adolescence*, 36: 465–476.

Prior, D. and Mason, P. (2010) A different kind ofevidence. Looking for 'what works' in engaging young offenders. *Youth Justice*, 10(3): 211–226.

Put, J. and Walgrave, L. (2006) Belgium: From protection to accountability. In: J. Muncie and B. Goldson (eds.), *Comparative Youth Justice*. London: Sage.

Reiss, A.J. (1951) Delinquency as the failure of personal and social controls. *American Sociological Review*, 16: 213–239.

Restorative Justice Council (2017) *Restorative Justice and Black, Asian and Minority Ethnic Children in the Youth Justice system A Restorative Justice Council Research Report*. London: RJC.

Richards, K. (2017) Responsibilising the parents of young offenders through restorative justice: A genealogical account. *Restorative Justice*, 5(1): 93–115.

Robertson, C. and Azaola, E. (2021) *Juvenile Delinquency: Why Do Youths Commit Crime?*. Harmondsworth, UK: Penguin.

Rutter, M. and Giller, H. (1983) *Juvenile Delinquency: Trends and Perspective*. Harmondsworth, UK: Penguin.

Salford, H., Cairns, L. and Marshall, J. (2017) Achieving child friendly justice through child friendly methods: Let's start with the right to information. *Social Inclusion*, 5(3): 53–63. Promoting Children's Participation in Research, Policy and Practice.

Sampson, R.J. and Laub, J.H. (1993) *Crime in the Making: Pathways and Turning Points through Life*. Harvard, MA: Harvard University Press.

Sampson, R.J. and Laub, J.H. (2005) A general age-graded theory of crime: Lessons learned and the future of life-course criminology. In: D.P. Farrington (ed.), *Integrated Developmental and Life-Course Theories of Offending*. New Brunswick, NJ: Transaction.

Sawyer, W. and Wagner, P. (2020) *Mass Incarceration: The Whole Pie 2020*. Northampton, MA: Prison Policy Initiative.

Schulze, C. and Bryan, V. (2017) The gendered monitoring of juvenile delinquents: A test of power-control theory using a retrospective cohort study. *Youth & Society*, 49(1): 72–95.

Schwartz, J., Walsh, A. and Beaver, K. (2019) The biosocial perspective: A brief overview and potential contributions to criminological theory. In M. Krohn, A. Lizotte, and G. Penly Hall (eds.), *Handbook on Criminology and Deviance* (2nd ed., pp. 89–111). New York, NY: Springer.

Sharpe, G.H. (2011) *Offending Girls: Young Women and Youth Justice*. Abingdon, UK: Routledge.

Sharpe, G.H. (2015) Precarious identities: 'Young' motherhood, desistance and stigma. *Criminology and Criminal Justice*, 15(4): 407–422.

Sharpe, G.H. and Gelsthorpe, L. (2015) Girls, crime and justice. In: B. Goldson and J. Muncie (eds.), *Youth Crime and Justice*. London: Sage.

Shaw, C.R. (1930) *The Jack-Roller: A Delinquent Boy's Own Story*. Chicago, IL: University of Chicago Press.

Sheldon, W.H. (1949) *Varieties of Delinquent Youth*. London: Harper.

Sherman, L.W., Gottfredson D., MacKenzie, D., Eck, J., Reuter, P. and Bushway, S. (1998) *Preventing Crime: What Works, What Doesn't, What's Promising*. Baltimore: Department of Criminology and Criminal Justice, University of Maryland.

Sherman, L.W. (2009) Evidence and liberty: The promise of experimental criminology. *Criminology and Criminal Justice*, 9(1): 5–28.

Skinner, B.F. (1938) *The Behaviour of Organisms*. New York: Appleton Century Crofts.

Smart, C. (1990) Feminist approaches to criminology; or postmodern woman meets atavistic man. In: L. Gelsthorpe and A. Morris (eds.), *Feminist Perspectives in Criminology*. Buckingham, UK: Open University Press.

Smith, D.J. (2006) Youth crime and justice: Research, evaluation and evidence. In B. Goldson and J. Muncie (eds.), *Youth Crime and Justice*. London: Sage.

Smith, D.J. (2010) *A New Response to Youth Crime*. Cullompton, UK: Willan.

Smith, D.J. and Ecob, R. (2007) An investigation into causal links between victimization and offending in adolescents. *British Journal of Sociology*, 58(4): 633–659.

Smith, D.J. and McVie, S. (2003) Theory and method in the edinburgh study of youth transitions and crime. *British Journal of Criminology*, 43(1): 169–195.

Smith, D.J., McVie, S., Woodward, R., Shute, J. and McAra, L. (2001) *The Edinburgh Study of Youth Transitions and Crime: Key Findings at Ages 12 and 13*. Edinburgh Study of Youth Transitions and Crime Research Digest No. 1. Available at: http://www.law.ed.ac.uk/cls/esytc/findings/digest1.htm.

Smith, R. (2005) Welfare versus justice – Again! *Youth Justice*, 5(1): 3–16.

Smith, R. (2011) *Doing Justice to Young People: Youth Crime and Social Justice*. Cullompton, UK: Willan.

Smith, R. (2016) *Youth Justice: Ideas Policy Practice*. Abingdon: Routledge.

Smith, R. (2020) Diversion, rights and social justice. *Youth Justice Journal*, 21(1): 18–32.

Smith, R. and Gray, P. (2019) The changing shape of youth justice: Models of practice. *Criminology and Criminal Justice*, 19(5): 554–571.

Smith, C. and Thornberry, T.P. (1995) The relationship between childhood maltreatment and adolescent involvement in delinquency. *Criminology*, 33(4): 451–481.

Snacken, S. and Dumortier, E. (2012) Resisting punitiveness in Europe? An introduction. In: S. Snacken and E. Dumortier (eds.), *Resisting Punitiveness in Europe? Welfare, Human Rights and Democracy*. London: Routledge.

Souhami, A. (2007) *Transforming Youth Justice: Occupational Identity and Cultural Change*. Cullompton, UK: Willan.

Soung, P. (2011) Social and biological constructions of youth: Implications for juvenile justice and racial equity. *Northwestern Journal of Law and Social Policy*, 6(2): 428–444.

Sowell, E.R., Thompson, P.M., Holmes, C.J., Jernigan, T.L. and Toga, A.W. (1999) *In vivo* evidence for post-adolescent brain maturation in frontal and striatal regions. *Nature Neuroscience*, 2: 859–861.

Stanley-Hall, G. (1904) *Adolescence*. New York: D. Appleton.

Stephenson, M. and Allen, R. (2013) *Youth Justice: Challenges to Practice*. London: Unitas.

Stephenson, M. and Allen, R. (2018) *Effective Practice in Youth Justice* (3rd ed.). Norwich: Unitas.

Sutherland, A. (2009) The 'scaled approach' to youth justice. *Fools Rush in … Youth Justice Journal*, 9(1): 44–60.

Sutherland, E.H. (1940) White-collar criminality. *American Sociological Review*, 5: 1–12.

Sutherland, E.H. (1947) *Principles of Criminology* (4th ed.). Philadelphia, PA: Lippincott.

Sutherland, E.H. and Cressey, D.R. (1960) *Criminology* (5th ed.). Philadelphia, PA: Lippincott.

Sutton, C., Monaghan, M., Case, S., Greenhalgh, J., and Wright, J. (2022) Contextualising Youth Justice Interventions: Making the Case for Realist Synthesis. *Sustainability: Special Edition "Youth Justice Research"*, 14(2). DOI: 10.3390/su14020854.

Tannenbaum, F. (1938) *Crime and the Community*. New York: Columbia University Press.

Taylor, C. (2016) *Review of the Youth Justice System in England and Wales*. London: Ministry of Justice.

Taylor, I., Walton, P. and Young, J. (1973) *The New Criminology: For a Social Theory of Deviance*. London: Routledge and Kegan Paul.

Taylor, I., Walton, P. and Young, J. (2013) *The New Criminology: For a Social Theory of Deviance*, 2nd edition. London: Routledge & Kegan Paul.

Taylor, J. (2003) An evaluation of probation practice in relation to masculinity and offending behaviour: Are we addressing the issue? Northumbria University, Unpublished MA Dissertation.

Taylor, J. (2019) Why you need to remain critical of ACEs (Adverse Childhood Experiences). https://victimfocusblog.com/2019/03/15/why-you-need-to-remain-critical-of-aces-adverse-childhood-experiences/

Telzer, E., van Hoorn, J., Rogers, C. and Do, K. (2018) Social influence on positive youth development: A developmental neuroscience perspective. *Adolescent Child Development Behavior*, 54: 215–258.

The Data First Project: An Introductory User Guide Beccaria, C. (1963, first English edition 1767) On Crimes and Punishment,translated by H. Paolucci. Indianapolis, IN: Bobbs-Merrill Educational.

Thom, R. Sales and J. Pearce (2007) *Growing Up With Risk*. Bristol: Policy.

Thomas, W.I. (1907) *Sex and Society*. Chicago, IL: University of Chicago Press.

Thomas, W.I. (1923) *The Unadjusted Girl*. New York: Harper and Row.

Thornberry, T.P. (1987) Toward an interactional theory of delinquency, *Criminology*, 25(4): 863–92.

Thornberry, T.P. (1994) *Violent Families and Youth Violence. OJJDP Fact Sheet 21*. Washington, DC: OJJDP.

Thornberry, T.P., Farnworth, M., Krohn, M. and Lizotte, A. (2023) *Rochester Youth Development Study Phase 1 Data, 1988–1992*. New York: Rochester (ICPSR 35167). Available at: https://www.icpsr.umich.edu/web/NACJD/studies/35167 (Accessed August 2024).

Thornberry, T.P., Huizinga, D. and Loeber, R. (2004) The causes and correlates studies: Findings and policy implications. *Juvenile Justice*, 10(1): 3–19.

Thornberry, T.P. and Krohn, M.D. (2003) *Taking Stock of Delinquency. An Overview of Findings from Contemporary Longitudinal Studies*. New York: Kluwer.

Thornton, A., Sidebottom, A., Belur, J., Tompson, L. and Bowers, K. (2019). On the development and application of EMMIE: Insights from the what works centre for crime reduction. *Policing and Society*, 29(3): 266–282.

Tisdall, K., Davis, J., Fry, D., Konstantoni, K., Kustatscher, M., Maternowska, C. and Weiner, L. (2023) *Critical Childhood Studies: Global Perspectives*. Bloomsbury Academic.

Tittle, C.R. (2000) Control balance. In: R. Paternoster and R. Bachman (eds.), *Explaining Criminals and Crime: Essays in Contemporary Theory*. Los Angeles, CA: Roxbury.

Tittle, C.R. (2018) *Control Balance: Towards a General Theory of Deviance*. London: Routledge.

Tompson, L., Belur, J., Thornton, A., Bowers, K. J., Johnson, S. D., Sidebottom, A., . . . Laycock, G. (2020) How strong is the evidence-base for crime reduction professionals? *Justice Evaluation Journal*, 4(1): 68–97.

Tonry, M. and Farrington, D.P. (1995) *Building a Safer Society: Strategic Approaches to Crime Prevention*. Berkeley: The University of Chicago Press.

Turnbull, G. and Spence, J. (2011) What's at risk? The proliferation of risk across child and youth policy in England. *Journal of Youth Studies*, 14(8): 939–959.

Ugwudike, P. (2025) *An Introduction to Critical Criminology*. Bristol: BUP.
Ungar, M. (2004) A constructionist discourse on resilience: Multiple contexts, multiple realities among at-risk children and youth. *Youth and Society*, 35: 341–365.
UNICEF (1989) *United Nations Convention on the Rights of the Child 1989*. Geneva: United Nations.
United Nations General Assembly (1985) *UN Standard Minimum Rules for the Administration of Juvenile Justice*. Geneva: United Nations.
United Nations General Assembly (1990a) *UN Guidelines on the Prevention of Delinquency*. Geneva: United Nations.
United Nations General Assembly (1990b) *UN Rules for the Protection of Juveniles Deprived of their Liberty*. Geneva: United Nations.
Van Eijk, G. (2016) Socioeconomic marginality in sentencing: The built-in bias in risk assessment tools and the reproduction of social inequality. *Punishment & Society*, 19(4): 463–481.
Van Eijk, G. (2020) Inclusion and exclusion through risk-based justice: Analysing combinations of risk assessment from pretrial detention to release. *The British Journal of Criminology*, 60(4): 1080–1097.
Vold, G.B., Bernard, T.J. and Snipes, J.B. (2002) *Theoretical Criminology*. Oxford: Oxford University Press.
Wacquant, L. (2009) *Punishing the Poor: The Neoliberal Government of Social Insecurity*. Durham, NC: Duke University Press.
Walker, J. and McCarthy, P. (2005) Parents in prison: The impact on children. In: G. Preston (ed.), *At Greatest Risk: The Children Most Likely to be Poor*. London: Child Poverty Action Group.
Walsh, T. and Fitzgerald, R. (2022) Youth justice, community safety and children's rights in Australia. *The International Journal of Children's Rights*, 30(3): 617–643.
Walton, P. and Young, J. (1998/2013) *The New Criminology Revisited*. London: Palgrave.
Ward, T. (2020) Why theoretical literacy is essential for forensic research and practice. *Criminal and Mental Health*, 31: 1–4.
Ward, T. and Maruna, S. (2007) *Rehabilitation*. London: Routledge.
Ward, T., Yates, P.M. and Willis, G.M. (2011) The good lives model and the risk need responsivity model: A critical response to Andrews, Bonta, and Wormith. *Criminal Justice and Behaviour*, 39(1): 94–110.
Webster, C. (2007) Criminal careers in theoretical context: Biography and history. In: A. France and R. Homel (eds.), *Pathways and crime prevention*, Cullompton: Willan.
Webster, C., MacDonald, R. and Simpson, M. (2006) Predicting criminality: Risk/protective factors, neighbourhood influence and desistance. *Youth Justice*, 6(1): 7–22.
Webster, C., Simpson, D., MacDonald, R., Abbas, A., Cieslik, M., Shildrick, T. and Simpson, M. (2004) *Poor Transitions: Social Exclusion and Young Adults*, Bristol, UK: Policy Press.
Welsh Government and YJB (2004) *All Wales Youth Offending Strategy*. Cardiff: Welsh Government. Available at: https://www.google.com/search?client=safari&rls=en&q=All+Wales+Youth+Offending+Strategy&ie=UTF-8&oe=UTF-8
Welsh Government and YJB (2014) *Children and Young People First*. Cardiff: Welsh Government/YJB. Available at:https://www.gov.uk/government/publications/youth-justice-strategy-for-wales-children-and-young-people-first
Welsh, B. C. and Farrington, D. P. (2012) The Future of Crime Prevention: Developmental and Situational Strategies. Washington, D.C.: U.S. National Institute of Justice.

Welsh, B.C. and Tremblay, R. (2021) Early developmental crime prevention forged through knowledge translation: A window into a century of prevention experiments. *Journal of Developmental and Life-Course Criminology*, 7(1): 1–16.

Welsh, B.C., Zane, S.N. and Rocque, M. (2017) Delinquency prevention for individual change: Richard Clarke Cabot and the making of the Cambridge-somerville youth study. *Journal of Criminal Justice*, 52, 79–89.

Werth, R. (2019a) Risk and punishment: The recent history and uncertain future of actuarial, algorithmic, and "evidence-based" penal techniques. *Sociology Compass*, 13(2): e12659.

Werth, R. (2019b) Theorizing the performative effects of penal risk technologies: (Re) producing the subject who must be dangerous. *Social and Legal Studies*, 28(3): 327–348.

West, D.J. (1982) *Delinquency: Its Roots, Careers and Prospects*. London: Heinemann.

West, D.J. and Farrington, D.P. (1973) *Who Becomes Delinquent?* London: Heinemann.

West, D.J. and Farrington, D.P. (1977) *The Delinquent Way of Life*. London: Heinemann.

Wigzell, A., Paterson-Young, C. and Bateman, T. (2024) *Desistance and Children*. London: NAYJ.

Wikström, P.-O. (2008) In search of causes and explanations of crime. In: R. King and E. Wincup (eds.), *Doing Research on Crime and Justice*. Oxford: Oxford University Press.

Wikström, P.-O. and Butterworth, D. (2006) *Adolescent Crime: Individual Differences and Lifestyles*. Cullompton, UK: Willan.

Wikström, P.-O. and Loeber, R. (2000) Do disadvantaged neighborhoods cause well-adjusted children to become adolescent delinquents? A study of male juvenile serious offending, risk and protective factors and neighborhood context. *Criminology*, 38(4): 1109–1142.

Wikström, P-O. and Treiber, K. (2017) Beyond risk factors: An analytical approach to crime prevention. In B. Teasdale and M.S. Bradley (eds.), *Preventing Crime and Violence, Advances in Prevention Science* (Vol. 2, pp. 73–87). London: Springer.

Wikström, P-O., Treiber, K. and Roman, G. (2024) *Character, Circumstances and Criminal Careers*. Oxford: Oxford University Press.

Wilcox, A. (2003) Evidence-based youth justice? Some valuable lessons from an evaluation for the Youth Justice Board, *Youth Justice*, 3: 21–35.

Wilson, J.Q. (1975) *Thinking About Crime*. New York: Basic Books.

Wilson, J.Q. and Herrnstein, R.J. (1985) *Crime and Human Nature*. New York: Simon and Schuster.

Winlow, S. (2002) *Badfellas: Crime, Tradition and New Masculinities*, Oxford: Berg Publications.

Wold, B. and Mittelmark, M. (2018) Health-promotion research over three decades: The social-ecological model and challenges in implementation of interventions. *Scandinavian Journal of Public Health*, 46: 20–26.

Yan, L. (2012) The exploration of the work of juvenile criminal offence. *Law and Society*, 1: 270

Ye, D.B. (2013) Establish mechanism for investigation and prosecution of minor offences. Academic Journal of Shanxi Provincial Committee Party School of CPC, 36(1): 80–83.

YJB (2021) *Strategic Plan* 2021 to 2024. London: Youth Justice Board.

Young, J. (1986) The failure of criminology: The need for a radical realism. In: R. Matthews and J. Young (eds.), *Confronting Crime*. London: Sage.

Young, J. (2007) *The Vertigo of Late Modernity*. London: Sage.

Young, J. (2011) *The Criminological Imagination*. London: Polity Press.

Young, J. (2016) Voodoo criminology and the numbers game. In: J. Ferrell, K. Hayward, W. Morrison, and M. Presdee (eds.), *Cultural Criminology Unleashed* (pp. 27–42). London: Routledge.

Youth Justice Board (2003) *Assessment, Planning Interventions and Supervision.* London: YJB.

Youth Justice Board (2010) *Process Evaluation of the Pilot of a Risk-based Approach to Interventions*. London: YJB.

Youth Justice Board (2014) *AssetPlus Rationale*. London: YJB.

Youth Justice Board (2016) *Participation Strategy: Giving Young People a Voice in Youth Justice*. London: YJB.

Youth Justice Board (2018) *Proposed Definition of 'Children First, Offenders Second. Board Information Paper*. London: YJB.

Youth Justice Institute (2020) Youth justice effective practice certificate. Available at: https://youthjusticeinstitute.co.uk/.

Zavala, E., Curry, T.R. and Morales, M. C. (2020) Explaining the cultural retention–delinquency relationship using differential support and coercion theory: A study of native-born and immigrant Latino youth. *Social Science Quarterly*, 101: 623–640.

Zehr, H. and Mika, H. (1998) Fundamental concepts of restorative justice. *Contemporary Justice Review*, 1: 47–55.

Index

actuarial: justice 52, 55; risk management 68, 70
adaptation 76–78
adolescent/adolescence: cognitive development 19–20; Edinburgh Study 84–86; offending 39; 'storm and stress' theory 20–21
adoption studies 18–19
adult-centrism 2; RFPP 58
Adverse Childhood Experiences (ACEs) 61, 68, 70; measurement 62
Age-Graded Life Course Theory (AGLCT) 84–86; Edinburgh Study 84–86; quasi-contextualised explanations of youth offending 86–87; *see also* Edinburgh Study
Age-Graded Theory of Informal Social Control 80; agency 81–84; turning points 81–83
agency 81–84, 87, 91
Agnew, R. 76–77
Algorithmic Risk Assessment (ARA) 60–61, 68, 70
androcentrism 2, 27, 32, 79, 101; of criminology 102
'anomie' 74, 76, 78
antisocial potential 38, 80
Artefactual Risk Factor Theories (ARFTs) 13, 36, 51, 55, 62–63, 81–82, 90, 92, 110; determinism 83–84; Developmental Risk Factor Theory 28–32; Integrated Development Risk Factor Theory 32–40; Rational-Contextual theories 38–40; reductionism 41, 66, 85–86; *see also* Developmental Risk Factor Theory; Integrated Development Risk Factor Theory; Rational-Contextual theories of youth offending
Bandura, Albert, Social Learning Theory 22
Baumgartner, Eric 102; on youth offending by boys 159–160
Beccaria, Cesare 13
Becker, H., on labels 96
Beijing Rules 127–128
Bentham, Jeremy 13
bias 2, 6, 8; Algorithmic Risk Assessment (ARA) 60–61; Biological Positivism 16–17; 'centrism' 41, 72; official statistics 5; psychosocial 28, 31, 56–58
biological determinism 20–21
Biological Positivist theories of youth offending 105; bias 16–17; genetic inheritance 17–19; neuroscientific 19–20; physical characteristics 15–17
Biopsychosocial theory 26–28
Bonger, Willem, 'Marxist Criminology' 98–99
brain: cortex 21; frontal lobe 19; imaging 19; 'use it or lose it' principle 19–20
Butterworth, D. 39–40

Cambridge Study 30–31, 54
capitalism 98–99
CASE studies framework 1–3, 153–154
Catalano, Richard 33, 53
causality 39; youth offending 56–57, 62
'Causes and Correlates' study 35–36
'centrisms' 28, 41, 72, 94; explanations of youth offending 78–79
Child First 10, 65–66, 112, 132, 138, 143–144; aligning with Child-Friendly Justice 151–153; challenges and opportunities 149–151; principles 133–137; tenets 132–133

Child-Friendly Justice 75, 112, 124–129, 151–153
childhood, psychosocial risk factors 84–86
'Children First, Offenders Second' (CFOS) principle 129–131
children's rights 125–129, 135–136; Beijing Rules 127–128; compliance with the UNCRC 128; sentencing 128; trial and sentencing 136
China, Child First principles 134–137
class: -centrism 2, 31, 79–80; middle 2; ruling 98; under 105; working 79, 98
Classical theories of youth offending 13–14
coercion 25, 98
Cohen, A. K., Subcultural Theory 77
Committee on the Rights of the Child (CRC) 125, 127–129
Community Crime Prevention 9, 54, 111–112, 143; Comprehensive Community Initiatives (CCIs) 116–117; context-related lessons 119; effectiveness 115, 117–119; socially disadvantaged contexts 116; theory of change 117–118; UK programmes 115–116
Compliance: UNCRC 128; children's rights **139**, 153
Comprehensive Community Initiatives (CCIs) 116–117
Concentric Zone Theory 74–75
conditioning 21–22
Constructivist Pathways Theory 87–89, 91, 110; contextualised explanations of youth offending 92–93; 'Pathways Into and Out of Crime' partnership projects 87–89; Teesside studies 89–90
context 3, 28, 92–93, 154; dynamic 1; reductionist definition 40; static 1; structural 80, 86–87, 89–91, 100; understanding youth offending and youth justice in 141–144, 154–155
Context-Mechanisms-Outcomes (CMO) 121–122
control, self- 25–26
Control Balance Theory 25
correlates 16–18, 21; youth offending 33, 56–57
Crawford, A. 53–54, 114–115
crime 9, 105; gendered theories 101–102; as social construction 9, 73–74, 93–94; socio-economic explanation 98–99; unreported 5
Crime and Disorder Act (UK, 1988) 63, 65, 130
criminal careers model 30–32
criminalisation 94–95, 104
criminogenic influences 15; adoption studies 18; brain development 19; capitalism 98–99; 'Causes and Correlates' study 35–36; correlations 16–17, 21; genetic inheritance 17–19; integrated Positivist theories 23–28; life events 81–82; meso-level 3, 12, 72, 85–86; neighborhood 78, 85; neuroscientific 19–20; place 74–75, 90; poverty 116; provocation 39–40; psychosocial 30, 39; stigmatisation 97; strain 76; temptation 39–40; twin studies 17–18
criminology: androcentrism 102; bifurcation 146–147; feminist 101–102; Marxist 98–100, 102–103
Critical Criminology 73, 93, 106, 110, 143; contextualised explanations of youth offending 103–104; gendered theories 101–102; Labelling Theory 94–98; Marxist origin 98–99; 'The New Criminology' 100–101; 'New Criminology Revisited, The' 101
critical theory 9

decision-making 38, 47, 52, 58
decontextualisation: youth justice 49–50, 63, 67–68, 70, 138, 140; youth offending 2, 8, 44–45, 58
desistance 83; 'knifing off' 83; life events 81–83; role of agency 81–84; structured role stability 83
determinism 78; Artefactual Risk Factor Theories (ARFTs) 83–84, 90; developmental 29–32, 83; environmental 75; reductionist 92; structural 83
Developmental Crime Prevention (DCP) 53, 114–115; effectiveness 54–55
Developmental Risk Factor Theory 36; criminal careers model 30–32; multi-factor developmental theory 29–30; reductionism 32
deviance 95, 100–101, 103
Differential Association Theory 23, 33, 77–78
diversion 113–114, 133, 135–136, 138, 152–153; *see also* punishment

dizygotic (DZ) twins 17–18
Drakeford, M., 'Young People and Youth Justice' 129–130
'dramatization of evil' hypothesis 95
Durkheim, E., 'anomie' 74, 77
dynamic context 1; youth offending 6

Ecological Systems Theory 3, 36–37
ecological validity 17, 57
Edinburgh Study: data collection 84–85; 'explanatory factors' 85–86; reductionism 86; *see also* Artefactual Risk Factor Theories (ARFTs)
effectiveness/'effective': Community Crime Prevention 115, 117–119; Developmental Crime Prevention (DCP) 54–55; intervention 65–66, 121–122, 163–164; youth justice 65–66, 150
EMMIE 121, 123, 143
ethnocentrism 2, 32
evaluation framework 145–146; EMMIE 121, 123; Realist Synthesis 120–124, 143, 161; 'What Works' 63–68, 111, 117–121
evidence/evidential 161; -based arguments 3; -based policy 45, 55–56, 144; -based risk management 51, 58, 63; -based youth justice 8, 54–55, 60–63, 120; -bases 148; reductionism 141, 145–147; *see also* 'What Works' framework
expansionism 73, 81, 111, 135, 138, 147–148, 161
experimental methodology 64–68, 110, 118–119; *see also* 'What Works' framework
explanations of youth offending 8–9; Age-Graded Life Course Theory (AGLCT) 80–87; androcentric 32, 79; Artefactual Risk Factor Theories (ARFTs) 28–40; bifurcation 146–147; Biological Positivism 15–20, 105; 'centrisms' 79–80; Classical 13–14; Constructivist Pathways Theory 87–93; Criminal Careers model 30–32; decontextualised 41, 43; developmental risk factor theory 28–32; Differential Association Theory 77–78; Ecological Theory 36–37; Edinburgh Study 85–86; Individual Positivist 23; Integrated Development Risk Factor Theory 32–40; integrated Positivist 23–28; Learning Theory 21–22; Neo-Classical 14; partial 2; Positivist 13–15; Psychological Positivist 20–23; Quasi-Contextualised Risk Factor Theory 80–93; Rational-Contextual theories 38–40; Right Realism 27; social constructionism 2, 6; Social Learning Theory 22; Sociological Positivist 73–80; 'storm and stress' theory 20–21; strain 76–77; *see also* criminogenic influences
explanatory reductionism 2, 6, 8, 12, 21, 72, 92, 142, 147–148; explanatory 12, 21, 92, 142; individualisation 12–13; *see also* reductionism/reductionist
explanatory utility 6, 17, 27–28, 30, 32, 36, 40–41, 43, 56–57, 78–79, 107, 110
Eysenck, Hans 23; Personality Theory 21

factorisation 57–58
family studies 17–18
Farrington, David 30–31, 37, 53; Integrated Cognitive Antisocial Potential (ICAP) theory 38
female offending 157–158
Feminist Criminology 101–102
free will 15, 75; Classical theories 13–14; Neo-Classical theories 14

gendered theories in Critical Criminology 101–102
General Theory of Crime 25–26
genetic inheritance 17–19
globalisation 50–51, 144
Glueck, S. and Glueck, E., 'Unraveling Juvenile Delinquency' 30, 81–82

Haines, K., 'Young People and Youth Justice' 129–130
Hazel 45–46
hegemonic masculinity 103
Hirschi, Travis, Social Control Theory 24–26, 33
Hope, Tim 115–116, 118–119
individualised approaches to intervention 2, 8, 58–59; ACEs (Adverse Childhood Experiences) 61–62; Developmental Crime Prevention (DCP) 53–55; Risk Factor Prevention Paradigm (RFPP) 55–56; 'What Works' framework 64–65, 68, 70

Individual Positivism 13–15, 74; integrated 23–27; reductionist explanations 28
Integrated Cognitive Antisocial Potential (ICAP) theory 38
Integrated Development Risk Factor Theory 32; 'Causes and Correlates' study 35–36; Ecological Theory 36–37; rational-contextual theories 37–40; social development model 33–34
Integrated Individual Positivism: Biopsychosocial theory 26–28; Social Control Theory 24–26
integrated Positivist explanations of youth offending: Biopsychosocial theory 26–28; social control theory 24–26
intervention/s 8, 20; children's rights 127–128; community crime prevention 9; Context-Mechanisms-Outcomes (CMO) 121–122; effectiveness 65–66, 124, 163–164; evidence-based 120, 161; individualised 59; Minimum Necessary 46, 113–114; preventative 122–124; programme theories 121–122, 162–164; 'What Works' framework 63–68; 'What's Unknown' 66–67; *see also* 'What Works' framework

Jeffery, C. Ray, Biopsychosocial theory of crime 26–27
justice: actuarial 52, 55; model 45–46; punitive 47–49; Restorative 47, 113, 148; 'welfare versus' 8, 44, 46, 68
juvenile delinquency: Cambridge Study 30–31; status frustration 77; Subcultural Theory 77

Key Elements of Effective Practice (KEEPs) 65–66; *see also* effectiveness/'effective'
'knifing off' 83, 87

Labelling Theory 94–98, 104; Becker on 96; criminalisation 95–96; criminogenic stigma 96–97; 'dramatization of evil' hypothesis 95
Laub, J.: Age-Graded Theory of Informal Social Control 80–84; 'Shared Beginnings, Divergent Lives' 82–83
learning: differential association 78; psychological 77–78; subconscious 22; theory 21–23
Left Realism 9, 73, 104–105; criticisms 107; 'relative deprivation' 106
life events 81–83; *see also* turning points
Lombroso, Cesare 23; 'L'Uomo Delinquente' 15–16

macro-level: criminogenic influences 86; racialisation 99; social system 3
Martinson, R. 48–49
Marxist criminology 98–100, 102–103
masculinity/ies 159–160; hegemonic 103
McAra 127–128
measurement: ACEs (Adverse Childhood Experiences) 62; crime 65; *see also* Scientific Methods Scale (SMS)
Mednick, Sarnoff, Biopsychosocial theory 26–28
meso-level: criminogenic influences 3, 12, 72, 85–86, 110; racialisation 99
micro-level: criminogenic influences 3, 12; racialisation 99
Minimum Necessary Intervention 46, 113–114
models: Social Crime Prevention 115; youth justice 113–114
monozygotic (MZ) twins 17–18
moral poverty 73, 105
multi-factor developmental theory 29–30

neighborhood 85; criminogenic influence 78
Neo-Classical Compromise 13, 23
Neo-Classical theories of youth offending 13–14
neo-correctionalism 51–53, 113
neo-liberalism 46, 48–49, 56, 113
neuroscience 19, 23; brain development in adolescents 19–20; 'use it or lose it' principle 20
'New Criminology, The' 100–101, 103

offending: criminalisation 94–95; 'dramatization of evil' hypothesis 95; early life risk factors 81–82; functionalist perspective 74; Labelling Theory 95–98; Realist perspective 104; sanctions 81; trajectory 81–82

official statistics 5; *see also* statistics

partiality 12, 43, 67, 72, 142; explanatory 2, 28, 60–61, 66, 68; reductionist 12, 28, 40–41, 92; responsive 68; *see also* bias
patriarchy 25, 101, 158
Personality Theory, 'storm and stress' theory 20–21
place, as criminogenic influence 75, 141
policing: community 116; statistics 5
policy/policymaking: ACEs agenda 61–63; Child First 132–137; criminal justice 49; evidence-based 45, 55–56, 144; *see also* evaluation framework, 'What Works' framework; youth justice
positive reinforcement 22, 27
Positive Youth Development Model 34–35
'Positive Youth Justice' 130–131, 135
Positivist explanations of youth offending 93; Biological 15–20; Individual 13–15, 23; integrated 24–28; Psychological 20–23; Sociological 73–80, 106; *see also* Biological Positivist theories of youth offending; integrated Positivist explanations of youth offending; Psychological Positivist theories of youth offending
positron-emission tomography (PET) scan 19
poverty 113, 116, 158; *see also* moral poverty
power 9, 94, 96–97, 103
Power Control Theory 25
predictors of offending 29–31, 51, 56–57; Adverse Childhood Experiences (ACEs) 61–63
preventative intervention 122–124
programme theories 121–122; child-centric 162–163
protective factors 30–31, 33, 35, 53, 81–82
provocation 39–40
Psychodynamic School of Psychology 22
psychological learning 77–78
Psychological Positivist theories of youth offending: Learning Theory 21–23; Personality Theory 20–21
psychosocial: bias 28, 31, 56–58; risk factors 39, 55, 62, 84; *see also* Artefactual Risk Factor Theories (ARFTs)
punishment 14, 27, 134; detention 136; in Western youth justice systems 47–49
'punitive turn', youth justice 47–51, 111

Quasi-Contextualised Risk Factor Theory 73, 87–89, 142–143; Age-Graded Life Course Theory (AGLCT) 80–87; Constructivist Pathways Theory 87–93; Edinburgh Study 84–86

racialisation 99–100
Randomized Control Trial (RCT) 65, 120
rational choice 13, 23, 27, 38, 73; Classical theories 13–14; Neo-Classical theories 13–14
Rational-Contextual theories of youth offending: Integrated Cognitive Antisocial Potential (ICAP) theory 38; Situational Action Theory (SAT) 39–40
Realism 79, 104
Realist Synthesis 120–121, 143, 161; Context-Mechanisms-Outcomes (CMO) 121–122; preventative intervention 122–124
reductionism/reductionist 10, 61, 73, 142; ARFTs 41, 66, 85–86; definition of 'context' 40; determinism 92; Developmental Risk Factor Theory 32; Edinburgh Study 86; evidential 141, 145–147; explanatory 2, 6, 8, 12, 28, 105, 108, 110, 147–148; of official statistics 5; partiality 12, 28, 40–41, 92; responsive 147; Risk Factor Prevention Paradigm (RFPP) 111; risk management 56–58; 'What Works' framework 117–118; *see also* expansionism
Referral Orders 122–123
reform, youth justice 59, 149–150
rehabilitation 48–49; individualised approaches 59; Risk Factor Prevention Paradigm (RFPP) 56
'relative deprivation' 106–107
responsibilisation 48–49, 56; neo-liberal 113
responsive: partiality 68, 142, 154; reductionism 147
Restorative Justice 46–47, 113, 148
Right Realism 27, 73, 104–105; explanatory theory of crime 105–106

rights-based approach to youth justice 151–152
risk 50; algorithmic assessment 60–61, 68, 70; -based theories of youth offending 28–32, 35–36, 39; management 51–53, 56–58, 63, 68; society 52; *see also* Algorithmic Risk Assessment (ARA); Artefactual Risk Factor Theories (ARFTs); Developmental Risk Factor Theory; Integrated Development Risk Factor Theory; Quasi-Contextualised Risk Factor Theory
Risk Factor Prevention Paradigm (RFPP) 53–59, 64, 111; adult-centrism 58; lack of explanatory utility 56–57; psychosocial bias 56; as reductionist risk management 57–58; technicisation 58
Rochester Youth Development Study 36

Sampson: Age-Graded Theory of Informal Social Control 80–84; 'Shared Beginnings, Divergent Lives' 82–83
scientific method 16–17, 74, 93
Scientific Methods Scale (SMS) 64–65, 117–119
self-control 22, 25–26
sentencing 47; children's rights 128, 136
Sharp, Gilly 102; on female offending 157–158
Sherman, Lawrence, 'Preventing Crime: What Works, What Doesn't, What's Promising' 64–68
Situational Action Theory (SAT) 39–40
Situational Crime Prevention 114–115
'Snakes and Ladders: Young People, Transitions and Social Exclusion' 89–90
social bonds 24–25, 80
social constructions 2, 159; crime 9, 73–74, 93–94; statistics 5; youth justice 8; youth offending 4, 6
Social Control Theory 24–26, 33, 83
Social Crime Prevention 53–54, 114; Community Crime Prevention 115–119
Social Development Model 33–34
social exclusion 89–90
Social Learning Theory 22, 33
Sociological Positivism 73, 106; adaptation 76–78; Concentric Zone Theory 74–75; Strain Theory 76–77; Subcultural Theory 77–78
somatotyping 16–17
static context 1, 162
statistics: crime 74; 'official' 5; police 5; as social construction 5; validity 57–58
status frustration 77, 100, 104
stigma/stigmatisation 96–97, 105
'storm and stress' theory 20–21
Strain Theory 76–78
structural context 80, 86–87, 89–91, 100
structured role stability 83, 87
Subcultural Theory 77–78; Cloward and Ohlin's version 78; Cohen's version 77; Sutherland's version 77–78
Sutherland, Edwin, Differential Association Theory 77–78

Tannenbaum, F., 'dramatization of evil' hypothesis 95, **108**
Teesside studies 89–90
temptation 39–40
theoreticism 146–147
theory of change 117–118, 120–121
Treiber, K., 'Beyond Risk Factors' 57
turning points 81–83
twin studies 17–18

United Kingdom: CCP programmes 115–116; Crime and Disorder Act (1988) 63, 65, 130; intervention effectiveness 122–123; National Deviancy Conference 100
United Nations Convention on the Rights of the Child (UNCRC) 125–129, 151–152
urban areas, as criminogenic influence 74–75
'use it or lose it' principle 20

validity: adoption studies 18–19; ecological 17, 118–119; statistics 57–58

Wales: 'Children First, Offenders Second' (CFOS) principle 129–131; *see also* United Kingdom
Walton, Paul 100–101
'welfare versus justice debate' 8, 44–46, 68
West, Donald 30–31

'What Works' framework 63–68, 111, 119–121, 145–146; reductionist approach 117–118
Wikström, Per-Olof 37–39; 'Beyond Risk Factors' 57
working class 78–79, 95, 98; underclass subculture 105

Young, Jock 100–101, 106
youth justice 9–10, 44, 75; actuarial risk management 52, 55; Algorithmic Risk Assessment (ARA) 60–61; children's rights 125–129; *see also* Child First; Child-Friendly Justice; in China 134–135; decision-making structures 47; decontextualised 8, 49–50, 63, 67–68, 70, 138, 140 *see also* punishment; Developmental Crime Prevention (DCP) 53–55; 'effective' 65–66, 150; evidence-based 8, 54–55, 60–63, 120; individualised approaches 59; justice model 45–46; Key Elements of Effective Practice (KEEPs) 65–66; neo-liberalism 49, 113; objectives 46; official statistics 5; preventative intervention 122–124; 'punitive turn' 47–51, 111; reform 59, 149–150; responsibilisation 48–49; Restorative Justice 113; rights-based approach 151–152; Risk Factor Prevention Paradigm (RFPP) 53–59; 'risk management' approach 51–53; sentencing structures 47; social constructions 6, 8; system types 47; systemic contextual influence 46–47; understanding in context 141–144; welfare model 45; 'What Works' framework 63–68
youth offending 9, 77–78; antisocial potential 38; by boys 159–160; in context 154–155; contextualised perspectives 3; correlates 33, 56–57; decontextualisation 8, 58; dynamic context 6; 'explanatory factors' 85–86; by girls 157–158; Integrated Cognitive Antisocial Potential (ICAP) theory 38; Labelling Theory 95–98; micro-level influences 12; official statistics 5; predictors 29, 51; protective factors 30–31, 33, 35, 53, 81–82; risk 50–51; as social construction 4, 6; twin studies 17–18; understanding in context 141–144; *see also* explanations of youth offending; juvenile delinquency
Youth Offending Teams (YOTs) 88, 160

zone of transition 74–75

For Product Safety Concerns and Information please contact our EU representative GPSR@taylorandfrancis.com
Taylor & Francis Verlag GmbH, Kaufingerstraße 24, 80331 München, Germany

www.ingramcontent.com/pod-product-compliance
Ingram Content Group UK Ltd.
Pitfield, Milton Keynes, MK11 3LW, UK
UKHW020004200926
475702UK00015B/2464
9781032806785